D1271922

Photo : Hartung, Pekin.

A DOMESTIC SCENE IN PEKIN

hours before, Sujimura had passed close to the camp of Tung Fu-hsiang's braves, near the entrance to the Temple of Heaven. And nothing had happened. But when he passed there once more, on his way back, the Chinese soldiers, for some reason, were in a different temper. They surrounded his cart, dragged him out on to the road, and beat out his brains with the butts of their rifles. Sujimura was the first foreigner to be murdered.

On the 14th of June, the Boxers penetrated into the Tartar City, by the gate called the Hata Mên. They killed the Chinese Christians who lived round the catholic church, that was situated near the gate, and set fire to their houses. The church also caught fire, and the Boxers threw their victims into the burning building and pushed them back with their bayonets when they tried to escape from the flames. During the night, foreigners in the Legation Quarter made an attempt to go to the rescue of these unfortunates, but in vain. As an example of the fate that awaited those who fell into the hands of the Boxers, the handful of volunteers, who attempted to rescue the Chinese converts, stumbled over the body of a Chinese woman who lay on the ground with her hands and feet tied with rope and her clothes soaked with petroleum. The Boxers had set fire to her and thrown her down to make a light for them along their path. She was half burnt to death, but still moaned a little and lived for about an hour.

The foreign Ministers had announced that they would pay a visit to Prince Ching, at the Tsung-li Yamen, on the morning of the 20th June, at ten o'clock 'if the Prince could receive them'. The German Minister, Baron von Ketteler, had written at the same time as the others, but he had omitted the phrase saying that he would come only if he heard that the Minister would receive.

No answer was received to any of these communications. Therefore the majority among the Ministers were of opinion that it was best not to go. The only one who thought otherwise was Baron von Ketteler, who had not made his visit to the Tsung-li Yamen conditional on his receiving a favourable answer from Prince Ching. His colleagues attempted to dissuade him, but he insisted on starting off, only to meet the same fate as Sujimura. Twenty minutes after his departure, his Chinese outriders returned breathless to the Legation saying that the Minister had been shot, and his Interpreter, Herr Cordes, grievously wounded.

From that moment began the siege of the Legations.

XIX

And there was a great battle in heaven. Michael and his angels fought with the dragon. And the dragon fought, and his angels. And they prevailed not. . . .

Revelations vii. 12.

N the 20th of June, the Grand Council met in the early hours of the morning in one of the Lake Palaces, to discuss the promulgation of a decree, ordering the destruction of all foreigners. Jung Lu was the only one to oppose it, maintaining that no good purpose could be served and no honour come to the imperial troops by attacking an isolated band of foreigners within the walls of the capital. Such an act might bring misfortune and entail the ruin of the dynasty.

Tzu-hsi answered that, even if she wished, she could no longer restrain the patriotic movement. Jung Lu had better urge the foreigners to leave the capital while there was yet time. If he had no other suggestions to offer, he might consider himself excused from further attendance on the Council.[1]

Jung Lu's courageous defence of the foreigners made him very unpopular in Peking. On one occasion, when he was passing under the Hu-mên gate, some Boxers surrounded his chair, shouting insults and threatening him as a 'Chinese traitor'. This was because he had tried to save the life of an Englishman, a Professor James, who had been caught and taken to the house of Prince Chuang, the Boxers prodding him all the time with the points of their bayonets. When

[1] *Note.*—Many of the details and conversations given in this chapter are taken from the 'Diary of His Excellency Ching Shan', first published in *China under the Empress Dowager*, by Bland and Backhouse. Ching Shan was a retired official, and had been tutor to Prince Tuan and to the Duke Lan. He was very intimate with the Boxer leaders, who used to visit him in his home in the Tartar City. He was killed (or forced to commit suicide) by his own son, En Ch'un, at the end of the siege, and his house was burnt to the ground.

Sir Edmund Backhouse has told how he saved the Diary when the house was already burning. The manuscript lay on the ground, among other papers that had been thrown aside as useless. But subsequently Doctor Morrison (at that time *Times* correspondent in China) expressed doubts as to the authenticity of the Diary, and suggested that Sir Edmund Backhouse himself might have compiled it, with the aid of his Manchu teacher. If this is so, Sir Edmund Backhouse appears worthy to be classed with the famous translator of Ossian's poems. If the Diary is apocryphal, it is a real work of art.

Mr. J. O. P. Bland did not enter into the controversy, but, as proprietor of the original document, he deposited it in the British Museum, so that sinologues might examine it, a facility of which many scholars have availed themselves. Mr. Bland also authorized a second publication of the text, by Mr. J. J. L. Duyvendak, whose translation was published in 1925, by Brill, of Leyden. This translation contains certain paragraphs which had been omitted from *China under the Empress Dowager*.

Jung Lu's men arrived to take the Englishman away, the Princes Chuang and Tuan had already had him beheaded. His head was then hung up in a cage, on the main beam of the Tung An Gate. Tzu-hsi ordered 500 taels to be distributed among the soldiers who had captured him. But she was greatly shocked to hear that many hundred Chinese converts to christianity (the so-called devil's disciples) had been put to death outside Prince Chuang's palace. She suggested that, if the Chinese catholics would recant and reform, their lives might be spared.

In hunting down the 'devil's disciples', as the Huguenots were hunted on the night of Saint Bartholomew, the Boxer leaders were not content to vent their blood-lust on the poorer classes. On the 26th of June, a group of sixty Boxers, led by Princes Tuan and Chuang, marched into the Palace itself, in search of fresh victims. When they reached the courtyard, on to which opened the Emperor's pavilion, they began shouting for him to come out. It was then about six o'clock in the morning, and Tzu-hsi was having her early tea. She heard the crowd approaching and the shouts of the Boxer soldiery, clamouring to kill. Without a moment's hesitation, she went out to meet them, and stood alone, at the top of a short flight of steps, her slight figure in its embroidered robes showing in strong relief against the darkness of the doors that were open behind her. By that time the courtyard was swarming with armed men, filled with the lust of animals who have tasted blood.

The Empress looked down upon them and her steady gaze met that of Prince Tuan, whose jaw dropped and whose knees shook beneath him. He had always been afraid of the Old Buddha. Then she began to speak.

She did not raise her voice; she did not bluster or threaten. Her words betrayed no fear and no anger, only an icy, measureless disdain. She asked if Prince Tuan had come to look upon himself as Emperor: 'if not, how dare he behave in this reckless and insolent manner? She would have him know that she, and she alone, had power to create or to depose the Sovereign, and she would have him remember that the power, which had made his son Heir-Apparent, could also wipe him out in a moment. If he and his fellow princes thought that, because the State was at a crisis of confusion, they could follow their own inclinations, they would find themselves seriously mistaken. She bade them depart, and refrain from ever again entering the palace precincts, except when summoned to her presence on duty. But they would first prostrate themselves and ask His Majesty's pardon for their insolent behaviour. As a slight punishment for their offences, she further commanded that the Princes be mulcted of a year's allowances. As to the Boxer Chiefs, who had dared to create this uproar in her hearing, they should be decapitated on the spot.'

At this point, she looked round towards the eunuchs, who stood by, half hidden among the lacquer columns. And she signed to them to fetch the guards from the outer gates. The eunuchs bowed to the ground and hurried off on their errand. Then the Empress turned and passed back through the doors, whence she had come. The Princes, who had borne themselves with so much pride a few moments before, slunk away without a word.

Tzu-hsi had quelled a riot, by sheer force of character and by the power of her dominant personality. It was no mere bluff that had made her speak as she did, and calmly order men to punishment, when any one of them might have felled her to the ground. She never doubted that it was hers to command and that she would be obeyed. China can boast of many great rulers, but none knew better than this Empress how to impose her will. In that brief imperious speech, from the courtyard steps, breathed the voice of old Asiatic conquerors: of Gengiz Khan, of Kublai and of Tamerlane.

The danger had been greater than she knew. With the pretext of seeking out the 'devil's disciples', Prince Tuan and his followers meant to strike at the Son of Heaven. If they had attained their object, in those days of utter confusion, it would have been easy for armed men, who enjoyed the favour of the populace in their campaign against the foreigner, to have brushed aside the women and the eunuchs, and to have seized the throne itself.

In her anger against Prince Tuan and his followers, Tzu-hsi almost raised the siege of the Legations. She sent for Jung Lu and authorized him to go to the foreign Ministers and to discuss terms. The attacking forces were called off amid a blare of trumpets. Under cover of a white flag, a Chinese soldier brought out a placard, nailed it to a board, and set it up opposite the British Legation, whence a group of sinologues, of various nationalities, began at once to decipher the Chinese characters, which they read with the aid of telescopes and field-glasses. Sir Robert Hart translated the message as follows:

'In accordance with the Imperial commands to protect the Ministers, firing will cease immediately and a despatch will be delivered at the Imperial canal bridge.'

The despatch was never delivered, but during the greater part of one day all firing ceased, and a certain amount of unofficial parleying went on, by shouting from a distance. The besieged learnt that the placard had been put up by order of Jung Lu, and that the Empress Dowager was much distressed and had expressed her opinion that the Boxers were fools. . . .

In Putnam Weale's *Indiscreet Letters from Peking,* there is a description of the motley crowd, outside the Palace gates, who stood gazing at 'foreign devils', whom they had attacked up till a few hours before:

There were jackets and tunics of every colour; trouserings of blood red embroidered with black dragons; great two-handed swords in some hands, men armed with bows and arrows mixing with Tung Fu-hsiang's Kansu horsemen, who had the most modern carbines slung across their backs. There were blue banners, yellow banners embroidered with black, white flags and red. . . . The Kansu soldiery of Tung Fu-hsiang's command were easy to pick out from among the milder looking Peking Banner troops. Tanned almost to a colour of chocolate by years of campaigning in the sun, of sturdy and muscular physique, these men who desired to be our butchers showed by their aspect what little pity we should meet with if they were allowed to break in on us. Men from all the Peking Banners seemed to be there with their plain and bordered jackets, showing their divisions; but of Boxers there was not a sign. Where had the famed Boxers vanished to?'

During the night, the attack on the Legations was resumed. Tzu-hsi had received news that the Seymour relief column had been repulsed and had retired to Tientsin. Once more the Boxers emerged from their lairs 'to eat the flesh and to sleep on the skins of the foreign devils'.

A few days later, all attacks ceased during the best part of an afternoon. Tzu-hsi had sent orders to stop all firing. She had a headache and the noise disturbed her.

For the Boxers and their leaders, she soon developed a great contempt. One day, while she was painting a design of bamboos on a panel of silk, she was informed that the Kansu Commander-in-Chief was waiting outside the Hall of Imperial Supremacy, demanding audience. It was Tung Fu-hsiang, who had been to see Jung Lu, to ask for the loan of the 'heavy artillery', which was under his orders. Jung Lu had kept him waiting for more than an hour, and then had refused to accede to his request.

Tzu-hsi did not like being troubled by these matters. When Tung Fu-hsiang kow-towed before her, she said:

'Well, I suppose you have come to report the complete destruction of the Legations? This will be the tenth time, since the end of the last moon.'

'I have come,' replied Tung Fu-hsiang, 'to ask Your Majesty's permission to impeach the Grand Secretary Jung Lu as a traitor and a friend of the barbarians. He has guns which my army needs. But he has sworn never to lend these guns, even though Your Majesty should command it.'

The Old Buddha replied: 'Be silent! You were nothing but a brigand to begin with, and if I allowed you to enter my army it was only to give you an opportunity of atoning for your former misdeeds. Even now you are behaving like a brigand, forgetting the Majesty of the Imperial presence. Of a truth, your tail is becoming too heavy to wag. Leave the Palace forthwith, and do not let me find you here again, unless summoned to audience.'

Tzu-hsi was beginning to find out that, whatever might happen in Peking, she could not count on the rest of China giving its support to Boxer violence. Even in Peking there were men brave enough to thwart the avowed policy of the throne. It was discovered that the character 'to slay' in the Imperial decree, ordering the extermination of all foreigners, had been replaced by the character 'to protect'. This had been done by two courageous officials, Yüan Chang and Hsü Ching-cheng. Tzu-hsi ordered them both to be decapitated.

Just before the sword of the executioner fell, Yüan said that 'he hoped the Sun might soon return to its place in heaven, and that the usurping comet might be destroyed'. Duke Lan, who was superintending the execution, recognized the allusion to a 'malign comet' and bade the condemned man be silent. But Yüan went on: 'In the years to come, my name will be remembered with gratitude and respect, long after you evil-plotting Princes have met your well-deserved doom'. Then, turning to his companion, he said: 'We shall meet again at the Yellow Springs. To die is only to come home.'

Duke Lan stepped forward, as if to strike him. But the headsman quickly despatched both prisoners.

As the possibility of failure became more apparent, Tzu-hsi began once more to rely on the advice of Jung Lu. The other members of the Grand Council left it to him to announce to the Empress that the foreigners had landed troops at Taku, that they had taken Tientsin, and that they were drawing nearer and nearer to the capital. Jung Lu was careful to avoid any suggestion that he had been wiser than the Empress herself. They discussed the possibility of the Court's retiring to Jehol, as in 1860. At first, the Old Buddha declared that, rather than leave the capital, she would commit suicide and oblige the Emperor to do the same.

The Grand Council met several times, but nothing was decided.

On the 14th of August, the news came that Tung-chow had fallen. The same evening, the Duke Lan burst into the Palace, followed by the Grand Secretary Kang Yi, to announce that a large force of turbaned soldiery were encamped outside the Tartar City in the enclosure of the Temple of Heaven. 'Perhaps,' said Tzu-hsi, 'they are our Mahommedan braves from Kansu, come to demolish the Legations?' But Kang Yi told her that they were foreign devils. They were in fact the Sikhs of the British contingent.

Next day, Tzu-hsi rose at dawn, after only an hour's rest, and dressed herself hurriedly in the common blue cotton garments of a peasant woman. For the first time in her life, her hair was done up in the Chinese and not in the Manchu fashion, a plain black satin band round the forehead instead of an elaborate head-dress. This small fact seems to have impressed Tzu-hsi more than the failure of her policy. 'Who would ever have believed,' she said, as she surveyed herself in a mirror, 'that it would have come to this?'

All the concubines had been summoned to appear at the Hour of the Tiger (3.30 a.m.). They were told that the Son of Heaven was about to leave his capital, but that none of them would accompany him at present.

The Pearl Concubine threw herself on her knees in front of the Empress Dowager, begging to be allowed to share the discomforts and perils of the flight. Tzu-hsi pointed out that it was prudent to limit, as far as possible, the number of persons who were to accompany the Court. But as the Pearl Concubine reiterated her prayer to be taken too, the Empress lost patience and exclaimed:

'I can do nothing for you. If you are not satisfied, throw yourself down a well!'

Taking these words as an order, two eunuchs approached the Pearl Concubine and wrapped her in a carpet. They threw her down the large well, just outside the Ning Shou Palace. The Emperor stood by, trembling with grief and wrath.[1]

Thus the Court left Peking, travelling in ordinary carts and with nothing to show that they carried the Son of Heaven and his suite. The Empress Dowager said to the carters: 'Drive your hardest, and if any foreign devil should stop you, say nothing. I will speak to them and explain that we are but poor country folk, fleeing to our homes.'

No one spoke to them, or molested them. But they had to wait a long time as they approached the Te-sheng Men, or Gate of Victory, on the north-west side of the city, for the way was blocked by the dense crowd of carts and palanquins of people who were passing out that way.

A few days later, one of the ladies of the British Legation, Mrs. W. P. Ker, was able to enter the Forbidden City and to visit the apartments of the Empress in the Ming Shou Palace. The Russians had placed guards at the outer gates, but the Russian General gave Mrs. Ker his signet ring, with an impression in wax on a piece of wood. The seals had to be broken on the massive brass lock, a foot long, and the door was sealed up again when the party came out.

[1] *Note.*—This version of the Pearl Concubine's death is taken from the *Unofficial History of the Ching Dynasty*, a work compiled by different Chinese authors. In the 'Diary of His Excellency Ching Shan' the Empress Dowager is represented in a more unfavourable light, as having given the order in a moment of exasperation and in spite of the Emperor's protests.

I quote Mrs. Ker's own words:

Tzu-hsi's room was just as she had left it. On the rich coverlet of the bed, lay an embroidered coat of black satin; beneath a pair of Manchu shoes. Near by were two large boxes of silk handkerchiefs, overturned: one box of pale yellow handkerchiefs and one of pale blue. A handful had been hurriedly snatched from each.

In the adjoining rooms, along the walls, were huge camphor-wood boxes, filled to the top with coats and trousers of every colour, embroidered with gold and with pearls; all were new, all were neatly piled. In other boxes were rich sable coats, and silk coats lined with white fox fur; untailored sable skins and fur of every kind, stored and ready for the winter.

Back once more to the Imperial road and to the K'ung Ning Throne Hall of the Empress, through a suite of many rooms, each one more magnificent than the other, divided not by doors but by wood-carvings, rose, sandal and peach woods all in different patterns: prunus, bamboo, peony and lotus, each side different.

Carved screens, tables, chairs and stools lined the walls, and on the tables lovely porcelain, jade, lacquer and jewel-trees.

On a long table, the length of one room, were dozens of foreign clocks, some handsome, others hideous, all ticking cheerfully, regardless of the ominous silence around. . . .

Coming out of these buildings, through the K'ung Ning Gate, we entered fairyland: the Yü Hua Yuan, a walled garden with lotus blooming on the lake, huge rocks with winding paths up to the pavilions, where seats were placed to give the loveliest views. Each turning brought into sight little cascades tumbling over rocks, and tiny ponds of gold-fish. Flowers were everywhere, and the background of shady trees.

And so we came to the Sheng Wu Mên (the Gate of Military Prowess) on to the Western Road, Tzu-hsi's *Via dolorosa*. Through this gate, in the early dawn, she had passed, and with her the Emperor Kuang-hsu, to the rough peasant carts waiting without. . . .

XX

The Marquis of Salisbury to Queen Victoria (Cypher Telegram) 10th June 1900: 'Humble duty. . . . We are hurrying up all the force available. Russia, not China, seems to me the greatest danger of the moment.'

IF all the forces at the disposal of the Chinese Government had been used against the handful of soldiers and volunteers, who defended themselves as best they could from behind a few walls and hastily built barricades, the siege might have been over in a few days, almost in a few hours. The Boxers were careful not to expose themselves to needless risk, and their officers never took the lead in an attack; they stayed behind and urged others forward. But they knew how to tire out the defenders with continual firing, with the springing of mines and the setting fire to neighbouring houses, when the wind made it appear likely that the flames would spread. They were always threatening a final assault that never came off, and they never stopped building offensive and even defensive works, always a little nearer to the object of their attacks. Such Fabian tactics were well adapted to wear out the foreigners' nerves, and to sap their power of resistance.

Although vague rumours occasionally reached them of dissensions within the Forbidden City, the besieged did not realize at the time that they owed their lives to the one strong man who dared befriend them, even against the Empress herself. It was at a much later date that the foreigners learnt of Jung Lu's obstinate refusal to lend what were inaccurately described as his 'big guns'. These guns were not really big (their diameter was two and a half inches), but they represented what was, in those days, the most modern and formidable of light artillery, having just arrived from Germany before the siege began. If they had been brought into action, the fate of the Legations would have been sealed in a few minutes. But Jung Lu was obdurate in his refusal, and when the relieving allied force eventually reached Peking, they were surprised to find a complete park of artillery (101 guns in all) which had never been used.

The siege centred round the British and American Legations, all the others having been burnt down. The former became the headquarters of the defence and a place of refuge for those Ministers and officials whose houses had been destroyed. Therefore the direction of affairs was assigned, by courtesy, to the British Minister. A census of civilians, who lived, or had taken refuge, in the Legations gave the following figures: Men, 245; Women, 149; Children, 79. Total, 473.

A separate siege, though also within the walls of the Tartar City, was sustained by the catholic mission of the Pei-tang, which was defended by the missionaries themselves, with the aid of about thirty soldiers and sailors, French and Italians, commanded by two young officers.

The damp heat of the rainy season; the anxiety of each individual for himself and others; hunger and indigestion; the flies; the mosquitoes; the stench of rotting corpses in the 'no-man's land' on three sides of the besieged Legations (starving dogs were the only scavengers); the mutual incomprehension of so many individuals of different nationalities, herded together in that cramped space; lack of medicaments for the sick and wounded; lack of information as to what was going on in the outside world, from which Peking was completely cut off: such were a few of the aspects of the siege, as seen from within. And of all the horrors, the worst was the hunger of the little children, for whom no suitable food could be provided. Sixty-six babies were brought into the Pei-tang for safety by Chinese converts seeking refuge. Sixty-six died.

In foreign countries and in the Treaty Ports of China, there reigned an anxiety almost equal to that of the besieged, as to whether relief could reach Peking in time. Most people, who had relatives in the Legations, mourned them as dead. Public opinion, the world over, demanded dire punishment on 'the Chinese' in general for this new violation of international law, and people recalled the burning of the Summer Palace. Despite his obvious unpopularity, the Chinese Minister in London continued to frequent the St. James's Club, as if nothing unusual were happening in the country he represented.

The American Minister in China was Major Conger

(he had fought for the North in the civil war), but the American citizen who enjoyed the greatest popularity among the besieged, was Fargo Squires, the fourteen-year-old son of the Secretary of the Legation. He was a forerunner of the ideal boy scout. Riding a small donkey, whose life was spared as long as possible by the Food Committee, he went everywhere and helped everybody, bearing messages and executing small commissions. It was difficult to go anywhere within the area of the besieged Legations, without meeting Fargo and his donkey doing their bit.

In recent years, American missionaries to the Far East have come in for a considerable amount of abuse. They are accused of being responsible, through the imprudent iconoclasm of their teaching, for most of the evils from which China is suffering to-day. But during the siege of the Legations, they won nothing but praise, and proved themselves tireless, fearless, practical and efficient. It was an American missionary, Doctor Gamewell, who prepared some of the most useful of the 'fortifications'. Though their ecclesiastical calling was generally an obstacle to the missionaries taking a place in the firing line, they did good work behind the lines. A siege is a test of character, and the American missionaries stood it well, better than some of the soldiers, who were often unreliable, not because they lacked courage, but because they lacked officers to command them. Many officers of various nationalities were killed or severely wounded during the first days of the siege, and they had to be replaced by petty officers, or by civilians, whose task was especially difficult, as the men did not trust them.

Among the Italians, the most popular was Don Livio Caetani. He was one of the few foreigners to be mentioned in the British Blue Book, 'as one who rendered special service to the defence'. A case of real heroism was that of Suor Vincenza, a little Italian nun, at the Pei-tang. One officer and several sailors owed their lives to her, when a mine was sprung, which buried them under the falling masonry.

The English community was the most numerous in Peking, and it furnished the greater part of the volunteers, drawn from the student-interpreters and junior customs officials. They formed a group of cheerful, patient fighters, not unlike their compatriots in South Africa, where at that time the war was entering its last phase. The English and the Japanese (under Colonel Sheba) bore the brunt of the fighting.

The least popular among the defendants were the Russians, owing to a widespread suspicion that the Boxer movement in China had been encouraged by their Government's agents. Both before and after the siege the foreign Ministers had an agreement among themselves to show a common front to the Chinese Government and not to negotiate singly. But it was known to them that the Russian Minister, Baron de Giers, held secret meetings at night with some of the Manchu princes. Once, during the siege itself, when de Giers passed through the crowd of refugees, who were collected in the British Legation compound, a voice from the crowd shouted after him:

"*Qu'est ce qu'il fait, celui là, parmi nous? Qu'il s'en aille avec les Chinois!*"

At one moment, the hostility to the Russian Minister was so manifest that he refused to attend a meeting of the Diplomatic Body, in Sir Claude Macdonald's house, and was persuaded to do so only when his French and Italian colleagues went to fetch him and accompanied him through the crowded compound to the meeting.

Similar suspicions were also current in Europe at that time, and they were confirmed by the death of Muraviev in St. Petersburg. It was rumoured that Muraviev's demise, in June, was brought about by a stormy interview with the Czar, who accused him of being responsible for the tragic events in Peking.

All is paradox in China, and all through the siege a certain amount of correspondence was exchanged between the foreign Ministers and the Tsung-li Yamen, with mutual assurances of their highest consideration. More than once, the Ministers were offered a safe conduct to Tientsin, and the offer was generally followed, within a few hours, by the most violent attacks.

On the 18th of July, Prince Ching sent to inquire after the health of the foreign Envoys, and on the 20th he forwarded to them, in the name of the Empress, a cartload of fresh fruit. On the 24th, hoping that the conflagration would extend to the buildings of the British Legation, the Boxers set fire to the famous library of the Han-lin Academy, thus destroying many of the greatest literary treasures of the Chinese people. The wind was favourable, and if the British Legation houses had indeed caught fire, there would have been no possibility of forming a second line of defence behind them. During many hours, long lines of soldiers, missionaries, diplomats, ladies, doctors, hospital patients, children and domestic servants passed up pails of water (and other vessels of the most intimate character), in order to keep the woodwork moist and the fire from spreading.

On the 30th of July, the Chinese Court sent a message of condolence to the Italian Minister, for the death of King

Humbert at Monza, the day before. The Chinese message of condolence was the only news that the Italian Legation received of the event and it did not say that the King had been assassinated. But the missionary, Padre d'Addosio, began at once to declaim against the evildoer 'who had lifted a sacrilegious hand against the Lord's anointed'. At the end of the siege, it became known that Padre d'Addosio had been right in assuming that it was a case of regicide. And people wondered if he was not indeed a Seer.

On the 31st of July, Prince Ching wrote to complain that shots were being fired from the foreign Legations into the town. On the 12th of August, he sent a proposal to open negotiations with the object of making peace 'and avoiding further misunderstandings'. That same evening, a last attack was made on the foreign Legations in the hopes of destroying them before they could be relieved. The Chinese appeared to think that if all foreigners in Peking could be killed off before the relieving troops arrived, the latter would consider it useless to advance any more, and would return whence they had come. The last attacks were carried out by regular troops. The soldiers were under the impression that they were defending the Emperor from the foreign devils, who had summoned their armies from abroad expressly to murder him. The Boxers were utterly discredited and strove to disperse before the Empress should turn and rend them.

There were sieges during the South African war (Mafeking and Ladysmith) which represented feats of arms of some military interest. But the military interest in the siege of the Legations was almost *nil*. The reader who follows events in Peking, in 1900, with the comfortable knowledge that all will come well in the end, is apt to be more impressed with the farcical than with the tragical elements in the story.

Yet few episodes in contemporary history were so harrowing both to the besieged and to their friends in the outer world. In those days, men and women were still alive who remembered the horrors of the Indian mutiny. It looked as if they must be repeated in Peking.

The Chinese do not take that almost humorous pleasure in torture that used to be a characteristic of the Red Indians. But they can be horribly cruel. To those who waited day after day for the relief that was always coming and never came, visions, born of the heat and misery and discomfort, rose naturally to fevered brains. The woman who had been found, bound and burning, to light the way for the Boxers, was one of many such horrors. Among the foreigners in Tientsin, who strove in desperate haste to overcome the difficulties in despatching the relief, there recurred a story of the first outbreak of the Boxer movement. Some European women, wives and daughters of missionaries in a town in the interior, had their breasts cut off, before they were turned out on to the city wall to die.

It was on the 14th of August, about three in the afternoon, that the Sikhs of the British contingent entered Peking by the western gate of the Chinese City and made their way to the so-called Water Gate, where the Jade Canal passes under the Tartar Wall by a subterranean tunnel.

The Russians actually arrived first at the outer wall of the Chinese City, and tried to make their way through the North-Eastern Gate. But they were temporarily held at bay by the Manchu Bannermen, who brought to bear on them a murderous cross-fire from the corner tower on the Tartar

Wall. When they eventually succeeded in breaking through, the Russians made their way to the north of the Forbidden City and occupied the Coal Hill.

The Japanese entered the town from the east. They proceeded straight to the Treasury and to the Tsung-li Yamen and occupied them both.

There is a story that, during the last hours of the siege, someone in the British Legation sniffed the air and remarked: 'Relief must be at hand. I *smell* Indian troops.'

This may be surprising to anyone who knows Peking, for the smell of the Chinese City and of the Jade Canal in summer would appear stronger than that of marching troops (and the Sikhs are a clean race !). The local *bouquet* comprises sesamum oil (much used in Chinese cooking), garlic, manure, beetroot and rotting corpses, besides what Sir Ernest Shackleton (speaking of China) called 'the smell of moth-eaten centuries'.

In the confusion of that so longed for moment, there are many different stories of what actually happened. One newspaper published the following account (erroneously mentioning Prince Tuan among the dead):

SHANGHAI, *Wednesday* (1.15 *a.m.*)

Lieutenant Keyes, Naval Aide-de-Camp to General Gaselee, is reported to have been the first member of the relief party to enter the British Legation in Pekin.

A great victory is reported over the Chinese at Teh-chou on Thursday. Prince Tuan was killed in the battle, the losses of the enemy amounting to 1,500 men. The Japanese drove the remainder of the Chinese back into Chihli.

The victories of the Allied Army in Peking are causing great alarm among the Chinese here. They think the Allies intend to cut off their pigtails and make them all soldiers.

Mrs. W. P. Ker describes the moment of the relief as follows:

The first man through the green door opposite the Counsellor's house was a Sikh. He rushed up to the lawn and then toured the compound: an unforgettable sight, naked to the waist, sweating like a pig, hair tumbling on his shoulders. He kept waving his rifle and shouting: 'Oorah!' There was no doubt about his joy at our relief. The next man was Tom Scott (Bengal Lancers), hard on the Sikh's heels; then the A.D.C., Captain Pell, and in a bunch with officers and men, that old darling, General Gaselee, about twenty-five yards behind.

Major Vaughan, cousin of the Headmaster of Rugby, *really* was the first man to reach the gate, but sat himself down in a ditch to light his pipe, and so got left.

While Mrs. Ker was watching the green gate opposite the Counsellor's house (this entrance is nearer than the main entrance of the Legation to the Water Gate), another member of the relieving party had arrived from the opposite side of the Legation. He too had entered the Tartar City by the Water Gate, but had then turned to the left, passing through the American and Russian compounds. The following is Sir Roger Keyes's story:

Major Scott of the 1st Sikhs, four or five of his men, Captain Pell, the General's A.D.C. and I were the first people to arrive at the Shuè (*water*) Gate under the Tartar City wall abreast of the Legation.

Some American Marines were pulling down the great wooden bars, which closed the entrance, and being very slim, I managed to slip through ahead of the others. I then ran up the bank of the drain and through a gate into the American Legation. Running through it and through the Russian Legation, I arrived on the lawn of the British Legation.

Sir Claude Macdonald had hurried down to the Shuè Gate, by another route, and I missed him, but he returned to the Legation some minutes later accompanied by General

Sir Alfred Gaselee and about seventy of the 1st Sikhs. Meanwhile I had been introduced to Lady Macdonald by Captain Wray of the Royal Marine Legation Guard, who was very astonished to see me.

When approaching the town, I had brought with me two flags: a Union Jack and a white Naval ensign. I left the Union Jack hoisted on the main gate of the Chinese City, which we blew open to gain access to the Tartar Wall. I gave the white ensign to Major Scott, to be hoisted in the Legation. And it now hangs in his regiment's Mess on the Indian Frontier.

I left my pony at the Water Gate, with a Naval Signalman, who accompanied me. He waited there until sufficient bars had been removed to allow horses through.

There is something of an anti-climax in this quiet finale to the thunderous drama of the siege. An officer stops to light his pipe, before entering the green gate. A young man asks to be introduced to the Minister's wife, as if at a garden party.

But one more life was to be sacrificed to Chinese hatred and superstition. There was a delay in sending off a relief column to the Pei-tang, and Padre d'Addosio was anxious to see his comrades of the French Mission and Suor Vincenza. So he started off, all alone, on a donkey. Tung Fu-hsiang's 'braves' still held the street to the east of the Forbidden City. They stopped Padre d'Addosio and dragged him into the courtyards of Prince Tuan's palace. And there they killed him.

So the prophecy came true, that he had made before the beginning of the siege. He earned his martyr's crown.

Thus ended the Boxer movement: the last attempt of the Chinese people to oppose by force the penetration of Western civilization; the last massacre of foreigners that had a manifest and premeditated government support.

Though the explanation of the outbreak appears simple

enough, there is still much unexplained, much that will never be known. Contemporary diaries and collections of letters are interesting but unreliable. They contain as much fiction as truth. Those who knew best what was happening and those who worked hardest wrote no Memoirs.

As time passes, new elements come to light, and some of these new sources of information are of unexpected interest. In 1933–4, Zanichelli of Bologna published the correspondence of Princess Radziwill (née Castellane) with General Count de Robilant, at one time Military Attaché at the Italian embassy at Berlin. The Princess mentions the gossip of the court of St. Petersburg after Muraviev's death: she confirms the rumours of Russian intrigues with the Boxer leaders. The following letter, written from her family estate in Poland, is dated 15th August 1900:

> . . . This evening a neighbour arrived here, who has just come from St. Petersburg. He sat next to me at dinner and I asked him to tell me all he had heard about the death of Muraviev. It is certain that it was suicide. With all the means in his power, Muraviev had urged upon the Czar a policy of aggression in China, against the advice of Witte, and this because *il avait cru jouer au plus fin.* Muraviev had long come to an understanding with the Chinese Prince Tuan, and was convinced that he could count on Tuan's friendship to obtain the gradual evacuation of all foreigners from China. At the same time the Russians would push on their railway in Manchuria, which would give itself to them *for love.* . . . The trick was to have been played within two years. Unfortunately Muraviev deceived himself. Tuan did not keep his promises. The movement broke out two years too soon. Manchuria did not behave as a friend, but as an enemy. Muraviev saw all his diplomacy turn against what he had foreseen, and himself betrayed by Prince Tuan, whom he had always described to the Czar as a friend. Not knowing

how to extricate himself, he committed suicide. All this is spoken of quite openly in St. Petersburg. . . .

The Princess Radziwill's letter is interesting because in it we find for the first time, a precise accusation confirming vague suspicions. And the conspirators are mentioned by name. But it would be a mistake to accept the gossip of a dinner-table as a reliable source of history. At the court of the Czar it was forbidden to speak of politics. Yet the ladies of St. Petersburg (when not occupied with more personal matters) talked of little else. And the more sensational news was the most appreciated. That Muraviev committed suicide is not proved. After a stormy interview with his master, he may well have had a fatal heart-attack.

But ' there is no smoke without fire ', and the suspicions of a Russian conspiracy with the anti-foreign leaders is not without foundation. It is certain that Muraviev and his agents viewed the Boxer rising as a chance to strengthen their hold on Manchuria. In seizing the opportunity they were not hampered by scruples of conscience. Yet it is unlikely that there was any preconceived plan of a Russian collaboration with the Chinese. Lack of scruple does not necessarily imply a Machiavellian intelligence.

History repeats itself. The attitude of the Czar's Ministers in 1900 was similar to that of the Soviet Government in 1926–7, when Chinese nationalist leaders worked in collusion with Russian emissaries and ' advisers ' from Moscow, with the object of ousting all other foreigners from China. The only difference was that, during the Boxer movement, the Russians strove to run with the hare and hunt with the hounds, posing as victims of Chinese treachery, though they were willing to take advantage thereof.

XXI

It is easier to gain than to secure the advantages of victory.

Chinese Proverb.

NLY while their nationals were in danger and their armies faced a common enemy, was it possible for France, Great Britain, Japan, Italy and the United States to act together in cordial collaboration. Even then, the relief of the Legations might have been effected sooner, if international jealousies had not prevented the Japanese advancing alone. The Allied expeditionary force represented states having divergent interests in the Far East. Once the danger to the Legations was over, these individual interests had to take precedence. Concord in international affairs is the exception and not the rule, though the Romans dedicated to it a temple on the Capitol, and the French the finest square in Paris. (It does not follow that it was ever easy to work in harmonious agreement with the Romans or with the French.) The practical impossibility for Western nations to maintain a common front becomes evident every time they have to face the anti-foreign policy of an Oriental power. In 1900, the jealousy between Russia and Japan foreshadowed the siege of Port Arthur and the battle of Mukden. The Russians withdrew their troops from Peking before a peace had been signed with China. Though they took part, with the other powers, in the negotiations for the Peace Protocol, they also conducted secret negotiations with the Chinese, in view—as ever—of furthering their own interests in Manchuria. But the Chinese, under the pressure of Russian threats, appealed to Japan and thus revealed that Russia had been playing a double game. For the moment, her ambitions were thwarted. The agreement reached on the question of Manchuria was very different from that which the Russians had hoped to obtain. It promised a gradual evacuation by the troops of the Czar.

Meanwhile, in Peking, political jealousies were reflected in the rivalry between foreign contingents, animated with the primeval lust for plunder. In 1860, the British and French troops had looted and burned the Summer Palace, but they had not molested the peaceful inhabitants of the towns and countryside. On that occasion, only the Emperor was despoiled of his possessions. But the later expeditionary force behaved differently. In the autumn of 1900, the gates of the Forbidden City were guarded by detachments of foreign soldiers and some show was made of respecting the Imperial domain. Nevertheless, many of the pavilions were emptied of their contents, and innumerable art treasures were carried off. But the personal treasure of the Empress was untouched. It was protected, not by thick walls and strong rooms, but by a flimsy silk partition. Had they but known it, the way to the Empress' treasury lay open to the Allied troops. But an optical illusion, similar to that which hides the doors behind the Buddha in a Chinese temple, produced the appearance of a solid wall. There was something symbolical of the subtle Eastern wisdom in the trick that protected the hoard of gold and jewels, not by locks and bars, but by the deception of a false appearance. No one dreamt that among those flimsy silk panels lay the riches that Tzu-hsi had accumulated since the days when she had confiscated all the ill-gotten wealth of Sun Shun.

Outside the Palace, the citizens of Peking suffered from the violence of the foreign soldiery, only a little less than if the town had been sacked by the Taiping rebels. The destruction of property was far in excess of the actual gain to the looters. Soldiers seeking buried treasure would wantonly destroy priceless collections of porcelain, never realizing that vases of celadon and '*sang de bœuf*' could be worth more than the silver taels that they had hoped to find hoarded in the cellars. At the worst, the looting was medieval in its cruelty; at its best, it was good humoured:

'That is a fine sable coat! Bring it along.'

'But there is a Chinaman inside.'

'Give it a shake. He will fall out.'

Which he did, only too pleased to escape with his life.

Amid the riot of looting, national rivalries became more acute. At one time the British command issued an order prohibiting the French from passing through the territory occupied by them at Tientsin. The tension between British and Germans reached fever-point, over so small a matter as the shooting of a mule, by a German sentry, on a dark night, the mule not having answered to the call: 'Who goes there?'

The arrival, at the end of September, of the German field-marshal, Count von Waldersee, had the effect of concentrating the command of the allied forces, but this formal unity did not add to the cordiality of international relations.

By her flight from Peking, taking the Emperor with her, Tzu-hsi had added to the difficulties of the foreign Powers. The 'Government' followed the Empress into the interior. She could sign decrees and issue proclamations, wherever she might be. On the other hand, the Chinese representatives in the peace negotiations could always hold up proceedings, in order to obtain the approval of the Court. These representatives were Prince Ching and Li Hung-chang. The former had left the capital at the time of the Emperor's flight, and it was with the greatest difficulty that he was persuaded (by Sir Robert Hart) to return. In Peking, he lived under Japanese guard, and declared himself so hard up that money had to be lent him for his personal expenses. Li Hung-chang had been summoned by the Empress from Canton, and after much delay he arrived in Tientsin, where he was given a guard taken from the Russian contingent. The fact that the two Chinese representatives appeared to be held as hostages by the Japanese and the Russians, gave rise to much suspicion among the other nationalities, who could not dispose of such pawns in their game.

Acting with what was—under the circumstances—remarkable solidarity, the foreign Powers exacted from China the reparations and indemnities which are embodied in the

Protocol of 1901. To guard against the danger of another attempt to wipe out the diplomatic community in Peking, it was decided that a special quarter should be set aside within the capital, defended by battlemented walls and a surrounding *glacis* and permanently garrisoned by Legation Guards; also that the railway line between Peking and the sea should be patrolled by foreign troops.

The Chinese and Manchu officials, guilty of having favoured the anti-foreign movement, were executed, ordered to commit suicide, exiled or degraded. Those who were already dead were posthumously degraded. Envoys of princely rank were sent to Germany and to Japan, to apologize for the murder of the Minister von Ketteler and Councillor Sujimura.

The fact of being a near kinsman of the Empress saved Prince Tuan from the death sentence he so richly deserved. He was stripped of his honours and sent in perpetual banishment to Turkestan. His son was deprived of his rank as Heir-Apparent. Once more the shade of Tung-chih remained without a ministrant at the family altar.

Li Lien-ying's pro-Boxer activities were well known, but the Chief Eunuch found a protector in the enemy's camp. The Russian Legation opposed the inclusion of Li's name on the black list that was presented to the Chinese by the foreign representatives, during the negotiations that preceded the signing of the Protocol. Baron de Giers did all in his power to help the Chinese in their attempts to evade promulgation of the 'Punishment Edict', as well as of the Edict that suspended all official examinations during two years (this suspension implied, for the Chinese Government, a considerable 'loss of face').

Besides Li Lien-ying, several other culprits found an official protector in the representative of the Czar. Count Lamsdorff, who had succeeded Muraviev as Russian Minister for Foreign Affairs, declared to the British Ambassador at St. Petersburg that his government took no interest in missionaries. As most of the foreigners who had been massacred in the interior of China were missionaries, Russia declined to associate herself with the other Powers in demanding the punishment of the assassins. By this attitude the Russian Government sought to obtain the consent of the Chinese to her policy of expansion in Manchuria.

The Chinese Government erected an expiatory monument, in the form of an arch of white marble (*pai-lo*), in honour of the German Minister, von Ketteler. It was put up over the Hata Mên street, at the point where the Minister had been killed. The Republican Government of China hastened to demolish the arch, when they saw fit to join the Allies and declared war on Germany, in 1917. The arch was then reconstructed elsewhere, after the inscription (in Chinese, German and Latin) had been removed. But even before it was taken down, and passers-by might still read how Baron von Ketteler had been traitorously done to death, the actual value of this monument as an object lesson was doubtful. If one asked one's rickshaw-coolie, for example, to whom that monument had been erected, he was almost sure to answer that the *pai-lo* had been set up to honour the memory of the Chinaman who had killed the German Minister.

All the ability, so characteristic of the Chinese, in glossing over unpleasant facts and adapting history to suit the requirements of their dynastic and national prestige, was brought to bear, with its accustomed success, on the inconvenient truths of the Boxer movement. Tzu-hsi herself supervised the preparation of the Annals (which however were never published till the close of the reigning dynasty) and bowdlerized them to her complete satisfaction. A 'revolution in the Palace' had compelled the Court to absent itself temporarily and to accomplish a tour in the West.

At an international ceremony in Peking, during the Allied occupation, a Chinese official, who was present, took it upon himself to make a speech in which he expressed, much to the astonishment of the foreign officers, his sincere gratitude to the Powers who had come to China's aid in putting down the Boxer rebellion.

When the time came for the evacuation of Peking by the international forces, it was decided that, during a transitional period, the foreign troops should remain in the capital, even after the entry of the Chinese regulars. The joint occupation was intended to prevent the spreading of a report that the foreign troops had fled on the approach of the Chinese. The precaution was justified. A town in the interior had been occupied by French troops. When these were recalled, permitting the Chinese to advance, the latter brought with them a large stone on which was engraved an inscription to the effect that, on their arrival, the foreign devils had fled in confusion and defeat. The stone was set up in the market-place to the great admiration of the townsfolk. But this event came to the knowledge of the French officer who had but recently departed. He sent back a Corporal of the Zouaves, who, although quite alone, intimated to the Chinese that they must demolish the stone. This they did, with perfect good-humour. Later on, they doubtless set up another stone, with the same inscription.

The Court remained absent from Peking until the Peace Protocol had been signed, and for some months after that. In those days, Li Lien-ying went in fear of his life. Only when he had been repeatedly assured by his correspondents in Peking that the Allies would not insist on his execution, did he cease from pointing out to the Old Buddha that it would be extremely dangerous to return.

The exile from her capital was accompanied, during the first few weeks, by discomfort and privations, which lent a note of real sincerity to the expressions of penitence and of sorrow that appeared in the Imperial decrees. There is a story of how, on one occasion, the Imperial cortège halted at a small village, where, for some reason, no food could be procured. After much fruitless parleying, the village barber stepped into the breach, and offered his scanty store. In gratitude for this timely help Tzu-hsi allowed her modest benefactor to join the Imperial cortège, meaning to reward him, when fortune smiled once more. The barber's name was Chang-hsun, and he became in time a military commander of some renown, with a following of 'braves', who were the terror of the countryside. After the Republic had been proclaimed in China, in 1912, Chang-hsun was one of the last to remain faithful to the fallen dynasty. He refused to cut off his pig-tail, and in the summer of 1917 made an abortive attempt (it was said, with the help of German agents) to replace the Emperor upon the throne. For one brief day, thanks to a village barber, the standards with the five-clawed dragon floated once more over Peking, in the fifth year of the

Republic. And it was noticeable how pleased the people were, to bring out the Imperial emblems.

At the beginning of her *hegira,* the Empress established herself at Tai-yuan Fu, capital of the province of Shan-si. This town had recently been the scene of massacres on a large scale. In the courtyard of the official Yamen, which was placed at the disposal of Her Majesty, fifty-seven missionaries had been put to death by the Governor, Yu Hsien. He had killed some of them with his own hand, after they had been expressly brought to Tai-yuan Fu from the surrounding district. Proud of the zeal which he had shown in carrying out the orders from Peking, Yu Hsien showed the Empress the great double-handed sword that the executioner (and he, himself) had used on the occasion of the massacre. Among those present, in the Empress' suite, was the son of Prince Tuan, the Ta A-ko, who in those days had not yet been degraded from his rank as Heir-Apparent to the throne. He caught up the sword and began running round the courtyard, imitating the action of the executioner in cutting off the heads of the foreign devils. But that ill-timed re-evocation of an unfortunate episode did not fall in with the Old Buddha's present mood, and the tactless boy was summoned to desist. A few days later, fearing that the foreigners might send a punitive expedition into Shan-si, the Empress decided to start off again on her travels, and to set up her Court at Hsi-an Fu, in Shen-si.

Meanwhile, the situation was improving. Reports from Peking showed how Prince Ching and the aged Li Hung-chang had taken advantage of the jealousies within the allied camp. Much to the astonishment of the Court, no cession of territory was demanded of China; the sum required for the payment of indemnities might be procured through the raising of the customs tariff; no sanctions were imposed with regard to the Empress and the Chief Eunuch. An Oriental invader would not have shown himself so magnanimous.

At Hsi-an Fu, the Court took up its normal functions, though living on a less luxurious scale. The receipts of taxes were brought there and collected by the eunuchs. The Court lived frugally, spending only two hundred taels a day on food. Tzu-hsi refurnished her wardrobe and let her nails grow long again. She had cut them short, at the beginning of her flight from Peking, as their length might have betrayed her social status!

One of the minor officials in the Imperial retinue celebrated each successive day of the Court's residence at Hsi-an Fu, in a short poem. And these poems were afterwards published in book form. The author bemoans in poetic phrase the sad fate of the Empress Dowager, and speaks feelingly of her sufferings. But his account of her daily activities does not correspond to the doleful tone of the commentary. Tzu-hsi is described as being always in good spirits and showing great benevolence towards the simple country folk.

The return journey from Hsi-an Fu to Peking was commenced in September 1901. The distance to be traversed was roughly seven hundred miles, but progress was very slow; not more than twenty-five miles a day. Roads in China are almost impassable after the summer rains, and the Imperial cortège was encumbered with much baggage. Such impedimenta had been non-existent on the day of the flight from the Forbidden City, but in a year's time the baggage train had grown to colossal proportions, comprising not only the personal effects of the Empress Dowager, the Emperor, the Empress and their attendants, but also the tributes in silks and jade and furs and bullion, which had come in from the provinces.

Forty years before, the youthful Yehonala's return journey from Jehol had been accomplished in haste, in fear of an ambuscade, and under the incubus of an uncertain future. This time, everything went pleasantly for the Dowager Empress. Halts at towns by the way were long and frequent, and at Kai-feng, in Ho-nan, the Court assisted at a theatrical performance, and a meeting was held of the Grand Council.

As the cortège advanced, it assumed an almost triumphal magnificence. Tzu-hsi and the ladies of the Court crossed the Yellow River in a barge, expressly built for the occasion, shaped like a dragon and richly gilded and lacquered. Garlands of flowers floated on the surface of the river, and, on the banks, the Imperial standards rose proudly against an autumn sky. Bonzes intoned litanies and burnt incense in honour of the Dragon who rules over the waters. On land, the roads were levelled and broadened to make travelling easier. The country-folk came in crowds to witness the unaccustomed sight of the Old Buddha and the Son of Heaven moving in state across the Empire.

The last part of the journey was accomplished by rail. This was the first time that a ruler of China had used such a means of locomotion. The Empress was in excellent spirits and insisted on superintending personally the disposal of her luggage in the railway trucks that had been allotted in its transport.

The presence of soldiers in the corridors of the train and even in her own special car did not appear to inconvenience or to displease her. But she noticed that an extra car had been added during a halt at a station, and, on inquiring the reason, she was told that it was for the benefit of Yuan-shi-kai and other high officials, who were now travelling with her and were inconveniently crowded. She promptly expressed her disapproval and had the car taken off again.

(Yuan-shi-kai's request for an additional car was characteristic of the attitude assumed by Chinese officialdom towards trains. In their opinion, every military commander or high official ought to have a car, and not merely a compartment, to himself. If he is a very important official indeed, he ought to have a special train.)

To prepare for the arrival of the Emperor and Empress Mother in Peking a new station had been set up, near the old terminus of Ma-chia-pu, to the south of the city. A gorgeous pavilion was constructed and furnished with thrones of gold lacquer, jars of cloisonné, and vases of fine porcelain. The road from the station to the Imperial Palace was lined with troops who knelt reverently as the cortège swept by. In conformity with the usual custom on such occasions, many of the foreign Ministers issued an order, warning their nationals against showing themselves in the vicinity of the station or along the road, where the Emperor and Empress might be expected to pass. But no one paid any attention to this official communication, and most of the foreigners who were then in Peking went up on to the wall, above the Ch'ien Mên gate, in order to watch the procession from the curved lunette that protected the gateway. At the beginning of the siege of the Legations, a fire had occurred in that spot, destroying a line of shops round the outer wall. Of the two towers, that rose from the wall itself and from the lunette, only the former

Photo: Hartung, Pekin.

THE CH'IEN-MEN: THE PRINCIPAL GATE OF THE TARTAR CITY AS SEEN FROM THE ENTRANCE TO THE IMPERIAL PALACE

remained standing. The outer tower had been gutted by the flames and only a part of the base remained, with a few deep, square windows, where once the Manchu archers stood at arms. It was here, among the smoke-blackened ruins, that the foreigners congregated. Among them was a young Italian midshipman, Don Rodolfo Borghese, who described the scene as follows:

> There was a strong wind and much dust. But all Peking had collected on the top of the wall, to enjoy the spectacle, which was really very fine and imposing. We could not have chosen a better place to watch it from. First to arrive were the Manchu Bannermen on their fiery little horses. Next came a group of Chinese officials in gala robes, and finally the imperial palanquins, which advanced at an almost incredible speed between the two lines of kneeling soldiers. The higher the rank of the person carried in a palanquin, the faster he should go. The Court chairs, on that memorable occasion, seemed to move as fast as the Tartar cavalry.
>
> When they reached the enclosure between the wall and the outer lunette, the chairs halted and the Emperor and Empress stepped down, to carry out the ceremony, prescribed by the Rites for a home-coming, that is to say, to burn incense and recite some prayers, in the tiny temple built up against the side of the wall. In that temple there was a shrine to the tutelary gods of the Manchus. As she got out of her chair, the Empress glanced up at the smoke-blackened walls and saw us: a row of foreigners, watching her arrival from behind the ramparts. The eunuchs appeared to be trying to get her to move on, as it was not seemly that she should remain there in full view of everybody. But the Empress was not to be hurried, and continued to stand between two of her ladies, who held her up under the arms on either side, not because she needed any support, but because such is the custom in China, when a great personage appears in public on a ceremonial occasion. The Emperor stood and waited a little distance off.

At last she condescended to move, but before entering the temple where the bonzes were all ready to begin the ceremony, she stopped once more and, looking up at us, lifted her closed hands under her chin, and made a series of little bows.

The effect of this gesture was astonishing. We had all gone up on to the wall, in the hopes of catching a glimpse, as she passed, of the terrible Empress, whom the West considered almost an enemy of the human race. But we had been impressed by the magnificence of the swiftly moving pageant, and by the beauty of the picturesque group, in palanquins of yellow satin flashing with gold. Something told us that the return of the Court to Peking marked a turning-point in history, and in our breathless interest, we forgot our resentment against the woman who was responsible for so much evil. That little bow, made to us who were watching her, and the graceful gesture of the closed hands, took us by surprise. From all along the wall there came an answering, spontaneous, burst of applause. The Empress appeared pleased. She remained there for a few moments longer, looking up and smiling. Then she disappeared within the temple.

Don Rodolfo Borghese was right. The return of the Court to Peking, after the Boxer troubles, was indeed a turning-point in history, and Tzu-hsi's little bow and smile marked the beginning of a new policy.

XXII

The East bowed low before the blast
In patient, deep disdain;
She let the legions thunder past
And plunged in thought again.

MATTHEW ARNOLD.

JUNG LU once asked the Empress Dowager what she would do if Peking were captured by foreigners (this conversation, which occurred during the siege of the Legations, is reported in Ching Shan's diary). The Empress, whose scholarship was seldom at fault, quoted a classic of the Han dynasty:

If the Emperor wishes to gain the allegiance of other countries, he can only do so by convincing their rulers that he possesses the three cardinal virtues of Government and by displaying the five allurements.

The three cardinal virtues of Government are: to simulate

affection, to express honeyed sentiments, and to treat one's inferiors as equals.

The five allurements are: Presents of chariots and rich robes, to tempt the eye; rich food and banquets, to tempt the palate; musical maidens, to tempt the ear; fine houses and beautiful women, to tempt the instinct of luxury; and the presence of the Emperor at the table of the foreign ruler, to tempt his pride.

Tzu-hsi's exceptional talent for governing was never so apparent as during those difficult years, after the tragedy for which she was in great part responsible. The animus against her among foreigners was, at one time, no less bitter than the feeling among the allied nations against Kaiser Wilhelm during the war. And yet her return to the capital was urgently desired even by her enemies. Everyone realized that only this strong-willed, misguided old woman could hold the tottering Empire together. On her part, she realized how great had been her mistake. Without regrets or hesitation, she began at once to set her house in order.

The little incident at the Ch'ien Mên, when Tzu-hsi bowed and smiled to the group of foreigners who were watching her from the wall, shows how she returned to Peking with the deliberate intention of effacing the catastrophic impression made on foreign opinion by her support of the Boxers. The ancient wisdom of the Sons of Han was hers. She could express 'honeyed sentiments' when the occasion required it.

The British authorities, with their vast experience of dealing with Oriental nations, foresaw that some attempt would be made by the Chinese to bring about that oblivion that comes to the lotus-eaters. In repairing the damage done to the Legation by Chinese artillery, they purposely omitted to restore a corner of the outer wall, which had been riddled with bullets. This corner still remains with the marks left on it by the siege. And on the half-ruined masonry is written: *Lest we forget!*

But mankind is quick to forget. The survivors of 1900 left Peking and were scattered over the world. The new arrivals found a China all smiles and sentiment. And Tzu-hsi took pains to make herself popular.

It is not surprising that foreigners fell under the charm of her personality. Their bitterness disappeared, their prejudices melted away, when an Empress laid herself out to captivate and to seduce. It was easy for her to capture the sympathies of the not very sophisticated women-folk of the foreign community. They would go to her receptions, animated by a sense of righteous indignation against the ruler who had committed such unpardonable crimes. They would feel the thrill of entering forbidden precincts, and be agreeably surprised to find themselves in the presence of a beautifully dressed old lady, with keen, shrewd eyes, the most gracious manner and the most winning smile. They would move through the pavilions of the palace, among silent eunuchs in embroidered robes, and they would gaze out over the lotus-covered lakes, while the breeze brought to them the muffled boom of temple bells. And then, as at the touch of some fairy wand, the lure of China would draw their thoughts away from all bitterness and resentment. That magic appeal to the senses, that veil of mystery, that charm of grandeur and riches and power undreamt of . . . how could poor little Mrs. So-and-so resist? She would drink it all in ecstatically, even though, to keep up her national prestige, she might pretend to be unimpressed. A few hours later would find her at her desk, writing against time to catch the mail, and straining her limited vocabulary to convey to Mother, or Sister, how wonderful it all had been!

Part of Tzu-hsi's policy of reconciliation became apparent in a new attitude towards Western learning and Western methods. Many of the reforms which Kuang-hsu had attempted in 1898, and which had been cut short in so ruthless a fashion, reappeared now under other names and were accomplished by order of the Empress. Her prestige was such, and her methods so well attuned to the mentality of her people, that even the powerful Manchu and Chinese bureaucracies dared not lift their heads in opposition. And probably the officials realized that, at heart, the Empress felt as they did about the vaunted changes, and that her action was inspired, not so much by the conviction that the reforms were desirable in themselves, as by the hope that they might serve to conciliate the foreigners and the more advanced elements of public opinion at home. This attitude towards Western learning was typical of what J. O. P. Bland calls 'the Chinese mandarin's adroitness in protective mimicry'. It was in harmony with the sentiments of the greater part of the Chinese people, who naturally preferred their own old changeless ways.

But whatever might be the feelings of the Empress and of her people, perforce the Old China was disappearing, and with it the men of the old régime. Li Hung-chang died at the conclusion of the peace, while the Court was on its way to the capital. He was accorded unprecedented posthumous honours. Jung Lu died in 1903. His merits in safeguarding the lives of foreigners during the siege were not recognized till long after his death.

In these two men, the Empress lost her most trusted councillors. And she, herself, was growing old. Using an old proverbial expression, the Chinese compared the last years of her reign to 'the sun descending the mountain sides'.

The little concubine of other days had become a personage of world-wide renown. Much of the past was forgiven. The present was more tranquil, less mysterious, less dramatic. Kuang-hsu was no longer a prisoner on the Ocean Terrace. He had his own quarters and servants, and was allowed a certain revenue from the public funds. The Empress Mother 'assisted' him in affairs of State.

In 1903 Tzu-hsi consented to have her portrait painted by an American, Miss Katherine Carl. The artist had to observe the prescribed rules, as set forth by Chinese authorities, in the pose of her subject and the reproduction thereof. An Empress had to be represented, seated on the throne, in the conventional attitude of the Audience Chamber. No detail of the magnificent robes might be omitted. The ideas of the Empress and those held by Miss Carl, on the art of portrait painting, were very different. Tzu-hsi was also a producer of those 'silent poems' which (in the Oriental simile) are pictures, and she was imbued with the traditional precepts of Chinese art. She would not allow that, in her portrait, there should be any shadows on the face, for the Chinese do not seek to obtain, by means of chiaroscuro, the appearance of a material solidity. Laurence Binyon writes: 'Not to represent facts, but to suggest a poetic idea (often perfumed, so to speak, with reminiscence of some actual poem), has ever been the Chinese artist's aim.'

The circumstances in which she worked and the necessity

of conforming to local traditions and prejudice, rendered the task of the foreign artist one of great difficulty; nevertheless, Miss Carl's portrait of the Empress Dowager is a fine picture of its kind. It was sent to the St. Louis exhibition and became the property of the American Government. When the framed painting started on its journey, it had to be carried in a vertical position. All those who saw it pass, bowed to the ground. Even the Emperor had to kneel before the finished portrait, as before the person it represented. A special train took it from Peking to the sea, where it embarked.

Miss Carl wrote a book of Memoirs, describing the days passed in the Palace, where she resided while engaged in painting the famous portrait. In her literary work, no less than in her painting, the author proves that she possesses powers of sympathetic observation. She makes it quite clear that she had fallen under the charm of her surroundings and that she was 'thrilled' at her own good fortune in being able to see the Empress daily at close quarters. Her narrative has all the interest of first-hand information, and is full of passages that give the personal touch. Here are some characteristic extracts, describing the Empress in her daily life:

Whether she has slept well or ill, she rises at six o'clock; for the morning is devoted to business, and she never misses an audience. On rising, she takes a bowl of hot milk, or lotus-root porridge; then her maids and tiring-women begin her toilet for the Audience. This is the '*grande toilette*' for the day, for full dress is worn by Chinese in the morning, and in the evening they wear simple gowns. When her toilet is finished, the young Empress and ladies having 'assisted' (from without) at her 'levee', she comes out into the Throne-room and receives their morning greeting. The

Emperor then comes to pay his respects to the Great Ancestress, and together they go in state, accompanied by all the Ladies of the Court, to the Audience Hall. The Ladies of the Court remain outside the great hall until the Audience is finished, when they accompany Her Majesty to the Throne-room. The business of the day is then over. Her Majesty lays aside her robes of State and gives herself up to duties connected with the Palace. . . . She would overlook the baskets of flowers and fruit sent to the Palace daily, select some to be sent as presents, and send others to the eunuchs of the kitchen to be cooked. Then she would look at new rolls of silk, just arrived from the Imperial looms, or examine new articles of toilet, fresh from the workshops of the palace-tailors. Sometimes she would play a game, of which she seemed very fond, and of which I know no counterpart. It was played on a large, square board, covered with white silk and painted in fantastic designs, representing Earth and Fairyland. The object of the game was to get an ivory chessman, representing 'man', into Fairyland. The length of the move was decided by throwing dice. There was no box for throwing the dice; they were taken in the hands and thrown into a jade bowl. The numbers uppermost were counted and the move made. She would play this game with the Princesses; and sometimes two of the high eunuchs, who were proficient, would be called in to make up the number. The game was played for money, but if Her Majesty won, the others did not pay. If, however, they won, she paid and at once. She was ever a cheerful giver. . . .

. . . .

The Empress Dowager only eats two solid meals a day—luncheon and dinner. These were exactly similar. The dishes, as far as I could see, were identical; but they were so numerous, and of such variety, one could change the menu by eating different dishes. The hours of these two meals were very irregular; in fact Her Majesty had no fixed hour for anything, except rising and attendance at the Audience Hall. 'Early rice', as the Chinese call luncheon, was served the Empress Dowager at any time between half-past ten and half-past twelve. 'Late rice', or dinner, was ordered with the same irregularity. She was very fond of nuts and fruits, and ate them between meals, when she drank tea, hot milk, and certain fruit juices.

. . . .

On one of our promenades in the park I saw a curious instance of her wonderful personal magnetism and her power over animals. A bird had escaped from its cage, and some eunuchs were making efforts to catch it, when Her Majesty and suite came into that part of the grounds. The eunuchs had found it impossible to entice the bird back into its cage; nor would it come upon a long stick with a perch attached, which they held up near the tree where it rested. The eunuchs scattered at the approach of Her Majesty and she inquired into the cause of their being there. The Chief Eunuch explained what they were doing and the Empress Dowager said: 'I will call it down.' I thought this was a vain boast, and in my heart I pitied her. She was so accustomed to have the whole world bow to her, she fancied even a bird in the grounds would obey her mandates, and I watched to see how she would take her defeat. She had a long, wand-like stick, which had been cut from a sapling and freshly stripped of its bark. She loved the faint forest odour of these freshly cut sticks, and in the spring often had one when she went out. They were long and slender, with a crook at the top. I used to think she looked like the pictures of fairies when she walked with those long, white wands. She would use them for pointing out a flower she wished the eunuchs to gather, or for tracing designs on the gravel when she sat down. To-day she held the wand she carried aloft and made a low, bird-like sound with her lips, never taking her eyes off the bird. She had the most musical of voices, and its flute-like sound seemed like a magical magnet to the bird. He fluttered and began to descend from bough to bough until he lighted upon the crook of her wand, when she gently moved her other hand nearer and nearer, until it finally rested on her finger!

I had been watching with breathless attention, and so tense and absorbed had I become that the sudden cessation, when the bird finally came upon her finger, caused me a throb of almost pain. No one else, however, of her entourage seemed to think this anything extraordinary. After a few moments she handed the bird to one of the eunuchs, and we continued on our promenade.

. . . .

Her Majesty was looking tired and anxious these days; her Audiences were unusually long, and despatches were arriving all day long. She would often go to the gardens immediately after the Audience, for solitary walks unattended by the ladies, and when she went out for a walk, accompanied by the Empress and the Princesses, she would sit distraught and abstracted before the finest views and those she loved most. She seemed absent-minded and when some eunuch with an official message would kneel before her, awaiting her order to deliver his message, she would recall herself with an effort. One day, when we were out, after days of this anxiety, and she was sitting alone in front of the 'Peony Mountain',[1] the Empress and Princesses standing in a group at a little distance, she looked a pathetic figure. Her strong face looked tired and worn. Her arms hung listlessly by her side, and she seemed almost to have given up. I saw her furtively brush away a tear. The days were so alike each other at the Palace, the Chinese dates being different from ours, I lost my reckoning until I had a Tientsin paper, and I saw that the date on which the Russians had promised to evacuate Manchuria had passed away and they were making no move towards doing so; and that there were rumours of war between Japan and Russia. This, then, must be what was weighing upon the mind of the Empress Dowager.

Miss Carl's description of the Empress, in a mood of sadness and discouragement, shows her to us at a moment of grave political anxiety.

The Russians had gone back on their word. In April

[1] *Note.*—The Peony Terraces were perhaps the most beautiful ornament of the Summer Palace. The flowers of a deeper hue were planted near the shore of the lake and the colours were graduated up the hill-side, so that the lighter hues were at the top. This arrangement gave the illusion of a landscape fading away into a far distance.

1902 they had signed an agreement, by which they undertook to retire, within a year, from the territories in Manchuria, occupied by them during the Boxer troubles. But despatches from the Governor of Mukden informed the Empress that the Russians were making no preparations to depart on the date agreed upon. Once more a storm was brewing in Manchuria. The Japanese were making preparations to take back by force the territories that they had already conquered in 1894 and had been obliged to restore to China. Their international status had been much improved after the stipulation, in 1902, of a Convention with Great Britain 'for the preservation of peace in the Far East, and of the integrity of China'.

In a difficult situation, there was no one left to whom Tzu-hsi could turn for advice. Li Hung-chang was dead. Jung Lu was dead. She must have felt very lonely in those days, and very old.

And doubtless she realized, though dimly, that for herself and for her Empire, the end was near. Foreign soldiers mounted guard over the Legations in Peking. Foreign troops were massing for the conflict that was to decide who should be supreme in the lands that had been the cradle of the Manchu race. The provinces where Nurachu had welded together his tribes to conquer China and found a new dynasty were traversed by foreign railways and garrisoned by foreign troops. And this because there was no longer, in Peking, an Emperor who could take command of his armies and lead them to victory. There was only an old Empress, sad and weary, in a eunuch-ridden Court.

War broke out, between Russia and Japan, in 1904, and the Russians were beaten on land and sea. The Czar had always declared, doubtless in all sincerity, that he did not wish for war. But he appeared to think that this declaration was sufficient. He never did anything to prevent war, and when it broke out, he could do little to ensure victory, but wept at the news of each successive defeat.

In June 1905, the belligerents accepted the mediation of the President of the United States. Two treaties followed: the Treaty of Portsmouth, by which Russia ceded to Japan the territories which she had occupied in Manchuria, and the Treaty of Peking, by which China signified her assent to what had been stipulated at Portsmouth. On the whole this solution appeared advantageous to China. It served to mask the fact that Manchuria had virtually ceased to be an integral part of the State over which a Chinese government ruled.

XXIII

When the tree falls, the shade is gone.

Chinese Proverb.

MONG the higher officials, no less than among the Court eunuchs, there were many who looked forward with apprehension to the day when the Empress Dowager should pass away and Kuang-hsu should take up once more the reins of government. It was in the natural order of things that he should survive his 'Great Ancestress' and resume the policy of reform, which had been brought to so brusque a termination in 1898.

In Miss Carl's memoirs, she gives a description of the Emperor, as she knew him, and she alludes to the possibility that he might be playing a waiting game:

His Majesty the Emperor Kuang-hsu was nearing the completion of his thirty-second year when I was first presented to him. I found him an interesting study, but not to the degree of Her Majesty the Empress Dowager, who has charm and is so fascinating. The Emperor is singularly devoid of this quality of 'charm' and has but little personal magnetism. . . . In person he is of slight and elegant figure, not more than five feet four in height. He has a well-shaped head, with the intellectual qualities well developed, a high brow, with large brown eyes and rather drooping lids, not at all Chinese in form and setting. His nose is high and, like most members of the Imperial Family, is of the so-called 'noble' type. A rather large mouth with thin lips, the upper short with a proud curve, the lower slightly protruding; a clear-cut, thin jaw, a strong chin a little beyond the line of the forehead, with not an ounce of superfluous flesh on the whole face, give him an ascetic air and, in spite of his rather delicate physique, an appearance of great reserve strength. . . . His luxuriant very long hair, a characteristic of the Manchus, is beautifully silky and glossy and always arranged with the greatest care. It is said he much dislikes being shaved, but tradition, immutable in China, does not allow a man under forty, even if he be the 'Son of Heaven', to wear a moustache or whiskers. Like all well-bred Chinese, he has small feet and hands, the latter long and thin and most expressive. The Emperor dresses with extreme neatness and great simplicity, wearing few ornaments and no jewels except on State occasions. His face is kindly in expression, but the glance from his rather heavy-lidded eyes is shrewd and intelligent. His manner is shy and retiring, but this does not seem to be so much from a lack of confidence in himself as from the absence of that magnetic quality which gives one an appearance of assurance.

He seemed to me the ideal of what one would imagine an Oriental potentate to be, whose title is the 'Son of Heaven'. There is a Sphinx-like quality to his smile. In his eyes one sees the calm, half-contemptuous outlook on the world of the fatalist. There is an abstractness in the subtility of his regard, an abstractness that embodies one's idea of the 'Spirit of the Orient'. At first it is difficult to tell whether this comes from a sense of power or from a knowledge of the lack of it, but that firm and fleshless jaw, that ascetic face and keen eye, show there must be reserve strength, that there can be no lack of power, should he wish to exert it. Over his whole face there is a look of self-repression, which has almost reached a state of passivity.

Does he dream of future greatness for his Empire ? Does he feel that though his first efforts at governing have failed, he can bide his time—that all things come to him who waits ? It almost seems so ! He appears to fully realize, now, that he made a mistake in the choice of his instruments and time, in his efforts for progress. But the look of eternal patience in the half-veiled regard of those large eyes seems to show that he will yet try to accomplish China's salvation—that he is but waiting his opportunity.

Kuang-hsu's original initiative in the matter of reform had received a new justification and a new encouragement from the victory of the Japanese over the Russians. Even the most reactionary of the Chinese and Manchu officials realized that the Empire of the Rising Sun could not have obtained a success in arms over a Western power, had it not assimilated the teaching of the West itself, especially in military and naval matters. Therefore it behoved China to follow her neighbour's example.

It was not, however, the fear of drastic changes that made certain officials and some of the Court eunuchs anxious as to the future (had not Tzu-hsi herself embarked on a policy of reform ?). It was the fear that the Emperor might revenge himself on those who had betrayed him in 1898, as on those who had ill-treated him in the bitter days of his misfortune.

There is no proof, or even any circumstantial evidence, to justify the suspicion that Kuang-hsu did not die a natural death. But on the other hand it was perhaps no mere coincidence that, when Tzu-hsi's health began to fail and it

Photo : Hartung, Pekin.

AN ALTAR IN THE IMPERIAL MAUSOLEUM

appeared probable that she would not live much longer, Kuang-hsu also should have sickened and died, on the 23rd of November, 1908.

On the last day, when he felt his end approaching, he wrote on a piece of paper the following words:

We were the second son of the Prince Ch'un when the Empress Dowager selected Us for the Throne. She has always hated Us. But for Our misery of the past ten years Yuan Shi Kai is responsible and one other. When the time comes, I desire that Yuan be summarily beheaded.

The Emperor's consort took the paper from his hand. His dying wish was not carried out.

When he lay on his death-bed and could no longer speak, those who assisted him noticed that he kept moving the first finger of his right hand, as if drawing circles in the air. It may have been an unconscious movement. But the first character of Yuan-shi-kai's name, *Yuan,* means 'round', or 'rotundity', or 'circle' (it is the same character that we find in the name of the Old Summer Palace). So the story got about how, till the very end, the Emperor kept repeating, with his dying gesture, that hated name: Yuan, Yuan, Yuan. . . .

The Rites prescribed that, at the moment of death, the Emperor should be clothed in the Robes of Longevity. But Kuang-hsu, in his last moments, refused to be disturbed. The ceremonial robes had to be put on after death.

Although her health, of late, had given cause for anxiety, it is probable that Tzu-hsi hoped to live many years after the demise of Kuang-hsu. Once more she chose a child as heir to the throne. Little Pu-yi, tenth of the Manchu Emperors, was the son of Prince Ch'un, who had married a daughter of Jung Lu. This Prince Ch'un was a brother of Kuang-hsu, and bore the same title as their father (the 'Seventh Prince'). At the meeting of the Grand Council, to discuss the election of a new Emperor, Yuan-shi-kai upheld the candidature of Prince Pu-lùn, pointing out the desirability of nominating an adult Emperor. But Tzu-hsi, as usual, imposed her own choice. By placing his grandson on the throne, she wished to render posthumous honour to Jung Lu.

The little Emperor's father, Prince Ch'un, was named adviser to the throne, and given some executive powers. He was very different, in appearance and in character, from his brother Kuang-hsu. After the signing of the Peace Protocol, in 1901, he had been charged with the mission of penitence to Germany, where he journeyed to present the apologies of the Chinese Government, for the assassination of Baron von Ketteler. The German Government desired that the Chinese Envoy, on this occasion, should perform the *ko-tow*, prostrating himself at the feet of the Kaiser. But Prince Ch'un bluntly refused (not without reason, as the German and other Envoys had always declined to prostrate themselves before the Son of Heaven). The Germans did not insist in their demand, and the fact of having got the best of this small argument gave to the Chinese delegation an air of success, somewhat out of keeping with their mission of penitence.

His mission abroad did not give to Prince Ch'un any greater breadth of view in political affairs; and it was well known that he shared some of his late brother's feelings toward Yuan-shi-kai. This explains why the latter would have preferred the selection of Prince Pu-lùn, to succeed to the throne, rather than the infant son of a man whose resentment might become dangerous in the near future.

The old problem of finding an heir to Tung-chih, which had given so much trouble in the past, was solved by a stroke of the pen. Tzu-hsi declared that the new Emperor should worship at the two shrines of Kuang-hsu and of Tung-chih. Such a thing had never been heard of before, but after so many years of reign, the Empress might well create a new precedent.

On the day after the death of Kuang-hsu, Tzu-hsi worked hard. She presided over the Grand Council and prepared edicts, in the new Emperor's name, by which she herself was given the title of Great Empress Mother. The old title of Empress Mother was passed on to Kuang-hsu's widow.

Tzu-hsi appeared to be completely recovered from her late indisposition. But she was suddenly seized by a fainting fit, and on coming back to consciousness, she realized that her end was near. She then gave out her last decrees, establishing the relative positions of Prince Ch'un, as Regent, and of the Empress Mother. She gave orders to prepare her own valedictory message to her people. When it was submitted to her for approval, she added the following paragraph with her own hand:

Looking back upon the memories of the last fifty years, I perceive how calamities from within and aggression from without have come upon Us in relentless succession. The new Emperor is an infant, just reaching the age when wise instruction is of the highest importance. . . . His Majesty must devote himself to studying the interests of his country and refrain from giving way to grief. It is my earnest prayer that he diligently pursue his studies and that he may hereafter add fresh lustre to the glorious achievements of his Ancestors.

Mourning to be worn for twenty-seven days only.

Here and Obey!

When the end drew near, they asked her, as the custom was, to pronounce her last words. She answered: 'Never again allow a woman to hold the supreme power in the State. It is against the house-law of Our dynasty and should be forbidden. Be careful not to allow eunuchs to meddle in Government matters. The Ming dynasty was brought to ruin by eunuchs, and its fate should be a warning to my people.'

So died, in her seventy-third year, Yehonala, surnamed Tzu-hsi, Great Empress Mother of China. Before her last breath was spent, they dressed her in the ceremonial Robes of Longevity, and, in dying, her face was turned towards the south.

Tzu-hsi's funeral offered a gorgeous spectacle: red robes of bearers, yellow robes of lamaist priests, silver and gold of rich embroideries. The Chinese bring to a funeral the colours of a sunset. From all over Asia came missions to render homage to the dead.

She was buried in the Eastern Tombs (the Tung-ling) not far from the tomb of the Emperor Ch'ien-lung.

Li Lien-ying, old and weary, preceded the Imperial bier to the region of the tombs, carrying the Empress' favourite dog, Moo-tan (peony), a yellow and white pekingese with a white spot on its forehead. Thus was observed a precedent set nine hundred years before, for on the death of the Emperor T'ai Tsung of the Sung dynasty, his little dog, T'ao Hua (peach flower), had followed the Son of Heaven to his last resting-place and had died of grief at the portal of the Imperial tomb. The next Emperor, Chen Tsung, had issued a decree, ordering the little dog's body to be wrapped in the cloth of an Imperial umbrella and buried alongside its master.

Tzu-hsi's dog is also supposed to have died of grief, but some say that Moo-tan was smuggled away during the interment and sold by one of the eunuchs.

For twenty years Tzu-hsi lay at rest in the forest. Then the tombs were broken into and their contents rifled. The looting of the Eastern Tombs was described in an article by Moore Bennet, in the *Illustrated London News*:

> The treasures buried with the Empress Dowager were tabulated at the time by the notorious eunuch Li Lien-ying, as follows: ' A mattress seven inches thick, embroidered with pearls, lay on the bottom of the coffin, and on the top of it was a silk embroidered coverlet strewn with a layer of pearls. The body rested on a lace sheet, with a figure of Buddha woven in pearls. At the head was placed a jade ornament formed as a lotus, and at the foot a jade ornament carved into leaves. She was dressed in ceremonial clothes done in gold thread, and over that an embroidered jacket with a rope of pearls, while another rope of pearls encircled her body nine times and eighteen pearl images of Buddha were laid in her arms. All the above were private gifts, sent by friends. Her body was covered by a sacred Tolo pall, a chaplet of pearls was placed upon her head, and by her side were laid 108 gold, jade and carved-gem Buddhas. On each of the feet were placed one water-melon and two sweet melons of jade, and 200 gems made in the shape of peaches, pears, apricots and dates. By her left side was placed a jade cut like a lotus-root with leaves and flowers sprouting from the top: on the right hand was a coral tree. The interstices were filled with scattered pearls and gems, until the whole spread level, and over all was spread a net-work covering of pearls. As the lid was being lifted to place in position, a Princess of the Imperial house added a fine jade ornament of eighteen Buddhas, and another of eight galloping horses.
>
> . . . .
>
> Besides the above, which were noted at the time, a vast quantity of gifts of lesser value, including porcelain, picture

drawings, bronze and silver ornaments, were placed in the 'Jewelled Chamber' or vault. . . .

All of this vast treasure has disappeared.

There is something harrowing in the profanation of a sepulchre. But when a tomb is supposed to contain untold wealth, its desecration becomes inevitable, in a country impoverished and brutalized by civil wars. Small wonder, then, that Tzu-hsi's tomb should have been violated in years of strife and famine. But if, as many believe, the Empress still haunts the places she frequented during her long life, it will not be to the despoiled pavilions of the Tung-Ling that her spirit will return, but to the quiet serenity of the Summer Palace and to the gardens she loved best. Here are the peach and cherry trees that she planted, grouping them in colourful masses, with a view to their place in the landscape. Long years after her death, their blooms open out to meet the spring, and reddening maples give warning of autumn.

Here, with rotting timbers half submerged, are the barges on which she took her pleasure. Along the wooded banks of lake and stream, kingfishers still hover and dip, their bright hues catching the dappled sunlight; woodpeckers mount in rapid spirals up the trunks of trees, and jays colour the air with blue, in garrulous flights through the coverts.

Here is the rockery where she sat and watched the sunsets. Though the shadows lengthen, a shimmering haze still rises from the plain, and where the plain ends, blue and purple outlines fade into the distance. From a Buddhist monastery, perched on the horizon, comes once in every hour the single note of an old temple bell, and echo repeats it to the Western Hills.

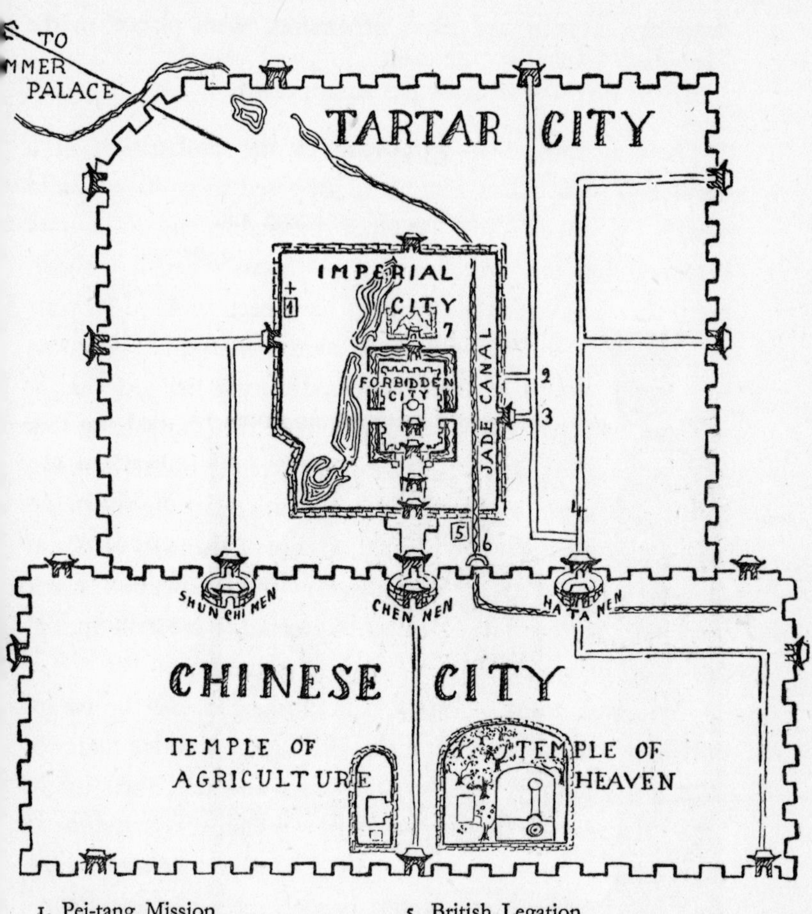

1. Pei-tang Mission
2. Pewter Lane
3. Jung Hua Mên
4. 'Morrison Street'
5. British Legation
6. Water Gate
7. Coal Hill

'he small circle in the centre of the Forbidden City represents the throne.

EPILOGUE

Still ending, and beginning still.

COWPER, *The Task.*

I

IN the Chinese language, different 'characters' (or, as we would say, different verbs) are used to express the idea of death, according to whom one is speaking of. In the case of the Son of Heaven, the Book of Rites prescribes the use of the character 'Peng', signifying ruin or downfall. This character is used for a mountain that crumbles, or an Emperor who dies. As Tzu-hsi was only a woman, the character Peng was not used to announce her death. Yet it would have been singularly appropriate, for one has the impression that, with her passing, something passed away, that the world will never see again.

The end of the Empire and the downfall of the Manchus

practically coincide with the death of Yehonala, for the three years that precede the declaration of a Republic have no history. The old prophecy had been fulfilled: a warrior woman had ruled over the Manchus and brought them to their doom. She had been a daring, even a warlike ruler, but she had miscalculated the strength of the forces which she had to face. Hers was the responsibility for the delay in adapting the administration of the Empire to the changing times, but it was a responsibility which she shared with the greater part of her subjects, both Manchu and Chinese. Indeed, it was because she possessed the defects as well as the qualities of her people, that her people loved her. She stood for the old philosophy, the old aloofness, the old disdain. When she died, the Old China went up in flames, like a Valhalla.

The end came unexpectedly. In October 1911, some Chinese troops mutinied at Wu-chang (one of the three cities situated at the meeting of the river Han with the Yang-tze-kiang). The rebels burned the house of the Viceroy, who, however, managed to escape, and they massacred the Manchu garrison, with their wives and children. It was said that the Manchu Bannermen were so degenerate, that, their Chinese servants having fled, they were incapable of saddling their horses, to go forth and do battle.

A colonel, Li-yuan-hung, was obliged, much against his will, to assume command of the mutineers and to proclaim the revolution, occupying the arsenal of Han-yang and the town of Hankow. In those first days, the movement was directed against the Manchus. But it would have been easy to suppress the revolt, if the rulers had shown some energy and had not abandoned their own adherents.

There was one person who might still have saved the Empire,

and this was Yuan-shi-kai. Had he been still at his post, the old favourite of the Empress Dowager might have continued in the tradition of the great Viceroys. He would have given protection and support to the Court, while China adapted herself to the times. But the heritage of hatred that the dying Kuang-hsu had left to his brother, the Regent, had fatal consequences. After the death of the Empress, Yuan was deprived of his official posts, which were distributed among the Manchu Princes. He then retired into his native province of Honan.

When faced by revolution, the Court turned once more to Yuan for help, and appointed him Generalissimo of the imperial forces. But this eleventh hour attempt to retrieve the fortunes of the Manchus was doomed to failure. Yuan accepted the command, but meanwhile the agitation for a republic had spread to the Treaty Ports. It might have been checked, if Yuan had been accorded sufficient financial backing; but this was not forthcoming. One can hardly say that the dynasty fell; it was pushed aside, and a republic set up in its place, no one knew whether as a permanent institution, or as a stop-gap.

On the 12th of February 1912, the Manchus abdicated. It was not a real abdication; the Emperor did not give up the throne; he transmitted the executive powers to Yuan-shi-kai, with instructions to restore the union between North and South and to form a Republican Government! During the negotiations which preceded this transfer of power, the Court obtained many promises: a civil list; the custody of the imperial tombs; the maintenance of certain privileges, among which the right to occupy a part of the Forbidden City. These promises were not kept. Very soon, the sums due to the Emperor ceased to be paid; the imperial tombs were left unguarded, except for a few old Manchu servants, whose allegiance survived their salary. For many years after the republican government had taken over Peking, a little Emperor kept up a little Court, in the north-western corner of the Forbidden City. His English tutor, R. F. Johnson, brightened the melancholy twilight of that gilded prison with the rays of Western learning. Thus the grandson of Jung Lu acquired a foreign education, which was destined to stand him in good stead in years to come.

For more than a decade, life within a few pavilions of the Forbidden City went on much as in other days: an image, in miniature, of past glories; an old-time picture on a Chinese fan. But in 1925, the Court was threatened by the so-called Christian General. The Emperor sought refuge in Tientsin. And for a time the fan was closed.

II

In the last years of the nineteenth century, many foreign missions in China were guilty of an excessive nationalism, and this did much to envenom popular feeling against them. After 1900, the character of the mission work as a whole began to change. The siege of the Legations sent a thrill of horror throughout the civilized world, and caused a renewal of missionary activity, especially among the American Protestant sects. It was felt that the Chinese people had sinned against the Holy Ghost and that they needed enlightenment. But the work of these new missionaries was not always beneficial, and their influence on political events was disruptive. The rival activities of divergent religious sects was in itself a danger: so much so that the Government in the Dutch East Indies wisely took precautions (that unfortunately could not be extended to China) forbidding the presence of missions of different denominations in the same locality.

The consequences of an inexperienced and not always disinterested missionary work have been described and analysed by J. O. P. Bland in *China. The Pity of It!* and he quotes (page 84) the following comment by Mr. Nathaniel Peffer:

'Every Mission School was an instrument of denationalization. The pupils were taught, not as Chinese children preparing to share in the life of the Chinese race, but as American schoolchildren. Of literature, the Chinese children learned English literature. Of history, they learned American history. . . . And it is not too much of a caricature to say that thousands of Chinese children grew to the age of sixteen without any clear knowledge that there had ever existed on this planet more than three men worthy of emulation: Christ, George Washington and Abraham Lincoln. . . .'

As a rule, the smaller the religious sect, the greater the spiritual intolerance. The longer experience and the more powerful organization of the Roman Catholic missions gave them a greater breadth of outlook.

In a lecture given in Rome, in 1934, a Catholic bishop, who for many years had been Apostolic Delegate of the Holy See in China, told his audience how the fall of the Empire had brought about a decadence in the religions of the East. Buddhism and Taoism had suffered from the political change. Many temples were abandoned:

'And we should be the first to deplore this fact. For every great religion is a manifestation of God. To see it disappear is mourning for the soul (*un lutto per l'anima*)!'

One almost heard an echo of Kipling's verses:

Oh ye who tread the Narrow Way
By Tophet-flare to Judgment Day,
Be gentle when the 'heathen' pray
To Buddha at Kamakura!

. . . .

And whoso will, from Pride released,
Contemning neither creed nor priest,
May feel the soul of all the East
About him at Kamakura.

. . . .

III

In the history of China, the fall of a dynasty has often been followed by a long period of chaos and civil war. After which a new Emperor would succeed in restoring unity. It is not surprising that the fall of the Manchus should have been followed by a period of dire confusion. But this time a solution was retarded by the ferment of democratic ideas and by the fact that China had entered, however unwillingly, into the *Weltpolitik*. In 1911, the Western powers had credits and missionaries to protect in China, and commercial ventures to encourage.

Had it been otherwise, had Asia been left to the Asiatics, it is probable that the fall of the dynasty would have coincided with another invasion from the North, similar to the invasion of the Mongols, in 1280, and to that of the Manchus, in 1644. This time, the invaders would have been the Japanese. Modern conditions prevented history from repeating itself. But not for long.

While China appeared to be disintegrating, Japan had known a real rebirth, and she assumed it to be her mission to bring order out of chaos, and not to allow the Chinese to do so for themselves.

In former days, the Kaiser had made 'the Yellow Peril' the subject for a picture, for which he worked out the composition, leaving the execution to more expert hands. The picture represented the Western powers, headed by Germany, ready to face the attacks of a fire-breathing dragon. The danger was never taken very seriously by statesmen in the West. But in the nineteen twenties, the same idea reappeared in another form. Lothrop Stoddard wrote *The Rising Tide of Colour*, and Father Wieger published *Le Flot Montant*. It was assumed that the tide of Western penetration had reached high water and was now on the ebb. An ingenious theory was expounded to prove that civilization flowed from East to West, and back again, throughout the centuries. Now would come once more the turn of the East to expand Westward, as when the Mongol and Islamic hordes invaded Europe, and Asia began with the Wends on the right bank of the Elbe.

Eastern people were offended, as well as economically injured, by the 'exclusion acts' of the United States and the British Dominions, as well as by the tactless refusal of post-war conferences to accord them a recognition of racial parity.

These common grievances and the lack of any effective support from the League of Nations to China, no less than the League's much trumpeted hostility to Japan, appeared at one moment to bring the two countries together, encouraging them to settle their differences. But much 'face-saving' on the part of the Chinese, and some bloodshed, may be necessary before China and Japan decide to work harmoniously in a common policy. Then indeed there might be an awakening of all Eastern Peoples.

IV

In December, 1911, the conspirator, Sun-yat-sen, landed at Shanghai, the same who had been held prisoner in the Chinese Legation, in London, in 1896. Young China, feeling the need of a national hero, made a great man of him, especially after his death in 1925. The cult of Sun-yat-sen has been given an almost religious form. But the 'three principles', enounced in his political will, offer a poor substitute for the old Confucian philosophy.

Sun-yat-sen was the first 'provisional' President of the new republic. The first real President (elected in 1913) was Yuan-shi-kai. He accepted nomination, although he was convinced that China ought to return to a monarchical form of government. Such being his opinion, it was only natural that he should attempt to restore the Empire, without the Manchus, and to found a new dynasty in his own family.

Yuan-shi-kai had good reason to believe that North China had remained imperialist at heart. He counted also on the support of the army, with which he was very popular. His aim was to create a constitutional monarchy, which should maintain the traditional sanctity of the Son of Heaven. At the winter solstice, Yuan, robed in the imperial mantle, proceeded to the Temple of Heaven, where he made the annual sacrifice, for the last time.

The inevitable opposition of the southern provinces might have been overcome. But the Japanese Government opposed its veto and Japanese agents stirred up trouble. The combined internal and external difficulties were too great. Yuan ended by renouncing the throne, and died shortly after, it was said, of a broken heart.

The presidency passed to Li-yuan-hung, the colonel who had first proclaimed the revolt against the Manchus. But the weakness of the civil administration, after Yuan's death, resulted in leaving all the power in the hands of the Tuchuns (military governors of the provinces). Thus it happened that the history of China, during fifteen years or more, is confined to rivalries among the 'War Lords'. Some of these were men of considerable ability, but their activity was mostly directed towards the carrying on of civil wars, which were never fought to a finish, the principal sufferers being the civilians in the captured towns, or on the countryside.

For many years China became a prey to rabble armies. The more distant provinces (such as Sze-chuan, well protected by encircling mountains) enjoyed a relative tranquillity, and became practically independent states. But the principal exception to the rule was Manchuria, whose history has ever been distinct, if not separate, from that of China.

After the fall of the Empire, Manchuria fell under the dictatorship of General (or Marshal) Chang-tso-lin, who later on extended his power over all the north of China and represented for some time the 'Chinese Government', with whom foreign diplomats had dealings. During the hey-day of his power, he gathered round him many of the other 'War Lords', but the southern provinces remained hostile. In 1927, the oft-predicted division of China into two separate States seemed about to take place. A 'nationalist government' was consolidating itself in Nanking and extending its rule up the Yangtze, while Chang-tso-lin's dictatorship was still strong in the north.

Had Chang-tso-lin been content with Manchuria, he might have continued to rule there undisturbed, for the Japanese had put a veto to the extension of China's civil wars north of the Great Wall. But, like the Manchus in the seventeenth century, his ambitions led him to Peking. And when the nationalist forces, coming up from the south, in 1928, forced him to retire once more into his native province, there was no longer a refuge for him there, even as there had been no refuge for the Manchus, when the Empire crumbled away. A bomb, placed on the railway line, on the outskirts of Mukden, blew up Chang-tso-lin's train. He died within a few hours.

Chang-tso-lin's death was kept secret for nearly a month, while his son, Chang-hsue-liang, made the necessary arrangement to take up the succession. Like his father before him, he made the mistake of mixing himself up with Chinese politics south of the Great Wall, and this gave to the Japanese a pretext for getting rid of him and creating, on the territory that once had been the domain of the Manchu tribes under Nurachu, a régime at the head of which they placed the late Emperor of China, the grandson of Jung Lu.

V

While the struggle between Chang-tso-lin, in the north, and the Nationalists, in the south, was still going on, a great many constitutional experiments were tried in various parts of China; among others an out-and-out bolshevist government, inspired by and directed from Moscow. This lasted as long as it appeared convenient to Nationalist rulers. When they deemed it necessary to open negotiations with the foreign powers, in view of stipulating new treaties, the Chinese Government abandoned its communist proclivities, and the political and military counsellors, who had been imported from Russia, had to take a hurried leave. They left behind them many elements of disorder, which helped to keep up the endemic conditions of internal strife.

Those who seek some thread of continuity among the changing scenes of Chinese history, since the fall of the Empire, will find it only in the gradual loss of prestige by western nations. The Great War destroyed the common front of the white race against the yellow, and the bolshevist revolution sent thousands of starving refugees into China. One saw white men in tattered uniforms begging at the doors of Chinese theatres, and white women offering themselves on the pavements of Chinese streets. The foreign educated students proved themselves the most active opponents of foreigners in general, in spite of individual friendships. The hysterical though well-meaning interference of the student class in home and foreign politics helped to perpetuate a state of uncertainty and confusion.

VI

The old hatred of the 'foreign devils' was a natural outcome of ignorance and fear. The new Chinese xenophobia was taught in the schools, in conformity with the political precepts of the Kuo-min-tang, that is to say, of the political party, who set forth to reorganize the country on a fresh constitutional basis. The thesis that China was an ill-used country, despoiled by 'imperialist' powers, was originally put forward by bolshevist advisers to the Chinese Government, and was taken up later by pacifist and humanitarian circles abroad, with the characteristic zeal of political amateurs.

But the West is getting to know China. Once it was only the Jesuit fathers who wrote the truth about the Chinese, and their reports were not meant to be circulated outside their Order. Nowadays one finds excellent books on Chinese life in the hands of the novel-reading public. This is all to the good. The better the Chinese are known, the easier will it be to deal with them. And there are no better critics of their own mistakes than the Chinese themselves.

Liang Chi-chao, a scholar of the old school, was one of those who, in 1898, showed sympathy with Kuang-hsu's attempts at reform. He died in 1929, and the trend of his philosophy was made known to the English-speaking world by his compatriot, L. T. Chen, in a volume on the *History of Chinese Political Thought*. The following passage is taken from the Preface:

'During the last two decades, China has tried to transplant, one after another, the political institutions of Europe to her own soil. Constitutional Monarchy has been tried, Republicanism, Confederacy, Sovietism: all have been tried, as though China desires to try every form in existence. In reality, nothing but the name has been introduced, and confusion is more confounded. For when an institution, whose roots are not among the people, is introduced from the top, it is like plucking the flowers of a neighbour's garden to embellish the dying branches of one's own tree; there can be no life. . . . The reconstruction of China's thought is not to be accomplished by the wholesale transplantation of the thoughts of another society; it must follow the natural development and must begin with the proper retention of elements of the old social heritage.'

The tragedy of China, in this period of transition, is that both the Old and the New are worthy of sympathy, yet would seem incompatible one with the other. Those who have had dealings with the new governing classes know that among them are many first-class men. And wherever the Old

China lives on, as in her agricultural classes, one finds the mellowed charm and the ancient wisdom of the Sons of Han.

The old China left a heritage of weakness, from which many of young China's difficulties have sprung. And the old psychological inheritance is lost, which was the sense of unbroken continuity with the past. Round the throne of Yehonala stood the ghosts of twenty dynasties. In the Edicts of the Old Buddha, her people heard the voice of all the Emperors of the past repeat with her the final injunction: 'Hear and obey!'

INDEX

INDEX

Aglen, Sir Francis, 142
Albazin, town of, ix, 76 *n.*
Alcock, Sir Rutherford, 59, 60
Alexander III, Czar, 201–2, 204, 227
A-lu-te, consort of Tung-chi, 104, 108, 113, 115, 117, 121–2, 133
Amur, River, ix
Anderson, Mr., 27
Anglo-Chinese convention, 39, 52
Anhuei, province of, soldiers, 115
Annam, 140
An-te-hai, "Little Ann", 46, 77, 82–3, 106, 128; executed, 84–7, 114
Arthur, Port, 167, 204

Backhouse, Sir Edmund, 180
Band of Patriotic Union, the, *vide* Boxers, the
Bannermen of the Guard, 32, 40–2, 51, 54, 197, 215
Barrow, Sir John, author of *Travels in China*, 35–6
Bauer, Colonel, 90, 111
Binyon, Laurence, 221
Bismark, Count von, 142
Bland, J. O. P., viii, 180, 220; author of *China, The Pity of It,* 243
Book of Rites, the, 161
Borghese, Don Rodolfo, 215–16
Boxers, the, 52, 71, 151, 168–71; the Rising, 175–200, 202, 209
Bruce, Hon. Frederick, 40
Burgevine, Mr., American adventurer, 89, 90, 92
Burlingame Treaty, the, 140
Burma, 140, 172
Byrne, Donn, author of *Messer Marco Polo*, 118

Caetani, Don Livio, 174, 193
Cantlie, Sir James, 147
Canton, 141, 147, 171
Carl, Miss Katherine, artist and author, 75, 221–2, 225, 229
Castiglione, Jesuit Father, 20
Chang-hsue-liang, 247
Chang-hsun, a barber, 210
Chang-tso-lin, General, 246–7
Chang, Yüan, 186
Chen Tsung, Emperor, 234
Chen-Mên gate, the, 214, 218
Cheng, L. T., author of *History of Chinese Political Thought*, 249
Cheng-lin, attached to the Yâmen, 60
Ch'ien lung, Emperor, viii, 10, 20, 35, 45, 48, 79, 146, 152, 171, 234
Chihli, province of, 141, 159, 198
China under the Empress, viii, 180
Ching dynasty, the, 31
Ching, Prince, 171, 177–8, 196, 206, 211
Ching Shan, H.E., his Diary, 180, 217
Chou, a eunuch, 109
Chou dynasty, the, 31

INDEX

Chow, Duke, 132
Ch'uan, Hung Hsiu, 91
Chuang, Prince, 180–1
Ch'un, Prince, brother of Emperor Hsieng-feng, 30, 44, 48, 52, 61, 113–14, 118; his son made Emperor, 119, 231–2
Ch'un, Prince, brother of Emperor Kuang-hsu, his son made Emperor, 231–3
Ch'unglun, 59, 60
Coleridge, Samuel Taylor, 34
Conger, Major, American Minister, 192
Cordes, Herr, interpreter, 178

D'Addosio, Padre, 174, 196, 200
Dàn, Madam, vii
De Giers, Baron, Russian Minister, 194, 207
De Luca, Luigi, vii
De Martel, Count, v
De Montauban, General, 29, 32, 39
De Robilant, Count, 201
Detring, Commissioner, 141–2
Diary of His Excellency Ching San, 180, 188 *n.*
Di Giura, Dr., vii
Dillon, E. J., 68
Discerning Concubine, the, 104
Dream of the Red Chamber, 14
Duyvendak, J. J. L., 180

Eastern Tombs, the, 124, 128; Yehonala buried in, 234–6
Elgin, Earl of, 24, 38, 46, 134
Empress, Mother, 13, 18, 58

Favier, Monseigneur, vii, 174
Flot Montant, le, by Father Wieger, 244
Footsteps in the Snow of a Solitary Goose, viii
Forbidden City, the, 17, 18, 22, 43, 77–8, 84, 105–6, 108, 116, 126–7, 191, 198, 200, 204, 213, 240–1
Forest of Pencils, the, *vide* Hanlin Academy, the
Fortnightly Review, the, 68
Franco-Chinese convention, 39, 52

Gamewell, Dr., 193
Gaselee, General, later Sir Alfred, 198–200
Giles, Professor, 35 *n.*, 42, 89
Gordon, Captain Charles G., later General, 36; Taiping rebellion, 93–8
Grand Canal, the, 3
Grand Council, the, 116, 126, 128, 159, 179, 186–7, 213, 233
Great Wall, the, 30, 31, 33, 247
Gros, Baron, French Plenipotentiary, 24, 38–40

Hakka, tribe, 91
Han dynasty, the, 217–18, 250
Hangchow, 2
Hankow, 239
Hanlin Academy, the, 93, 155, 195
Han-yang, Arsenal of, 239
Hannekin, Admiral von, 141–2
Hart, Sir Robert, 97–8, 142, 173–4, 183
Hartington, Marquis of, later Duke of Devonshire, 61
Hata-mên gate, the, 155, 177
Hata-mên street, 208

History of Chinese Political Thought, by L. T. Chen, 249
Hoi-an-hu, 127
Hong Kong, 147, 161
Hsien-feng, Emperor, 12, 14, 19, 20, 29, 30, 43, 45–6, 52, 87, 92, 105, 122, 127–9; flight to Jehol, 31; his death, 47–9, 51; funeral ceremonies, 53–4, 57
Hsi-an-Fu, the Court at, 211–12
Hsü Ching-cheng, 186
Hua-Feng, 104
Huei-cheng, father of Yehonala, 2, 3, 4
Humbert, King, 196
Hu-mên gate, the, 180
Hunan, province of, 1

Indiscreet Letters from Peking, by Putnam Weale, 184
Influence of Sea Power on History, by Admiral Mahan, 145

Jade Canal, the, 6, 33, 197–8
James, Professor, 180
Jehol, 30–33, 46, 48, 51–2, 105, 127–8, 186, 213
Jesuits, the, 123
John Chinaman, by E. H. Parker, 59
Johnston, Reginald F., author of *Twilight in the Forbidden City*, 151–2, 168; Tutor to the Emperor Pu-yi, 241
Jung Lu, cousin of Yehonala, 6, 13, 33, 53, 82, 99, 104, 106, 116, 119, 126–7, 146, 151, 158–9, 171, 179–81, 183–6, 191, 217, 220, 226, 232, 247

Kai-jeng, in Ho-nan, 213
Kaiping, coal mines, the, 159
Kang-hsi, Manchu Emperor, 48, 76, 79, 82, 146
Kang-Yi, the Grand Secretary, 187
Kang Yu-wei, a reformer, 149, 151, 156, 160–1
Kansu, 187
Ker, Willy, vii
Ker, Mrs., vii, 188–9, 199
Ketteler, Baron von, 177–8, 207–8, 232
Keyes, Lieut., later Admiral Sir Roger, 198–9
Kiangsu, province of, 90
Kiau-chau, 166
Kienlung, Emperor, 60
Kierulf, Danish shopkeeper, 130–1
Kipling, Rudyard, 243
Korea, 140, 146, 156
Kuantung peninsula, 167
Kuang-chin-wan, occupied by the French, 167
Kuang-hsu, Emperor, 2, 122, 127, 130, 146, 148, 189, 233, 240; his marriage, 132–4; Reform plans, 149–158, 220, 228–30; deposed by Yehonala, 160; imprisoned, 161–4, 221
Kubla Khan, 183; his Court, 119
Kuei Ching, 109–10
Kung, Prince, brother of Hsien-feng, 30, 39, 40, 44, 46, 52, 56–7, 59, 61, 66–7, 83, 85, 87–8, 103, 113–14, 117–18, 126, 146, 150
Kung-hing lake, the, 135, 145
Kung-hing gate, the, 189
Kuo Sung-tao, Chinese Minister in London, 103
Kuo-min-tang party, the, 248
Kwei-hsiang, *vide* Chow, Duke

INDEX

La Femme qui commanda à cinq cent mille hommes, by C. Pettit, viii
Lamb, Harold, 130
Lampson, Sir Miles, v
Lan, Duke, 170, 180, 186–7
Lang, Captain, R.N., 141
Lattimore, Owen, 167
Le Fils du Grand Eunuque, by C. Pettit, viii
Liang Chi-chao, philosopher, 249
Liao-lung peninsula, the, 167
Li-huan-hung, Colonel, 239; President of the Republic, 246
Li Hsiu Ch'eng, the Patriotic Prince, 92
Li-Hung-Chang, 60, 93–6, 98, 106, 115, 118, 126, 140–3, 145, 156, 158, 171, 206, 211; his death, 220, 226
Li Hung-hao, Tung-chih's tutor 113
Li Lien-ying, Chief Eunuch, 43, 48, 79, 106–9, 128, 134, 137, 145, 162, 170, 207, 234–5
Life of Queen Victoria, by Lytton-Strachey, viii
Li-po, Chinese poet, 35
Little Chao, *vide* Yehonala
Liu-ko-chao, 86
Liu Poo-chin, Commodore, 141
Lung Yü, Empress, 132–3
Lustrous Concubine, the, 133

Macao, 164
Macartney, Lord, 35, 60
Macdonald, Sir Claude, 171, 194, 199
Macdonald, Lady, 20
Ma-chia-pu, Peking, 214
Macmurray, J. van A., v
Mahan, Admiral, author of *Influence of Sea Power on History,* 145
Man-chu-kuo, 92
Manchuria, 92, 139, 167, 204, 226–7, 246
Manchus, the, 4, 10, 21, 23, 31–3, 46, 48, 52, 60, 66, 69, 70, 76, 83, 88, 90–3, 104, 113–14, 124, 126, 146–7, 149, 156, 167, 180, 194, 206, 215, 226, 229–31, 238–40, 243, 247
Marco Polo, 119
Messer Marco Polo, by Donn Byrne, 118
Mesny's Chinese Miscellany, 108
Ming Dynasty, the, 80, 92, 99, 234
Ming Shou Palace, 188
Mongols, the, 243–4
Morrison, Dr., *The Times* correspondent, 4, 180
Mufan, kinsman to Yehonala, 11, 12
Mukden, 9, 14, 204
Muraviev, Count Michael, 167, 195, 201–2, 208
Muyanga, *vide* Mufan

Nala, a tribe, 8
Nanking, 16, 141; destruction of, 99
Newchwang, a Treaty port, 143
Ning Shou Palace, the, 188
Nurachu, a Chieftain, 8, 31, 226, 247

Odes, Book of, 1
Oudendÿk, W., v

Palace of Mind Nurture, the, 116–17
Pa-li-kao, 32; Chinese defeated at by Allied forces, 28, 29
Pân Chieh Yü, Lady, 42, 45
Pân, Lady, 20, 70

Pao-ma-chang, vii
Paoyün, attached to the Yamên, 60
Parker, E. H., author of *John Chinaman*, 59
Pearl Concubine, the, 133, 187–8
Peffer, Nathaniel, 242
Pei-tang mission, the, 191–2, 194
Peking, ix, 2–4, 16, 17, 22, 27, 32, 36, 49, 51–3, 55–9, 90, 93, 101, 116, 118, 127, 130, 141, 145, 147, 155, 159, 175, 207, 209–12; Summer Palace at, 27, 29; attack by Allied forces, 29; the Boxer rising, 175; siege of the Legations, 178, 194–7; flight of the Emperor, 206; the Court returns, 213–16; Treaty of, 227; Republic Government at, 240
Peking Gazette, the, 123
Pell, Captain, 199
Pettit, Charles, author, viii
Pewter Lane, in Peking, 4–7, 9, 11
Pichon, Monsieur, 174
Pi Mo Yen temple, viii
Polo, Marco, 87
Portsmouth, Treaty of, 227
Pu-chun, Prince, son of Prince Tuan, 165–6, 182, 211
Pu-lùn, Prince, 113–14, 117, 232
Pulling the Strings in China, by W. F. Tyler, 141
Pu-yi, son of Prince Ch'un, 231; elected Emperor, 232–3, 240–1

Radziwell, Princess, 201–2
Rising Tide of Colour, The, by Lothrop Stoddard, 244
Rites, Book of, 238
Roberts, Issachar J., Baptist missionary, 91, 97
Ros, Signor, at Italian Legation, 84
Rosthorn, Mr., vii
Rosthorn, Mrs., vii

Sakota, sister to Yehonala, 11, 13, 32, 53–5, 61–2, 65, 85, 87, 101, 117, 127–8; made Empress of the Western Palace, 21, 46–7; appointed co-Regent, 56; created Tzu-an, 79; her death, 129
Salisbury, Marquess of, 103, 147, 190
Salvago Raggi, Marchese, Italian Minister, 161, 174, 195
San-ko-lin-sin, Prince, 27
San-Mun, Bay of, 167
Scott, Major, 1st Sikhs, 199, 200
Scott, Tom, Bengal Lancers, 199
Seal of Legally Transmitted Authority, 51, 56
Seoul, 157
Seymour relief column, 175–6, 184
Shanghai, 89, 96–7, 149, 161, 198, 245
Shansi, province of, 84, 211
Shantung, province of, 83–4, 86, 166–7, 171
Shan-yu, the Great Khan, 19
Sheba, Colonel, 194
Shên Kwei-fên, attached to the Yamen, 60
Sheng Wu Mên gate, 189
Shufeldt, Commodore, U.S.A., 140
Shun, Su, 29, 30–2, 44, 46–9, 52–3, 55–7, 205
Siam, 140
Sino-Japanese War, the, 141, 145, 156

Squires, Fargo, 193
Staunton, Sir George, 90
Strachey, Lytton, viii
Su Shun, conspirator, 44–8, 50, 53
Sujimura, the Japanese Chancellor, 176–7, 207
Summer Palace, the, 27, 29, 33–5, 134–7, 139, 146, 231; destroyed by Allied forces, 36–9, 52, 204; feasts at, 136–7
Sung dynasty, 234
Sun-yat-sen, 147, 156, 245
Sze-chuan, province of, 246

Ta A-ko, *vide* Pu-chun, Prince
Tai-yuan Fu, the Empress at, 211
Taipings, the, 22; rebellion, 36, 89, 90–6, 172, 205
Taku forts, the, 24, 186; the Bar at, 175
Tamerlane, the Tartar, 8, 76, 130, 134, 183
Tang dynasty, the, 122
Tao-Kwang, Emperor, 9, 12, 13, 80, 114, 166
Teh-chou, 198
Temple of Agriculture, 170
Temple of Heaven, 170, 245
Temple of the Threefold Duties, 125
Tenney, Dr., vii
Te-sheng Men gate, the, 188
Thatched House Club, the, viii
Tientsin, Treaty of, 23–5; city of, 106, 126, 146, 158–60, 175, 186, 197, 205–6; the Arsenal, 176
Ting Ju-chang, Admiral, 141–3
Ting Pao-chen, 83–4, 87
Ting Pao-chuan, Governor of Shansi, 84–5, 87
Tombs of the Emperors, 124–5
Tonking, 140
Travels in China, by Sir John Barrow, 35
Tsai-chih, Prince, 113–14, 117
Tsai Yuan Conspiracy, the, 44, 90
Tsai Yuan, Prince, 30, 44, 46–7, 55–7
Tseng Kuo-fan, General, 22, 92–3
Tsi-nan Fu, 84, 114
Tsing-kiang Pu, Taotai of, 3
Tsin-tao, port of, 166
Tsung-li Yamên, 59, 66, 96, 101–2, 163, 171, 177–8, 195, 198
Tsung, Emperor T'ai, 234
Tuan Hua, Prince, 30, 44, 55, 57
Tuan, Prince, 165–6, 180–3, 198, 201, 207, 211
Tun, Prince, 166, 170
Tung Fu-hsiang, General, 170, 184–5, 200
Tung Sün, poet, 60
Tung-chih, Emperor, son of Yehonala, 101–5, 109–11, 114–15, 122–3, 127, 133, 207, 233; his death, 112–13, 120
Tung-Ling, *vide* Eastern Tombs
Twilight in the Forbidden City, by R. F. Johnston, 151–2
Tyler, William F., author of *Pulling the Strings in China*, 141–3
Tzu-an, *vide* Sakota
Tzu-hsi, *vide* Yehonala

Unofficial History of the Empress Tzu-hsi, by Mr. Pâ, 2
Unofficial History of the Ching Dynasty, 188 *n.*

Valley of the Lions, 43
Vaughan, Major, 199
Victoria, H.M. Queen, viii, 107, 190
Vincenza, Suor, vii, 194, 200
Vitale, Baron, vii, 161

Wade, Sir Thomas, 60
Waldersee, Count von, 207
Ward, Mr., American adventurer, 89, 90, 92
Water Gate, the, Peking, 197, 199
Weale, Putnam, vii
Wei-hai-wei, 143, 145, 167
Weng Tung-ho, Kuang-hsu's tutor, 126, 148, 151
Wieger, Jesuit Father, 90; author of *Le Flot Montant*, 245
Wilhelm, Kaiser, 218, 244
Witte, Count Sergius de, 201
Wu-chang, mutiny at, 239
Wu-ko-tu, an ex-Censor, 123, 125

Yangtze River, vii, 2
Yeho, a tribe, 8
Yehonala, the last of the Empresses, vi, viii, ix, 26, 34, 36, 42, 61–2, 80, 93, 97, 104–5, 110, 113–14, 117, 119, 152–3, 163–5, 179, 180, 186, 196, 204–5, 217, 227–9, 240, 250; her birth, 1; early home, 4–7, 11; ancient prophecy, 9, 15; enters the Imperial harem, 13–14; bears the Emperor a son, 21; made Empress of the Western Palace, 21; her influence at Court, 22–3, 29, 30; flight to Jehol, 31–3; Su Shun conspiracy, 44–8, 50, 53; Regency decries invalid, 51, 56; journey to Pekin, 53–5; appointed Joint Regent, 56; audience ceremonials, 64–7; appearance and dress, 69–75; extravagances, 76–77, given the title of Tzu-hsi, 79; her favourite An-te-hai, 82–88; ascendancy of Li Lien-ying, 106–8; nominates Prince Ch'un's son as Emperor, 118; consults Li-Hung-Chang, 126; death of Tzu-an, 129; retires to the Summer Palace, 134; war with Japan, 146; attempted arrest of, 156–9; deposes the Emperor, 160, 166; acts as Regent, 161; supports the Boxers, 170; quells a riot, 181–2; siege of the Legations, 183–5, 195; flight from Pekin, 187–9, 206; her return, 210–14; triumphal entry into Pekin, 215–16, 218; her personality, 219–20; her portrait, 221–2; daily routine, 222–5; death of the Emperor, 231; becomes the Great Empress Mother, 233; death of, 234; her tomb, 235–6
Yellow River, the, 192
Yen-Shou-Mao, the Court painter, 18, 19
Youan-ti, Emperor, 18, 19
Yu Hsien, Governor of Shansi, 211
Yuan Ming Yuan, *vide* Summer Palace
Yuan-shi-kai, 4, 156–8, 171, 214, 231, 233, 240; President of the Republic, 245
Yung-lo, Emperor, 99
Yunnan, province of, 4

Zanichelli of Bologna, 201

THE LAST OF THE EMPRESSES

BOOKS BY THE SAME AUTHOR

in Italian

NOVELLE DI YEN CING

Serie I. Le Cinque Tigri
,, II. La Gabbia d'Avorio
,, III. L'Albergo dell'Eterna Sfortuna

STORIA D'INGHILTERRA

Volume I. 1837–1856
,, II. 1856–1885
,, III. (*in corso di stampa*)

I VOLI DEL LEONE ALATO

(per i ragazzi dai dieci ai sessant'anni)

PRINCIPESSA IN TARTARIA

(Commedia per marionette)

YEHONALA

Storia dell'Imperatrice Tzu-hsi e del trapasso dalla Vecchia Cina alla Nuova

in English

THE MAKER OF HEAVENLY TROUSERS (*a novel*)

(Book Society Recommendation)

(Methuen)

THE EMPRESS

[*Frontis.*

THE LAST OF THE EMPRESSES

and the passing from the Old China to the New

BY

DANIELE VARÈ

LONDON

JOHN MURRAY, ALBEMARLE STREET, W.

First Edition . . . 1936

Made and Printed in Great Britain by Butler & Tanner Ltd., Frome and London

PREFACE

LETTER TO THE FIVE MINISTERS

SIR MILES LAMPSON (*Great Britain*); COUNT DE MARTEL (*France*); J. VAN A. MACMURRAY (*U.S.A.*); K. YOSHIZAWA (*Japan*) and W. OUDENDŸK (*Holland*), *one time Ministers to China*

SAVILE CLUB,
December, 1935.

MONSIEUR LE MINISTRE ET CHER COLLÈGUE,
In how many diplomatic Notes have we addressed each other thus, and concluded with an assurance of our highest consideration ? I use the formula once more, to offer you my YEHONALA. There is still room for a book on the Empress who held the fate of China in her hands for more than half a century. The passing from the Old China to the New occurred in her lifetime.

We came together in Peking: six of us, of different nationalities, as Secretaries of our respective Legations. The Empire had just fallen. We watched the afterglow, where the sun had set.

To understand what was going on, it was not necessary to learn the History of China, as set forth in Father Wieger's *Textes Historiques*. It was enough to study the events of the past seventy years. We sought them in the Club Library's 'Far Eastern Section'.

Many people who had known the old China were still living in Peking: Sir John Jordan, in his quiet study, surrounded by despatch-boxes, with little paper tags sticking out of them, marked URGENT (it always seemed an anachronism that anything should be 'urgent' in China); Sir Francis Aglen, in the I.G.'s pavilions, next to me; Basil Kroupensky, arranging Gargantuan picnics, with gallons of champagne; Sidney Barton, organizing the 'Peking Volunteers' during the War; Miss Carl, living again, in memory, the days she had passed with the Empress; Dr. Morrison, in his house in 'Morrison Street'; the Bredons (Lady Bredon was the last to keep up a carriage with ma-fus wearing the official hats of other days); the Kers (Willy Ker deep in Chinese translations, and Mrs. Ker mothering the student-interpreters); 'Putnam Weale'; Baron Vitale, with his Manchu wife; Luigi de Luca, then a young man directing cotillons and theatricals; Suor Vincenza, still running the pharmacy in the French hospital, as she had done for forty years; Monseigneur Jarlin, pacing the sunny cloisters of the Pei-tang; old Dr. Tenney, beloved of many Chinese statesmen, whose teacher he had been; Dr. di Giura, at the Italian Legation Guard; the Rosthorns, Madame Dàn; *tai-pans,* missionaries and interpreters . . . From these and such as these, we were always hearing of good old times, when one travelled to Peking in barges, and palanquins were used in the north, as they are to-day above the Yangtze gorges.

Only the winter dust-storms were ever there, as links with the past, and the 'Spring Flowering' (a veil of misty blossoms on brown hillsides), and summer rains and autumn garnerings, not to mention the ten thousand smells that greeted us, like old friends, when we walked on the Wall and passed out of the City gates on our way to Pao-ma-chang or to the hills.

A happy uniformity in our diplomatic careers brought us back to Peking, all six of us, after an interval of a few years. By this time we were full-fledged 'Ministers Plenipotentiary'. Friends of other days, seeing us return to the former haunts, called us 'Ye olde Firme'.

Our knowledge of China extends over some twenty years, and we are not unworthy of being classed among the Old China Hands, whose Doyen (see how the official terms recur in our phraseology!) may be found on Wednesday mornings at the Thatched House Club, in the person of J. O. P. Bland.

From the inspiration of *China under the Empress Dowager* was born my desire to write a book on the same subject, more than twenty years after the publication of Bland and Backhouse's *magnum opus.* I am indebted to Mr. Bland for his kind permission to use the translation of several Chinese documents and for much friendly encouragement.

It is not possible to compile a Life of Yehonala, such as Lytton Strachey wrote of Queen Victoria, without describing her surroundings and contemporary events. Charles Pettit has attempted to do so in *La Femme qui commanda à cinq cent millions d'hommes,* but I feel that he has brought the Empress to the level of his own creation, *Le Fils du Grand Eunuque.*

Too much mystery surrounds the Forbidden City for us to write of its inmates with assured authority. Even when the facts are known, there are two or three versions, each giving a different rendering of what occurred. This vagueness is like the nebulous parts of a Chinese painting; it has a charm that it might be a mistake to dispel. Nor is it certain that the historian, could he lift the veil, would discover the truth. In the East, facts are no less difficult to interpret than to ascertain.

It was in a Buddhist temple in the Western Hills that I wrote the first chapters of this book. The temple is named Pi Mo Yen. In the eighteenth century, a Manchu General, cousin to the Emperor Ch'ien-lung, stayed up there, like myself, and wrote a book. (His was a book of travel, with the quaint title *Footsteps in the Snow of a Solitary Goose.*) Close by were the Hunting Park and the tower whence the

Emperor used to watch his army manœuvring in the plain. All around were signs of a past magnificence.

In a valley, not far from my temple, was a brick stairway, leading up the hillside, and an arch, surmounted by a belfry in foreign style. In the belfry hung three bells, adorned with the arms of the Romanoffs and a double-headed eagle. This is all that remains of a town, once situated on the River Amur, where now stands the town of Albazin. Formerly Russian, it passed under Chinese sovereignty in the year 1688, after the Treaty of Nertchinsk. The Emperor of China, K'ang-hsi, was much interested to hear that a foreign city had been included in his dominions, and expressed a desire to see it. But he had not the time (nor the inclination) for so long a journey. So the town itself, with its inhabitants, was brought to the Western Hills where the Son of Heaven might visit it at his leisure.

Yehonala was the last to possess such a grand mentality. In this sense she may be called The Last of the Empresses.

I have written what I learned and what I thought about her, after the fall of the Empire over which she reigned, while the spell of her personality still seemed to emanate from the Forbidden City.

My book may bring back, to those who knew it, some of the glamour that was Peking.

This time I conclude with no formal assurance, but you will find one more proof of our old friendship in these lines.

D. V.

CONTENTS

PAGE

I The Birth of Yehonala—Journey to Peking—A Little Girl in Pewter Lane 1

II A Prophecy—The Manchus in China—Muyanga's Stammer—Yehonala enters the Harem . . . 8

III The Throne that faces South—The Emperor and his Concubines—The Birth of an Heir—The Empresses of the Eastern and of the Western Palaces—The Coming of the 'Foreign Devils' 16

IV The Seizure of the Envoys—Battle of Pa-li-kao—Rivalry between Su Shun and Yehonala—Flight of the Court to Jehol 26

V The Burning of the Summer Palace—The 'Outer Barbarians' obtain the Right to send Ministers to Peking 34

VI A Conspiracy at Jehol—The 'Autumn Fan'—The Death-bed of an Emperor 42

VII The Seal of Legally Transmitted Authority—The Empresses and the Regents travel separately to Peking—The End of the Conspiracy . . 50

VIII The Staff of the Tsung-li Yamen—Sidelights on the Audiences—Brief Disgrace of Prince Kung 58

IX The Charm of Yehonala—Her Dresses—Her Extravagance—Her Morals 68

X Chinese Names—Yehonala is given the Title of 'Tzu-hsi'—The Court Eunuchs—The Death of An-te-hai 78

CONTENTS

PAGE

XI The Tai-ping Rebellion—Gordon and Li Hung-chang—Sir Robert Hart and the Customs Service—The Porcelain Pagoda 89

XII End of the First Regency—The Diplomatic Body received at Court—The Chief Eunuch, Li Lien-ying—Tung-chih and the Eunuchs . . 101

XIII Death of Tung-chih—The Choice of a Successor . 112

XIV The Emperor Kuang-hsu and the Sacrifices on the Altar of Tung-chih—Suicide of Wu-ko-tu—Tzu-hsi becomes Sole Regent after the Death of Tzu-an 121

XV Kuang-hsu and his Foreign Playthings—His Marriage—Tzu-hsi goes into Retirement at the Summer Palace—The Mid-Autumn Festival . 130

XVI The War with Japan—W. F. Tyler's Reminiscences—Kuang-hsu's Attempts at Reform 139

XVII Kang Yu-wei's Projects—Yuan-shi-kai's Betrayal—Tzu-hsi resumes the Government of the Empire 154

XVIII The Boxer Movement 165

XIX The Siege of the Legations (from without) . . 179

XX The Siege of the Legations (from within)—Russian Complicity 190

XXI The Allies in Peking—The Peace Protocol—Return of the Court to Peking 203

XXII A New Spirit at Court—The Portrait of the Empress—Miss Carl's Memoirs—Russians and Japanese in Manchuria 217

XXIII The Death of Kuang-hsu and of Tzu-hsi—The Violation of the Tombs in 1929 228

Epilogue. The Fall of the Empire—The Foreign Missions in China—Internal Chaos and Japanese Penetration—The First Presidents and Chang-tso-lin—The Nationalists and the Students—The Old China and the New 238

LIST OF ILLUSTRATIONS

FACING PAGE

THE EMPRESS . . . . *Frontispiece*

THE SUMMER PALACE AT PEKIN* 1

A SEPULCHRAL PILLAR* 12

PEKIN: A CORNER OF THE TARTAR CITY* 30

A COLUMN OF A PAVILION AT THE IMPERIAL MAUSOLEUM* . 64

A PRIEST* 78

A CORRIDOR AT THE SUMMER PALACE* 116

THE SUMMER PALACE AT PEKIN* 134

THE SUMMER PALACE* 156

A DOMESTIC SCENE IN PEKIN* 176

THE CH'IEN-MEN: THE PRINCIPAL GATE OF THE TARTAR CITY AS SEEN FROM THE ENTRANCE TO THE IMPERIAL PALACE*. 214

AN ALTAR IN THE IMPERIAL MAUSOLEUM* 230

PLAN . . . . *page* 237

* *Photo: Hartung, Pekin.*

The portrait of The Empress reproduced on the wrapper and as Frontispiece is an authentic portrait existing in the Temple behind the Coal Hill in Pekin.

The initial capital letters at the beginning of each chapter are drawn by Elisabeth M. Varè (E.M.V.).

Photo : Hartung, Pekin.

THE SUMMER PALACE AT PEKIN

I

The highest towers rise from the ground.
Chinese Proverb.

NO one knows where she was born; possibly in Hunan, or perhaps in Anhuei. But wherever the birth occurred, we may be certain that all hygienic precautions were lacking. No doctor, but at most an experienced woman, will have assisted in 'receiving life'. The child being a girl, her arrival cannot have provoked any enthusiasm among her parents and other relations. In the Book of Odes it is said that, if the new-born babe be a girl, it needs no softer cushion than a brick. But daughters are not so unwelcome to the Manchus as they are to the Chinese, and possibly someone may have quoted the adage: 'When cinnabar is not to be had, even red earth is of value.'

She was a daughter of Huei-cheng, a captain in the second of the eight Banner Corps. As a child, they called her 'the Little Chao'. In her youth she bore the name of Yehonala, which was that of her clan.

Her father held one of those military appointments that the Manchus in China reserved to themselves in order to keep an eye on the civilian magistrates of the subject race. It would appear that he had two daughters and one son, but history makes no mention of the son, except incidentally at the time of the Emperor Kuang-hsu's marriage in 1889.

Huei-cheng died when Yehonala was still a child. Unlike the majority of military officials in China, he had amassed no great fortune, which seems to prove that he must have been either a very honest or a very incompetent man. Shortly before, or soon after, his death, his family proceeded northwards, to seek the hospitality of relatives in Peking. They travelled by barge along the Grand Canal, the artificial waterway, which connects Peking with Hangchow and the towns of the Yangtze River. In recent years, China's waterways have been allowed to silt up, adding greatly to the danger of floods, and the Grand Canal is only navigable for short tracts here and there. But travellers by rail, looking out through the carriage windows, may still observe square sails moving among the rice and millet fields. And men and boys still earn a precarious living by towing the barges from a path along the bank, when the wind is not favourable.

There is a story about the journey of Huei-cheng's family to Peking, a story on which the more conscientious historians have cast a doubt, attributing it to the malicious gossip of the Manchu Princes at court. But it is given as authentic in an *Unofficial History of the Empress Tzu-hsi*, by Mr. Pâ.

One of the principal towns on the Grand Canal is Tsing-kiang Pu. All barges stop there to replenish their stores and to pay toll. On the barge which carried Huei-cheng's widow and her daughters, there happened to be travelling also a friend of the local Mandarin, that is to say of the Tao-tai of Tsing-kiang Pu. The two cronies met and passed a convivial night together, playing a game called *Wei-chi*, in which the Tao-tai was the loser. Next day, he sent a messenger on board the barge with money to pay his debt. But either the letter-carrier (*tingchai*) made some mistake, or the Yamen official, in writing the creditor's address, used the wrong characters, for the letter went astray. And the widow of Huei-cheng received, much to her surprise, a large sum of money, with the compliments of the Tao-tai of Tsing-kiang Pu.

Never suspecting that there might be a mistake, the poor woman sent for a public letter-writer, and with his help compiled a laboured epistle, expressing in conventional terms made sacred by long usage, her heartfelt gratitude for the generous gift and her best wishes for the donor: 'Might he live for many many years, and might his descendants be counted in hundreds'.

The Mandarin's first impulse was to send and ask for the money back. But his companion of the night before dissuaded him, saying: 'Better leave it alone! This woman and her daughters are on their way to Peking. They are Manchus, and the girls are pretty. In a few years they will be of an age to enter the harem of the Son of Heaven. At present, they know you for a kind-hearted man, who has befriended them in time of need. Why make enemies by giving them a grievous disappointment?'

The Mandarin somewhat reluctantly agreed. He let the widow keep the money, and paid his debt for the second time. In after years he had cause to be thankful that he had done so.

When they reached the capital, Huei-cheng's family went to live with their relations in the Hsi-la Hu-tung, or Pewter Lane. It is an unpretentious little street, running east and west, in the Tartar City, and owes its name to the fact that it was then a meeting-place for bearers of utensils and ornaments made of pewter. These were sent to the Court as tribute from various provinces, principally from Yunnan.

Pewter Lane is one of the side-streets that run out of the Wang-fu-ching Ta-chie, or 'The big road to Prince Ching's well', which foreigners now call Morrison Street, because the former *Times* correspondent, Dr. Morrison, lived there until he became Political Adviser to Yuan-shi-kai.

It is not certain which of the houses in Pewter Lane was the home of the future Empress of China. In any Western country, they would have marked her habitation with a tablet. Here no one remembers, and no one seems to care.

But gentlefolks' dwellings in Peking are all much alike, save that some are larger than others and have gardens, with a lotus-pond and an artificial mound, where in April the wistaria falls in perfumed cascades from the roof of a belvedere. The palaces of the Manchu Princes only differed from the neighbouring houses because of some outward sign of authority, such as two marble lions, one on each side of the entrance, or two lacquered poles, symbolizing the power of life and death. Even the temples are built on much the same plan and with the same architectural features. All the houses in Pewter Lane consist of separate one-storeyed pavilions, built round courtyards which follow one another in a straight line from south to north; sloping roofs with ornamental tiles at the corners; windows of rice-paper stretched over wooden lattices; outer walls which hide all that is within; outer gates with heavy wooden panels, painted scarlet, with brass knockers (two lions' heads, each with a ring held in the mouth); a walled screen to face one on entering: it is meant to keep out the evil spirits. In one of the first courtyards, called the Court of Ancestors, there is a large bronze censer, in which, on certain dates, incense is burned. And the perfumed smoke floats on the quiet air, so that the lacquered pillars of the house seem to rise up out of cloud, as in a Chinese painting.

A little girl with almond-shaped eyes and her hair in two plaits down her back; small for her age, but quick witted and quick tempered; full of curiosity and determined not to miss anything that might be going on in the house or down the street—such a child must the Little Chao have been, when she dwelt in Pewter Lane.

One may see other little girls now, in that same street, dressed in black silk jackets and red trousers, and generally carrying a baby pick-a-back on their shoulders. Sometimes they stand with the servants and dogs on the doorstep, watching a funeral go by, or a wedding procession; more often they crowd round the itinerant vendors of puffed-rice candy, or sugared walnuts and ripe haws and grapes on little slivers of bamboo.

Chinese children are attractive little people, with impassive faces and sparkling black eyes. They seldom laugh or cry, and seem to bring to the problems of life a characteristic philosophy and a wisdom beyond their years. The children in Pewter Lane must have learnt a lot about the ways of men, in their own courtyards and in the immediate neighbourhood. The Forbidden City was close by, a few hundred yards beyond the Jade Canal. One could see the yellow-tiled roofs gleaming in the sunlight and the hawks hover round the towered Gate of Western Flowering. Behind those walls was the source of all power, of all riches, of all honour. Men called him the Son of Heaven.

Like all well-brought-up children in China, the Little Chao began her education by learning to recite from the Book of the Three Characters, a trisyllabic poem that begins:

Jen-je-chu
Hsin-pen-shàn.
(at the beginning of man
the heart naturally good)

and later on she learnt the twenty-five examples of filial piety.

One can imagine her, when lessons were over, scampering down the lane after her cousin Jung Lu, as he sallied forth to catch dragonflies in an old butterfly net, along the banks of the Jade Canal, or to fly a big kite (shaped like an eagle) from the open spaces near the city walls. And later, hurrying home in the dusk (lest she should be scolded for being out after dark) and cowering against a wall, to avoid a blow from the outriders of a Prince's palanquin, or the protruding shaft of a covered cart, that bore one of the Palace eunuchs along the narrow lanes.

Those who have observed the street life of Peking may conjure up many visions of Little Chao, in the days when she and Jung Lu played together as children in Pewter Lane. Such visions need not be wholly fanciful, for she must have known the life of the people, Manchu and Chinese. She must have seen hawkers with their portable stoves, cooking in the street, while lean dogs sniffed around them; barbers shaving chins and heads in the open; vendors of seed oils and bearers of fresh manure; and little groups of bird lovers in sunny corners, showing off the tricks of their pet starlings and jays.

She must have frequented the covered market, close to her home (the best toy shops in Peking are there), and doubtless she accompanied her elders to the fair at the Loong Fu Ssè, which is held on the ninth and nineteenth of every lunar month. There the Manchu housewives buy hair ornaments and shoes with high cork soles, covered over with white kid; story-tellers recount in sing-song the deeds of legendary kings (as well as the latest gossip), and puppet-shows draw crowds of children, like any Western Punch and Judy. But in Yehonala's young days, no 'foreign devils' were to be met in the streets of Peking, nor were there any rickshaws.

The fact of having acquired some personal knowledge—even at so early an age—of the realities of life, as known to her subjects, gave to Yehonala, in later years, a notable advantage over those members of the Imperial family, who had been brought up from infancy in the seclusion of the palace.

A child's experience of a modest household, with its little economies and expedients to keep up appearances, would not seem of much use as training for one who was destined to rule over a fourth of the human race. Yet it served as a corrective to that ignorance of the world as it is, which has so often been the ruin of an Oriental despotism. Like her subjects, Yehonala knew nothing of the Barbarians who lived beyond the Four Seas. But she knew her own people well.

II

Ancestral voices prophesying war

COLERIDGE, *Kubla Khan.*

YEHO and Nala were the names of two tribes, united much against their will under the rule of a chieftain called Nurachu. He it was who fused the Manchus into one nation, and with them conquered China, founding the dynasty which reigned in Peking from the year 1644 down to our own times.

The name ' Yehonala ' recalls the days when warlike hordes caused the earth to tremble at the coming of a Gengiz Khan, or a Tamerlane, and after the death of their chief dispersed once more over the windswept grasslands of northern Asia.

Soon after Nurachu had succeeded in imposing his rule on the independent tribes, a story began to get about and to be repeated with a sense of ominous foreboding. There are two versions of this story; one tells of a marble stele bearing an ancient inscription; the other mentions a sooth-sayer, who prophesied. The inscription, or the prophecy, contained a warning against a woman of the Yehonala tribe, who would reign over all the Manchus and bring them to their doom.

Time passed and the prophecy was forgotten until 1911, when the Empire fell. Then only did the Manchus think of connecting the inscription on the wooded banks of the Tsùngari with a little girl in Pewter Lane, and of linking up the tribes round a seer in Mukden with a proud old Empress on the Dragon Throne. In the legend of a warrior woman, who materialized in Yehonala, we can observe a symptom of that sense of insecurity that the Manchus never lost during their domination in China. Their dreams were haunted by the fear of another conqueror ousting them, as they had ousted the Mings. Manchuria was ever regarded as their old home, where they might again seek refuge in times of stress (in a sense, this idea was realized with the creation of Manchu-kuo). Up till the middle of the nineteenth century, in the reign of Tao-kwang, the Emperor used to make periodical visits to the cradle of his race. He would worship at the shrines of his first ancestors, and deposit the records of successive decades in the dynastic archives.

Porcelain and jade and jewels were stored at Mukden, and treasure was hoarded against a rainy day. Even the dried-up wells in the old palace grounds were used to store up treasure. A mud furnace was built at the edge of each well and silver ingots were melted and poured down, until it was full to the curb with a cylinder of pure metal. The well was then cemented over and another prepared in the same way. The wells at Mukden were called the 'silver cheeses', and the Manchu Emperors meant to nibble at them in the lean years that might return. But when these years came indeed, the hoarded treasure of the Son of Heaven had long since been rifled by sacrilegious hands.

The Manchu army was divided into eight 'Banners', of which the first three formed the bodyguard of the Emperor. But all the Manchu people numbered less than three million souls, and though the population of China was then only half what it is now, the Manchus had to impose their rule on nearly two hundred million Chinese. This was possible owing to their military qualities and feudal administration. They made use of the ablest Chinese as civil governors and officials, allowing the people to live on undisturbed in the time-honoured traditions of the Celestial Empire, imbued with the Confucian system of ethics and the ancient Taoist philosophy.

In order to keep the provinces in subjection, the Manchus built themselves walled cities, within the Chinese towns. In Peking itself there is a 'Tartar City', partly superimposed on the old Chinese town.

At first, the Manchus had few dealings with the subject race. There were no mixed marriages, and Chinese women were not allowed to enter the imperial harem.

But in time, China absorbed the Manchus, as the Roman Empire absorbed the barbarians who invaded it. Tribute-fed soldiers lost their Spartan virtues. They had no aptitude for commerce, or for the arts of peace. The golden age of the Manchu dynasty ended with the reign of Ch'ien Lung, last of a series of conquerors and benevolent despots. The later Manchu Emperors were no less degenerate than the later Merovingian kings. Their history might be described in

Wagnerian terms as a *Götterdammerung*. In this twilight of the Gods, the figure of Yehonala stands out against the gathering darkness, like one bright star at sunset.

The house in which Yehonala went to live on her arrival in Peking belonged to a kinsman, an official, whose name in Chinese was Mu-fan, and in the Manchu language Muyanga. He was afflicted by a most painful stammer. Having been given an appointment to the Board of Works, he was received in audience, so that he might express his thanks to the Emperor. Kneeling before the Son of Heaven he spake, or attempted to speak, the following words:

'This glory and good fortune for my descendants is all a gift of Your Majesty.'

But owing to his unfortunate stammer, he stuck at the words 'this' and 'is' (in Chinese: *chù* and *shì*), with the result that his speech sounded like the clucking of a hen:

'Chù, chù, chù, chù . . . Shì, shì, shì, shì . . .'

The Emperor roared with laughter, and for this small absurdity poor Mu-fan has gone down in the history of his race.

A certain reflected glory came to him from the fact that his eldest daughter had been chosen as consort for the Emperor's son. She died shortly after her marriage, without children. When Yehonala came to live in Pewter Lane, a younger sister was living in the house. Her name was Sakota, which had been the name also of the elder sister, who had died.

As daughters of Manchu Bannermen, Yehonala and the younger Sakota had their names inscribed on the list of girls, from whose ranks were chosen the wives and concubines of the Emperor. The list contained information regarding the family tree, the date of birth and the physical characteristics of the various girls, also any data obtainable concerning their nature and education. The first selections were usually made by provincial magistrates; a series of preliminary examinations served to discard the obviously unfit. Those who emerged successfully from the semi-finals were brought up for examination by the Chief Eunuch and the Empress Mother. It was the latter who made the ultimate choice and decide upon the rank to be attributed to each girl chosen. The final tests were the most severe and the most intimate. In some cases the girls were made to run a certain distance, in order to ascertain if their perspiration was normal.

The imperial bridegroom had no say in the matter until the girls that had been chosen for him entered the Palace for good. Then their names were engraved on tablets of jade, which were placed on an ivory table at the entrance to the Emperor's private apartments, known as the Chamber of Divine Repose. On retiring, the Emperor would turn over the tablet of the consort or concubine to whom he wished to accord his favours. Later on a eunuch would carry her, wrapped in a coverlet of red silk (wadded if the night was cold), along the corridors and through the minor courts of the Forbidden City, till he laid her naked at the foot of the Emperor's bed.

In 1852, the reigning Emperor was Hsien-feng, eldest of the nine sons of the late Emperor Tao-kwang, who had died in 1850. Hsien-feng was a widower since the death of his first consort (Muyanga's daughter, the elder Sakota) and the rites forbade another marriage during the period of mourning,

Photo : Hartung, Pekin.

A SEPULCHRAL PILLAR

which lasted twenty-seven months after the late Emperor's death.

One consequence of the unavoidable delay in providing other consorts and concubines for Hsien-feng was that, in the meanwhile, the younger Sakota and Yehonala reached an age when the probability of their being selected became greater. As sister to a former consort, Sakota was especially eligible, and Yehonala was growing more beautiful every day. Girls in noble Manchu families lived a life of great retirement, learning how to keep house, how to weave, how to embroider and to make their own clothes. Marriage was arranged by the parents and negotiated by means of intermediaries. Even so, it would seem that Yehonala's thoughts as to her own future centred round a less exalted bridegroom than the all-powerful but nebulous personality that graced the Dragon Throne.

When the period of Court mourning was over, sixty Manchu girls, among whom were the two inmates of Muyanga's house in Pewter Lane, were summoned to the Palace, to be inspected by the Empress Mother (Tao-kwang's widow) and the Chief Eunuch. Twenty-eight girls were chosen and classed in four groups, according to the grade assigned to them. Yehonala was placed in the third grade, styled *kuei jen'* (honourable person). Sakota was given the second rank (*P'in*).

One wonders what were Yehonala's feelings on leaving Muyanga's house for the imperial harem. The day-dreams of a girl of sixteen may well paint the future with the colours of the rose, but it is generally believed that, before being chosen as concubine for the Emperor, Yehonala had been betrothed to her cousin Jung Lu, and that the two young people suffered by reason of the inevitable abandonment of their matrimonial plans. This vague rumour gives us the starting-point of a real love affair, which lends to the formal history of Yehonala, as imperial concubine and as Empress, a touch of human pathos, a note of high romance. In an Oriental form and in an Oriental setting, we have again the old old story of Lancelot and Guinevere.

In the north-eastern corner of the Forbidden City, there is a row of one-storeyed pavilions, roofed over with blue tiles. Here the eunuchs prepared a habitation for the newly chosen concubines. The pavilions centred round two courtyards, whose walls were frescoed over with scenes from a Chinese story, called *The Dream of the Red Chamber.* A finer story was about to open in those same pavilions: the story of a little concubine, who was to add her name to those of the great Asiatic rulers. Yet the times appeared singularly inauspicious.

When Yehonala entered the harem, Hsien-feng was twenty-five years old: a sickly, degenerate youth, who strove to drown in pleasure and in vice the sense of his own responsibility and the fear of the dangers that threatened his Empire. Of these dangers, the most formidable was the Tai-ping rebellion, which had started in the southern provinces and now threatened to extend all over the country and to found a new Empire, with its capital at Nanking. The Manchu policy of hoarding treasure at Mukden appeared well justified by the trend of events. The days of adversity were at hand, for the eunuch-ridden Court was incapable of resistance, and the prestige of the throne was shaken. Among the people it was said that 'the dynasty had exhausted the mandate of heaven'. The day was approaching when a warrior woman of the Yehonala tribe should rule over the Manchus and lead them to their doom.

But Yehonala was to do more than this. She was to give to the old China one last blaze of glory, one more imperial figure set high in splendour above the teeming millions of a boundless realm.

III

. . . up and down the city are beautiful palaces and fine houses in great numbers. The whole city is arranged in squares like a chessboard, and disposed in a manner so perfect and masterly, that it is impossible to give a description that would do it justice.

The Travels of Marco Polo.

MONG the many expressions which, in the Chinese language, correspond to our word 'Emperor', there is one, *Nan Mien*, meaning 'The Face which is turned towards the South' (*Nan* = south; *Mien* = face). In China, anyone who gives audience to a subordinate should be seated with his back to the north. All living things were subordinate to the Emperor of China. Officially, his face was ever turned towards the south.

Peking, the 'northern capital' (as opposed to Nanking, the 'southern capital'), conforms to the rule, and is backed by a semi-circle of mountains, which face the plain towards the south. In the centre of the town is the throne, round which the earth is supposed to gravitate like the heavens round the Polar Star. The Chinese have a proverb: 'All the stars in heaven salute the north.'

The traveller who approaches Peking by the road that leads northwards from the open country, first passes under the outer walls of the old Chinese town. Though jostled by the busy crowd, and choked by the dust that rises from the feet of camels and of mules, he has the sensation of treading the flags of a *Via Sacra,* towards the seat of an overwhelming majesty. Passing under successive walls, in an unswerving line from south to north, the road leaves the crowded streets and passes into the seclusion of an imperial domain. That same road leads to the throne itself, whence the Son of Heaven might gaze, through wide-open gates, out over his empire.

Reading certain Memoirs, in the style of Pierre Loti, one has the impression that Peking, in the last century, was all lacquer and gold and dust. Nowadays there is less lacquer, and less gold, but more dust. Whereas, under the Empire, one could only guess at what was hidden behind the pink walls, where dwelt the Son of Heaven, now one may visit palaces within palaces, and gardens within gardens. Some of the most picturesque pavilions are grouped round three artificial lakes, and their red columns and many-coloured roofs are reflected in the water. The Forbidden City is not a palace, but a citadel, vast, mysterious labyrinthine. The Emperor was the only adult male who might live within its precincts, together with the women and the eunuchs. Among the women were the wives and concubines of the reigning Emperor, the widows of past Emperors and two thousand girls, who remained there for a period of several years, as household servants. The number of eunuchs varied, but it was over two thousand.

This gynecæum was entrusted to the care of the Empress Dowager. Within the Forbidden City, she enjoyed an authority superior to that of the Emperor, whose minor concubines were not so much the secondary wives of the Son of Heaven as servants to the senior Empress.

The Tartar Chiefs of olden days conquered thrones, but lived in the saddle. They could resist the influence of the harem and deny to their women any part in the affairs of State. But this was made difficult by the life of seclusion, prescribed for Emperors who had ceased to lead their armies in war. And the eunuchs knew how to enervate the generous impulses of youth, and how to offer unhealthy excitement to old age. Their power in the State waxed or waned with their personal ascendancy over the ruling Sovereign. At the time we speak of the eunuchs were all-powerful.

When Yehonala first entered the Forbidden City, it was summer, and from the bridge that crosses the moat, opposite the Gate of Military Prowess, one could see the velvety leaves and pink chalices of the lotus above the water, and dragonflies afloat on the drowsy air above the floating flowers.

To be the concubine of an Emperor did not necessarily imply the privilege of being known to him. A story, typical of the harem, was that of the Emperor Yuan-ti, of the Han dynasty, who had so many concubines that he never saw the greater part of them. He saw their portraits, by the Court painter, Mao Yen-shou. Therefore, the concubines gave presents to Mao, in order that he might make them appear beautiful and inspire the Emperor with a desire to have them brought to him. The loveliest of the concubines was Cha Chun, but she did not trouble to bribe Mao Yen-shou, thinking it would be all right if he painted her as she really was. Out of spite, Mao painted a portrait of her that failed to do justice to her beauty, and so the Emperor knew her not.

In those days, there came to the Court of Peking, for the first time, the Shan-yu, who reigned over the Turkomans of Hiung-mu (he was known in Europe as the Great Khan of the Huns). Wishing to bind closer the ties of friendship with this powerful neighbour, Yuan-ti decided to offer him a wife. And he gave him Chao Chun, whom he had never seen.

When the bride appeared before him with her husband, who had come to take leave, Yuan-ti was struck dumb with astonishment. He had not known that his harem contained a maiden of such transcendent loveliness. And now Chao Chun was his no longer.

As soon as the Shang-yu had departed, Mao Yen-shou and the concubines who had bribed him were committed for trial, and that same day they were beheaded in the market-place. But Yuan-ti was haunted by the memory of Chao Chun's beauty and by regrets for a happiness that might have been his.

One afternoon Yehonala sat sewing out of doors, in a part of the Summer Palace known as ' the deep recesses among the plane trees '. And she sang a little song that she had learnt as a child in the south. The Emperor passed by, along a rustic path, and heard her singing. He stopped and asked whose voice it was. When she was brought to him, he saw for the first time his little concubine of the third grade.

From that day onward, the jade tablet with Yehonala's name used to be turned over on the ivory table, whenever Hsien-feng retired to his private apartments.

History had handed down the names of other favourite concubines, such as 'the Perfumed Concubine' of the Emperor Ch'ien Lung, whose portrait was painted by the Jesuit father Castiglione. And the annals of the T'se dynasty tell of the Lady Pàn, a favourite of Hsiao Pao Kuan, who danced before the Son of Heaven on a golden floor, encrusted with jewels that formed a design of lotus flowers. As he watched her dance, the Emperor exclaimed in delight: 'It is as if the lotus opened at the touch of her little feet!'

Such legends are not without their charm. But records of advancement within the harem are not tales of pure romance. The Emperor was the source of riches that others might enjoy; his the power that might be wielded also, by those whom he delighted to honour. No mere love drama was enacted on those summer nights, when Yehonala was carried through the silent courtyards, and laid her on the Emperor's bed. The fate of Asia was shaped within the sleeping palace, while crickets chirped in the willow trees, and the Bell Tower boomed out the passing hours over the Tartar City.

Yehonala held the Emperor in thrall, yet managed to avoid the jealousy of her colleagues, and entered easily into the graces of the old Dowager Empress (who died in 1855). Only those Manchu princes, who had been companions of the Emperor in his dissolute habits, regarded the new favourite with suspicion, for their power at Court was diminished, as a consequence of Hsien-feng's infatuation for his concubine.

Yehonala's future was assured from the moment when she gave the Emperor a son. In the dynastic law of the Manchus, the fact that the boy was born to a concubine and not to an Empress did not constitute an impediment to his succeeding his father on the throne. It was indispensable only that the mother should be of a Manchu family, inscribed in one of the eight Banner Corps.

The happy event was hailed as a good omen. It put new life into the tottering Empire and seemed a presage of better days to come. In Hunan and in Kiang-hsi, the imperial troops gained signal victories over the Tai-ping rebels.

After the birth of an heir to the throne, Yehonala rose to the first grade among the concubines. She was known as 'the Ye concubine'. A year later, she was given the title of Empress of the Western Palace. Sakota, who continued to take precedence, assumed the title of Empress of the Eastern Palace. She also had a child by Hsien-feng, but its arrival made no difference to anybody, for it was a daughter and died young.

From the moment when, as favourite concubine of the Emperor, Yehonala began to have access to documents of State, it became her custom to read the reports from the provinces and to offer advice on all important questions. Very soon, a consultation with the Ye concubine became a necessary preliminary to all decisions in government matters. In her complex character we find a combination of womanly qualities (and womanly defects) with a remarkable business capacity. She was thoroughly at home in the sensuous surroundings of the harem, but she could shine also in the Council chamber and, when dealing with matters of State, she gave proof of possessing what we might call a bureaucratic mind. She loved order and system and the knowledge of precedents applied to official correspondence. She was impatient of delay, and though observant of forms she resented exaggerations of formalism. With so many natural gifts, so much aptitude for government and such personal charm, it was natural that Yehonala should carry all before her. Her situation at Court was not without its dangers, but these were not immediately apparent. In the first flush of success, there was no one to oppose her. She was the most influential person in the Forbidden City. It was her misfortune to have lived in a period of transition, when China was on the threshold of momentous changes, and the experience of the past was of little value in facing new problems in foreign affairs. The old classical education could and did produce courageous, honest and able administrators, but the Court eunuchs were ignorant, servile and corrupt. And it was through them that Yehonala had to gather information. Many of the political mistakes committed by her came from the fact that she did not possess sufficient elements to judge a situation correctly. Her mistakes were all the more dangerous because of her exceptional ability. An Arab proverb says: 'Allah protect us from the error of the intelligent.'

The first opportunity for Yehonala to intervene in questions of State arose in the matter of ensuring a capable commander for the imperial troops who were fighting the Tai-pings. Her influence was exerted in order to obtain the nomination of General Tseng Kuo-fan. This general had already proved his worth in the never-ending campaign that was being waged against the rebels in the southern and central provinces. He was a Chinese and not a Manchu, and had not possessed up till that time any influential friends at Court. He had retired from active service at a most inopportune moment, in order to go into mourning for the death of his father. This procedure was in strict conformity with the Rites, but it had the effect of putting fresh heart into the rebels. Things might have gone badly for the imperial troops, had not Yehonala brought pressure to bear on the Emperor, and persuaded him to exempt his best general from the duties of family mourning, allowing him to proceed once more to the front.

Yehonala's intervention was less fortunate when directed against the advance of the 'foreign devils'. Her advice of uncompromising resistance was not based on any real knowledge of the forces with which she had to deal.

In 1860 the thunder of foreign guns was heard within a hundred miles of Peking. The Plenipotentiaries of England and of France came to demand from the Chinese Government that it should carry out the terms of the Treaty of Tientsin, signed in 1858 and violated the following year by the refusal of the Chinese to allow foreign representatives to enter the country.

In certain books and magazine articles about the Far East, one often finds mention of 'the traditional isolation' of China under the Empire. The expression is misleading. Only the Manchu Cæsars of the decadence, conscious of their own weakness, strove to bar the door of China to all comers. The desire for isolation was a symptom of decay. But all Emperors of China considered other monarchs as their vassals and foreign Ambassadors as mere bearers of tribute, with whom there could be no necessity to negotiate.

On the other hand, England and France assumed it to be their right to maintain diplomatic relations with China, as with any other country, and they insisted on their demand to keep a Resident Minister at Peking. In 1858, the Chinese had consented. But next year, when the British Minister arrived at the mouth of the Pei-ho, the Chinese forts opened fire on his ship.

The consent of the Chinese government to receive a Minister Plenipotentiary in the capital had been given to Lord Elgin. So he was sent out once more to demand redress for the violation of the treaty. He was accompanied by the French Plenipotentiary, Baron Gros. The two Ministers were backed by an armed force of twenty thousand men. They did not attempt to enter the mouth of the river, under the fire of the Taku forts. A landing was effected farther north, and the forts were then attacked and taken from the land side. After which, the Allied army started on its march to Tientsin.

At Yehonala's suggestion, the Emperor sent an envoy, named Chi Ying, to speak with the Allied commanders in order to persuade them to go away, and to resume negotiations elsewhere. Chi Ying naturally failed in his mission, and subsequently received a silken cord, which signified permission to hang himself. Yehonala is also supposed to have dictated the following edict, which set forth the policy of the Chinese Court in foreign affairs:

Last year the Barbarians endeavoured to force the entrance to the Pei-ho, but in twinkling of an eye their ships were sunk and thousands of their bodies floated on the water for a distance of one league from the shore. I thought that this lesson would have rendered them more circumspect. But a year after their defeat they have returned, more numerous and more insolent than before. Taking advantage of the low tide, they disembarked at Pei-tang and then attacked the Taku forts. But, like true barbarians, they attacked from the rear.

Our soldiers, being accustomed to meet their enemies face to face, did not expect so much cowardice and perfidy.

Proud of a success that ought to make them blush for shame, they have now attacked Tientsin. My anger is about to strike and exterminate them without mercy. I command all my subjects, Chinese and Tartars, to hunt them down like savage beasts. Let the villages be abandoned, as these wretches draw near. Let all provisions be destroyed, which they might secure. In this manner, their accursed race will perish of hunger, like fish in a dried-up pond.

A price was set on the head of every barbarian. For the head of an Ambassador, a sum equivalent to about five hundred pounds; for the head of a general, three hundred.

IV

Punica fides

SALLUST, *Jugurtha.*

IN less than half a century, China, considering herself outside and above any *comitas gentium*, twice violated the fundamental law in foreign relations, which gives immunity to official envoys. The first of these episodes occurred in 1860, when the youthful Yehonala had just emerged from the shadows of the harem into the light of history.

During a halt in the advance of the Anglo-French forces towards the capital, thirty-eight persons (officers and interpreters) proceeded from the Allied camp to the Chinese headquarters, bearing a safe-conduct. They arrived punctually at the pre-arranged hour, with the object of discussing the terms of an armistice, as a possible preliminary to peace. They were captured, bound and hurried off in carts to the

Summer Palace, near Peking, where they underwent such harsh treatment that twenty of them died. The Emperor and his Court were there at the time, and were directly responsible. One of the survivors, a Frenchman, described the event as follows:

'When we had all been tied up, they poured water on to the ropes that bound us, to tighten them. Then they carried us off and threw us down in a courtyard, where we lay exposed to the cold by night and to the sun during the day. At the end of the second day, they gave us two small pieces of bread and a little water. In the daytime anyone who liked might come and torment us. At night they placed an official by the side of each of us. If we spoke a word, they stamped on us and gave us blows on the head. If we asked for food or drink, they filled our mouths with filth. The rest cannot be told. Mr. Anderson died after ten days. The ropes had cut into his hands and the worms crawled in his wounds. Gangrene ate away the flesh, till it exposed the bones of the fore-arm. His dead body lay for three days among the survivors.'

As soon as the Allied commanders realized that their envoys, who had gone to the Chinese camp to arrange for an armistice, had met with treachery and could not be expected to return, they prepared to resume the advance on Peking. A decisive encounter took place at Pa-li-kao, on the canal that connects Tung-chow with the capital. The Chinese army was commanded by a Mongol prince, named San-ko-lin-sin (the British Tommies spoke of him as 'Sam Collinson'). In this chieftain were centred all the hopes of the Court of Peking, and San-ko-lin-sin was confident of his own ability to drive the foreign devils into the sea. The Tartar cavalrymen, who rallied to his standard, came from no degenerate garrisons in pleasant Chinese towns. They were imbued with the old spirit of the clans that Nurachu had welded together: a survival of the Asiatic hordes, who had carried their horned standards into India, and Persia and Europe itself.

When the Allies had approached within two miles of the bridge that crosses the canal at Pa-li-kao, they saw a large mass of cavalry advancing towards them in perfect formation. The men were mounted on the vigorous Mongolian ponies, such as are now bred in North China and are probably the descendants of those with which the Huns invaded Europe. Behind the horsemen, one could descry the lines of infantry, and farther off, efficiently distributed among the trees, was the artillery. The advancing cavalry changed its formation without a spoken command or note of bugle. Orders were transmitted in silence, by means of waving flags. Though the fire of the French artillery cut long furrows in their massed formation, the Tartar horsemen never flinched, but closed up their lines and came on undaunted, with banners fluttering in the breeze. If the Chinese artillery had been as efficient as the cavalry, the outcome of the battle might have been very different. But their guns were trained high, and no one troubled to correct the aim. Unsupported as they were, the Tartar horsemen were powerless against foreign infantry and artillery. After seven hours' fighting they had to retire over the bridge, which was defended by six guns, all firing into the air, like the others.

The battle was practically over and San-ko-lin-sin's army in full retreat, but his own standard-bearer stood alone, like

Horatius on the bridge, among a pile of corpses. He was a Tartar of gigantic stature and carried a banner of yellow silk, with Chinese characters in black. With this banner, he transmitted the last orders of his chief. The fire of the allied guns swept around him; he appeared unconcerned. His fine figure, outlined against the sky, might have been a symbol of China's hopeless resistance to the impact of the West.

General de Montauban cried out: '*Ah! Le brave homme! Je voudrais bien qu'on ne le tuât pas. Sauvez le!*'

Three soldiers sprang forward in an attempt to take the Tartar giant prisoner. But even as they did so, the gunfire, which had spared him so long, cut him down as with the sweep of a scythe. The yellow banner was swept away, with the arm that held it.

The Allied forces crossed the bridge and, after a few hours' march, arrived within sight of the walls of Peking. They were not strong enough to attempt to take the town by assault, so they advanced to the north, in the direction of the Summer Palace, thinking to find there the remains of San-ko-lin-sin's army. But the enemy had retired farther west, and the Palace had been abandoned.

The failure of her policy of defiance to the foreign devils weakened Yehonala's position at Court. The timid Emperor, whom fear made unreasonable, appeared to consider that the defeat of his army was in some way her fault. And he gave ear to rival counsellors. Among these, the most influential was Su Shun, a member of the Imperial clan (not that of Yehonala) and foster-brother to the powerful

Prince Tuan Hua. The figure of Su Shun might have stepped out of the Book of Esther. Although there were no Grand Viziers at the Court of China, he had succeeded in acquiring a similar and no less lucrative position. Without assuming any office of importance, and remaining always in the shadow of two powerful patrons, the Princes Tsai Yuan and Tuan Hua, Su Shun acted in their name and to his own personal advantage. He accused high officials of extortions and peculations, which he, himself, was the first to commit. The Son of Heaven let him have his own way, and he would hold his victims in prison until they ransomed themselves with all they possessed.

Su Shun had acquired a certain hold over the Emperor, in days when they had been companions in many a drunken orgy. But his influence had waned, as Yehonala's grew in strength. At the Court of an absolute monarch, there is no more dangerous rival for a favourite minister than a favourite wife. It was Yehonala who stood in the way of Su Shun's acquiring all the power in the State. Had it been possible, he would have made away with her. Not daring to strike directly at the Empress of the Western Palace, he began by striking at her friends, and sometimes she found herself powerless to help them. But as long as Yehonala could exercise a direct influence on the vacillating mind of the Emperor, she held her own.

It was in the danger represented by the advancing foreigners, that Su Shun saw his chance. He proposed that the Court should retire to Jehol, an autumn residence and hunting lodge, situated in the mountains, outside the Great Wall. The two brothers of the Emperor, Kung and Ch'un, would remain in the capital, and to the elder, Prince Kung, might

Photo : Hartung, Pekin.

PEKIN: A CORNER OF THE TARTAR CITY

be entrusted the difficult task of negotiating with the foreign devils.

Yehonala opposed this suggestion. She pointed out that the mighty walls and fortified gates of the Tartar City (each protected by an external lunette) could be easily defended and that the foreign devils had invaded China with a very small army, compared with the resources of the country that they had presumed to defy and to attack. All of which was perfectly true. The decline of the Ching dynasty, once so warlike, was never so manifest as at that moment, when, at the first threat of danger to the Son of Heaven, it was proposed that the descendant of Nurachu should retire beyond the Great Wall into what had been the domain of the Manchus, before their conquest of China.

After much hesitation, and at the very last moment, the Emperor agreed to take refuge in flight. The Court left in haste and disorder, recalling to scholarly minds a precedent of the Chou dynasty, when the Son of Heaven fled from his capital 'his head covered with dust'.

The departure of the Court to Jehol was a masterly move on the part of Su Shun. Within the precincts of the Forbidden City, it was not always easy for an official, or even for a Prince of the Blood, to approach the Son of Heaven, whereas this was always possible for an Empress or a concubine, when the palace eunuchs were faithful to her interests and obedient to her commands. But circumstances altered greatly in the informal life of a hunting-lodge among the hills.

A long line of carts and palanquins threaded its way along the narrow track that stretches away towards the mountains, north-east of Peking. The track passed through the millet fields and fields of indian corn, which had been harvested a month before, and the paths were heavy with mud after the autumn rains. In the confusion of the hurried departure, Yehonala could not find her little son. In the palanquins, as in the Peking carts (which are closed, with a cover resembling the *felze* of a Venetian gondola), the person carried remains unseen from the road. This rendered the search difficult, especially as the bearers, outriders and eunuchs were all in a state of terror, fearing an attack from the foreign devils, who were advancing from Pa-li-kao in a north-westerly direction. At last, a message came from the Empress of the Eastern Palace, to say that the boy was in the palanquin with her. And Yehonala found him asleep in Sakota's arms.

This episode served to intensify the painful impression of that ignominious flight. Yehonala had lost authority among a crowd of frightened people, who had forgotten the rigid discipline of the Court. Every mile of the journey from Peking represented an advantage gained by her rivals and an added danger for herself.

But riding in the fields, on either side of the imperial cortège, were men who showed no haste or fear, the Bannermen of the Guard, Manchus of the Yehonala clan, whose name the young Empress bore. These were the comrades of the Tartar cavalrymen, whose unflinching courage under fire had won the admiration of General de Montauban. They were devoted to the Empress of the Western Palace, who was known to them for her beauty and for her courage. These soldiers had nothing in common with the timid courtiers, who accompanied the Emperor in his flight. Su Shun had chosen with care the officials, who might follow the Court to Jehol. But he had not selected the officers of the military escort. And commanding that escort was a young captain, by name Jung Lu, the same who in former days had played with Little Chao along the banks of the Jade Canal, when she lived in Muyanga's house in Pewter Lane.

As they came nearer to the Great Wall, the cavalcade proceeded at a more tranquil pace and threaded its way among those barren hills, that are so characteristic of Chinese landscapes and have the deceptive appearance of a painted screen.

Here we must leave Yehonala, to seek her again, later on, at Jehol. On the plain that the imperial cortège had traversed only a few hours before, one might see the flash of bayonets in the sunlight. The Allies passed round the north-eastern corner of the town, seeking what remained of San-ko-lin-sin's army. But the enemy had retired to a safe distance. The Allied commanders decided to fix their camp at the foot of the Western Hills. The tents were pitched alongside the outer wall of the Summer Palace, where three pagodas rose up like cypresses in the clear autumn sky. After the flight of the Court, the Palace itself had remained empty. The guardians and caretakers had followed the Emperor's example, and fled.

Within sight of the Allied camp, rose the fairy-like pavilions of the imperial domain. The call of foreign bugles on the hillside broke the silence of empty halls, scented with aromatic woods, beautified with pictures, glorified with velvets, with lacquer and with gold. In the Summer Palace were treasures that had been collected by Manchu Emperors of seven generations.

And no one there to guard them.

V

In Xanadu did Kubla Khan
A stately pleasure-dome decree,
Where Alph, the sacred river, ran
Through caverns measureless to man,
Down to a sunless sea.

COLERIDGE.

ONE knows something of Yehonala, if one knows the Summer Palace. It was there, if the story is true, that the Emperor first heard her singing, in the 'deep recesses among the panel trees'.

The pleasure dome, described by Coleridge, never existed. The verses came to the poet in a dream, and he wrote them down on waking. But the real Summer Palace possessed a haunting beauty, worthy of a poet's dreams. In those days it was called the Yuan Ming Yuan ('round', 'luminous', 'garden'), a classical allusion, meaning 'The garden where the intellect become rounded', that is to say, more complete. The Summer Palace to-day is sometimes called Wan Shou Shan, or 'Mountain of ten thousand longevities', and sometimes I Ho Yuan, or 'Garden of intimate harmony'.

The I Ho Yuan is a reconstruction of an older palace built by the Emperor Ch'ien Lung. Yehonala loved those lakes and streams and distant views of mountains. In the evening she used to go to a rockery, situated on rising ground, and would watch the sun setting over the Western Hills, while a eunuch recited to her the verses of Li-po:

> The birds have all flown to roost in the tree,
> The last cloud has just floated lazily by,
> But we never tire of each other, not we,
> As we sit there together—the mountains and I![1]

There is a description of the old Summer Palace, in the days of its splendour, in Sir John Barrow's *Travels in China*, published in 1804. The author accompanied Lord Macartney on his mission to the Court of Ch'ien Lung and takes some pains to make it clear that he was not impressed by anything he saw. Indeed, he waxes indignant over the scant comfort and the unswept condition of the rooms that were assigned to him. He calculates that the grounds of the Yuan Ming Yuan covered about sixty thousand acres (ten English miles in diameter), and compares it to Richmond Park,

> to which, however, they add the very great advantage of abundance of canals, rivers, and large sheets of water, whose banks, although artificial, are neither trimmed, nor shorn, nor sloped like the glacis of a fortification, but have been

[1] Translation by Professor Giles. The Chinese poet, Li-po, lived in the years A.D. 705–62.

thrown up with immense labour in an irregular and, as it were, fortuitous manner, so as to represent the free hand of nature. . . . The views appear to have been studied; the trees were not only placed according to their magnitude, but the tints of their foliage seem also to have been considered in the composition of the picture. . . .

According to Sir John Barrow, there were thirty distinct places of residence for the Emperor within the enclosures of the Summer Palace, each composing a village of no inconsiderable magnitude, for lodging the officers of state, eunuchs, servants and artificers. He does not mention the row of palaces, built in European (baroque) style, according to the designs of Jesuit fathers. These were erected to give the Emperor some idea of how foreign kings lived, in their own country.

After the flight to Jehol, Yehonala was destined never again to see the wonders of the Summer Palace, as she had known them in her youth. When she returned to Peking, all that was left was a vast expanse of hilly ground, covered here and there with smoke-blackened ruins, which were reflected in the lakes and winding streams.

Among the British officers that took part in the military operations in China, was Captain Charles George Gordon, subsequently known as 'Chinese Gordon' for the part he played in suppressing the Tai-ping rebellion. He wrote to his mother from the allied camp near Peking:

Owing to the ill-treatment the prisoners experienced at the Summer Palace, the General ordered it to be destroyed, and stuck up a proclamation to say why it was so ordered. We accordingly went out and, after pillaging it, burned the whole place, destroying in a Vandal-like manner most valuable property which could not be replaced for four millions. We got upwards of 48 pounds apiece prize money before we went out here; and although I have not as much as many, I have done well. Imagine D . . . giving sixteen shillings for a string of pearls, which he sold the next day for five hundred pounds!

The people are civil, but I think the grandees hate us, as they must after what we did to the Palace. You can scarcely imagine the beauty and magnificence of the places we burnt. It made one's heart sore to burn them, in fact, these palaces were so large, and we were so pressed for time, that we could not plunder them carefully. Quantities of gold ornaments were burnt, considered as brass. It was wretchedly demoralizing work for an army. Everybody was wild for plunder.

All that is left to-day of the old domain are the artificial hillocks and waterways, and the ground strewn with blocks of marble, huge bricks, and fragments of majolica. Residents in Peking, who are fond of shooting, will tell you that it is a good place for snipe. This is the 'Old Summer Palace', as distinct from the New. Even the small outlying part of the ancient whole, which Yehonala reconstructed, and which is now shown to strangers, covers more ground than Hadrian's Villa, near Rome.

To view the events in their correct perspective, one should remember that the premeditated act of setting fire to the pavilions came as a final episode in the looting of all that was most precious in the Yuan Ming Yuan. The first to despoil the palace, after the arrival of foreign troops, were the Chinese themselves, the place having been utterly abandoned. The foreign soldiery saw the Chinese climbing over the wall, by means of ladders, and thus discovered that looting had begun, after which it became impossible to prevent them doing likewise. Their commanding officers interfered to put a certain order in the proceedings, so that every man, as far as possible, should have an equal share. The decision to set fire to the buildings was taken, after Lord Elgin had ascertained, from the survivors among the envoys, the fate of those who had not survived.

Everything pointed to the Court's being responsible for the cruelties committed. The English representatives might have insisted on the punishment of those who had accomplished the deed. In this case the Court of Hsien-feng would have got off cheaply enough. Examples of vicarious punishment are not unusual in China. But in setting fire to his *Domus Aurea,* Lord Elgin struck at the Emperor himself, *nella roba e nell'onore.* It is thus (in a man's belongings and in his honour) that, according to Machiavelli, an injury should be inflicted.

When one knows the facts and the circumstances, one can but admit that Lord Elgin's was the only way. And one's sympathies go out to the dour little Scotsman, who was not afraid of being accused of vandalism, when he gave the grim order to burn and to destroy. War would become ten times more horrible, if the envoys who engage in the preliminaries of peace are not to be held sacred. And what would they have cared, those torturers of unarmed messengers, for large sums paid out in indemnities, or severed heads that rolled to the foreign devil's feet ? Only in those smoking ruins was there an unmistakable sign of a power greater than China's; a power that from the end of the world could mete out justice and avenge its dead.

The French Plenipotentiary, Baron Gros, would not associate himself with his British colleague in the burning of the Summer Palace, though the French soldiers had taken an active part in the looting (a famous necklace of black pearls was taken home by the General de Montauban). Baron Gros feared that the final act of reprisal might interfere with the negotiations for peace. But the French historian, la Gorce, takes a favourable view of Lord Elgin's decision:

> With Asiatic peoples, nothing convinces more than mere brutal strength; nothing succeeds like the *fait accompli.* Lord Elgin's somewhat risky decision was fully justified by the result. 'I fear,' wrote Baron Gros, 'that this act of useless and savage vengeance will so frighten Prince Kung that he will take flight and disappear into Manchuria.'
>
> But the Prince did not fly. On the contrary, it was then, and then only, that he understood the uselessness of further subterfuges. The flames were still mounting upwards, when a despatch from the Chinese Plenipotentiary was brought to the French camp; the first despatch that expressed, in clear and unequivocal terms, the formal acceptance of the Allies' proposals. At last they held something positive. Baron Gros seized the opportunity with enthusiasm. Lord Elgin did so with considerable hauteur.

The Anglo-Chinese convention was signed on the 24th of October, the Franco-Chinese convention on the 25th. At that time, the Allies held one of the gates of the town in order to make impossible any treachery towards those who entered the capital. Lord Elgin was living in a temple outside the walls. On the day appointed, he proceeded to the Tribunal of Rites in a palanquin carried by sixteen Chinese bearers robed in scarlet. His horse was led behind him, and the members of his suite rode on either side. British troops lined up to keep order, as the Chinese crowds pressed forward to see 'the Great Barbarian'. A military band played *God save the Queen,* as Lord Elgin's palanquin was carried right into the pavilion where the signature of the Conventions was to take place, and where Prince Kung was waiting on a raised platform. Two chairs stood, one on each side of the table where the official documents were placed in ornamental boxes. Lord Elgin's credentials were first read out, and then the Imperial edict which authorized Prince Kung to use the seal of State. There were no speeches, no compliments and no greetings; only a formal bow on arriving and on departure. When the documents had been exchanged, Lord Elgin rose and went away, as he had come, Prince Kung accompanying him to the door.

Baron Gros, who performed the same ceremony next day, was more affable. He presented Prince Kung with portraits of the Emperor Napoleon, of the Empress Eugenie and of the Prince Imperial. He excused himself for not being in full uniform, as his baggage had been lost in a shipwreck off Ceylon. Prince Kung replied that he also was not in full dress: 'Your uniform was destroyed by water, and mine by fire.'

This was his only allusion to the burning of the Summer Palace.

After the signature of the Conventions, it was no longer possible to put off the evil day when official representatives of the 'outer barbarians' should take up their residence in the capital. The first foreign Minister Plenipotentiary was Mr. Bruce (Lord Elgin's brother), who arrived in Peking in March 1861. His presence was so much resented that several influential persons suggested transferring the Court permanently to Jehol. But such a decision would have caused considerable financial loss to the Manchu Bannermen, whose principal allowance (payable while they acted as a bodyguard to the Emperor) ceased automatically when the Court was not in residence in Peking. Therefore the officers of the Peking garrison, and the Manchu Bannermen in general, exerted all possible pressure to bring the Emperor back.

VI

O fair white silk, fresh from the weaver's loom
Clear as the frost, bright as the winter snow,
See! Friendship fashions out of thee a fan.
At home, abroad, a close companion thou,
Stirring at every move the grateful gale;
And yet, I fear, ah me! that autumn chills
Cooling the dying summer's torrid rage
Will see thee laid neglected on the shelf,
All thought of bygone days, like them, bygone.

By THE LADY PAN CHIEH YÜ. *Translation by* PROFESSOR GILES.

YEHONALA'S interests coincided with those of the Manchu Bannermen. She also had reason to wish for a speedy return to Peking.

The Court had taken up its quarters at Jehol, in a palace known as 'The Mountain Lodge where you avoid the heat', and it had brought into the pure mountain air all the baneful atmosphere of the Forbidden City, ever laden with suspicion and intrigue. The natural beauty of the hills served as a background to mysterious dramas, in which concubines and princes faced each other in deadly rivalry. At night, on the terraces overlooking the Valley of the Lions, Court astronomers questioned the heavens, and noted portents foreshadowing calamity. In the sky above the southern ranges, a comet outshone the stars.

On his splendid couch, inlaid with cloisonné, the Emperor lay dying. He sought relief from the pains that racked his limbs, by frequent massage at the hands of a young eunuch, named Lu Lien-ying. The Courtiers hid their indifference to his sufferings under a mask of abject veneration, and meanwhile they busied themselves with a question that in the East is ever fraught with danger: the question of a regency.

As in the days of Marco Polo, the imperial couriers travelled between Peking and Jehol with silver hawks on their caps (the insignia of their office). They wore leather belts hung with bells, so that one could hear them on the road, far down the valley.

The Emperor had asked for information concerning that special breed of foreign devil, known as *In-guo* (English people), who seemed to be even more tiresome than the others. One day a messenger brought him a long report, written on yellow paper and bound with yellow silk; in this document the history of the British nation was set forth in brief. But, after glancing through the manuscript and reading a few pages here and there, Hsien-feng dropped it with a sigh and the weary comment: 'They seem to be always at war, or going to war, with somebody!'

Other messengers travelled up and down the southern road, without their approach being heralded by the sound of bells: messengers from the Princes and the Chief Eunuch to their adherents in the capital. They bore secret reports and confidential news concerning the rival forces that faced each other across the bed of the dying Emperor. The struggle between Su Shun and Yehonala grew more bitter, as Su Shun advanced in the Emperor's favour, and Yehonala's position became less secure.

'The Tsai Yuan Conspiracy' is the name given by historians to the attempt made by Su Shun and his patrons to assume the supreme power, by obtaining from Hsien-feng a decree which should invest them with the quality of Regents, during the minority of the heir to the throne. They laid their plans to prepare for a Council of Regency, composed of the two Princes, Tsai Yuan and Tuan Hua, with Su Shun in a minor capacity. The brothers of the Emperor and the two Empresses were to be excluded from any participation in affairs of State. Such an exclusion had a sinister significance. Other decrees were in course of preparation, ordering the arrest of the Princes Kung and Ch'un, for having signed the conventions with England and with France and admitted the presence of foreign Envoys in the capital.

The conspirators made their preparations in secret, for it was uncertain how long the Emperor might live. As long as he lived and was well enough to think for himself, no one could be sure of holding his favour.

In Hans Andersen's fairy tale, *The Nightingale*, the author describes an Emperor of China, who lay dying on his magnificent bed, abandoned by all the courtiers. They had gone to greet his successor. Death was pressing on the Emperor's chest, and all around were the ghosts of his past deeds. But suddenly, through an open window, came the sweetest music. The nightingale sat on a branch outside and, as she sang, the ghosts faded away and Death himself departed. There is an unconscious touch of realism in this story, except, of course, for the end.

To Hsien-feng, lying in his costly pavilion, all lacquer and silk and gold, there came through open windows the rustling of leaves in the forest and the voices of woodsmen calling to one another in the valley. He could hear the short tread of donkeys on mountain paths and the murmur of the river in its bed. Cocks crowed and dogs barked in distant farms. In the early morning and again at sunset, came the twittering of birds.

It is not probable that, if the courtiers had left him for dead, like the Emperor in the fairy-tale, Hsien-feng really would have got well while the birds sang outside his window. But, at any rate, he might have passed away in peace. To the end, Su Shun tormented him with insinuations against the Empress of the Western Palace, recalling the story of an unfaithful concubine, in the time of Ch'ien Lung, who was sent to the Cold Palace, where Princes of the Blood were imprisoned.

The ancient Chinese simile of 'the autumn fan' dates from a poem, written in the first century before Christ, by the Lady Pan Chieh Yü, whom the Son of Heaven had loved and then forgotten. Like a fan in autumn, Yehonala was laid upon the shelf. To be removed from power, in the Orient, often means to step down from a throne into a grave. On the Emperor's birthday, when he held a last levée to receive the congratulations of the Court, the Empress of the

Western Palace was not permitted to be present. Her son was taken from her and entrusted to Tsai Yuan's wife. Such were the episodes in a silent warfare, no less portentous for the fate of China than the struggle between Lord Elgin and Prince Kung on the broader stage of international politics.

Never in her long life did Yehonala prove herself so wise, so prudent and withal so brave, as during those ominous days when the Son of Heaven lay dying and her own future hung in the balance. One false step would have cost her her life; an opportunity missed, or an action delayed, would have meant the triumph of her enemies and her own ultimate doom. But Yehonala made no mistake. Nor was she slow to act, and to act in secret.

To the vigilant eye of Su Shun she appeared ever tranquil and resigned. Thus she succeeded in lulling any suspicion that she might be meditating a counter-move, to thwart his plans. But after Hsien-feng's birthday, she sent off a secret message to Prince Kung, to inform him of what was happening at Jehol, and to ask him to despatch reinforcements of Manchu troops of her own clan. The connivance of the Chief Eunuch, An-te-hai, made it possible to send off this message, which was delivered, not only in Yehonala's name, but in the name of the two Empresses.

A story is told of how Yehonala succeeded in obtaining the consent of her imperial colleague to sending a secret messenger to Prince Kung. The difficulty lay, not in reaching an agreement (for a common danger threatened the two Empresses), but in discussing the situation without arousing the suspicion of Su Shun's spies. There is no privacy for an Empress in Eastern lands, and no solitude.

Eunuchs and waiting women were always near Yehonala, ready to offer a fan, or a handkerchief, or a comfit box. Only out of doors was it sometimes possible to keep them a little distance off. Indoors, there were watchful eyes and attentive ears behind every silk partition.

It happened one afternoon that the two Empresses were walking together in the garden, surrounded by the Court and under the surveillance of those who had been instructed to follow their every movement and to listen to every word they spoke. As the group proceeded down a narrow path, where only two could walk abreast, they came to a large bowl of goldfish. When they reached it, the Empresses stopped and remained there for a minute or two, idly bending over the water. They smiled and spoke in low-pitched voices, seeming only to admire the beauty of the golden fish. But in those brief moments, Yehonala made the proposal that Sakota accepted.

One might not speak in the future tense of the death of a Chinese Emperor. But, as one of his titles was 'Lord of Ten Thousand Years', one might say 'when ten thousand years have passed'. The euphemistic phrase was pronounced more and more often, till one day Hsien-feng appeared indeed to be nearing his end. Then Su Shun and the two Princes turned everyone out of the Emperor's room and submitted to him the decrees appointing a council of regency. Prince Tsai Yuan was to be its president; the other two were to be members. A special decree forbade Yehonala to exercise any control over the child Emperor.

Hsien-feng died on the following day, or, to use the orthodox Chinese expression, 'he mounted the Dragon for the long journey'.

Strange tales have gathered round that death-bed (this often happened when a Chinese Emperor passed away). In the dynastic laws of the Manchus, there is no law of primogeniture. K'ang-hsi, the second of the line, had thirty-five sons and twenty daughters. He changed the order of succession several times during his long life, and thus caused bitter family feuds. His son, Yung Chên, wrote with his own hand the name of the prince whom he chose to succeed him, and placed the paper in a sealed casket, in the presence of the Court. When the Emperor died and the casket was opened, it was found to contain the name of Ch'ien Lung, the fourth son of the deceased.

Hsien-feng had only one son to succeed him and he did not deem it necessary to officially designate him as his heir. All he did was to ensure—or attempt to ensure—that, after his death, the Empress of the Western Palace should not have any part in the government of the country. If necessary, she should be made to commit suicide.

According to one version of this story, the Emperor placed his written order in the hands of Su Shun, and the latter hid it in the imperial bedchamber, under or inside one of those hard, flat cushions that cover the Chinese *kangs*. The secret was discovered by the eunuch, Li Lien-ying, who nursed the Emperor and used to massage his limbs. Li Lien-ying did not dare to steal the written order, but he mentioned it to the wife of Prince Ch'un, who was Yehonala's younger sister. She had come to Jehol, shortly after the arrival of the Court. Either she stole the order, on being admitted to the bedchamber when Hsien-feng was nearing his end, or this was done by Yehonala herself. When Su Shun looked for it, the document had disappeared.

The death of Hsien-feng marks the end of an epoch, for he was the last Emperor of China to reign in Peking, before the coming of the foreign diplomats. Up till 1861 the governments of Europe and America received no direct official information about events in the capital of China. After that date, they had the reports of their Ministers, and though the latter might not be in direct communication with the Court itself, they were 'the men on the spot' and as such could keep up a daily contact with people who were willing to act as informants.

In a sense, the Chinese idea was justified that the presence of foreign officials in Peking constituted a contamination and a sacrilege. For those foreign officials committed, with almost every mail home, a crime of *lèse majesté*, criticizing and blaming the policy of the Son of Heaven. The old seclusion might be maintained behind battlemented walls, and the old mystic super-philosophy; but the aloofness and the mystery were no more. Peking might be visited and described by 'foreign devils' from all over the world. In that unveiling the greatest of Eastern cities lost something of its own soul.

VII

The bright moon is not round for long
The bright cloud is easily dispersed.
Chinese Proverb.

DEATH had come to the Emperor when the star of Su Shun was in the ascendant, but that star soon reached its zenith. The conspirators had been appointed regents. So much they achieved, but the Emperor being dead, they could no longer seek shelter behind his authority. They had to face the opposition of their rivals and hold their own as best they might. Of all their opponents, the most formidable was the young Empress of the Western Palace. Su Shun proposed that she should be done away with. But the Princes Tsai Yuan and Tuan Hua were afraid that Yehonala's death might bring matters to a head, before they had the situation well in hand.

The decrees appointing the Regents took effect at Jehol and were transmitted to Peking for promulgation. But it was immediately noted that the documents lacked a proof of authenticity that should have been given them by the imprint of 'The Seal of Legally Transmitted Authority'. At the moment when the dying man had signified his assent to the last decrees that bore his name, the Seal could not be found. It is probable that the Emperor was too far gone to notice the omission.

It became evident, later on, that Yehonala must have hidden the seal. By this simple expedient, she invalidated all the documents that transferred the supreme power from the Son of Heaven to the regents of his choice. A mere signature would not have been sufficient to give effect to the Emperor's wishes.

A Chinese seal consists of a group of formalized ideograms, used as a device, which can be printed on paper to authenticate a document. This imprint takes the place of a signature. Using the word 'seal', not to signify the impression itself, but the implement for making it (more properly called matrix), we may add that Chinese seals of State are incised (often with great skill) on ivory, jade or gold. They are large and heavy. Each seal is kept on a table by itself, and, in the days of the Empire, used to be covered with cloth of gold. The pigment used is cinnabar in the form of a vermilion paste. Violet or purple colours are used when the signatory is in mourning.

After the death of Hsien-feng, the Regents might have denounced the theft of the most important Seal of State. But they feared to create a scandal, by accusing Yehonala, who enjoyed much personal prestige among the Manchu Bannermen. Su Shun and his patrons did not belong to the clan of Yehonala, and though they had with them a bodyguard of their own clan, it was outnumbered by the adherents of the young Empress. Thus the Regents were masters of the situation only as long as they did not attempt, in Jehol itself, any open act of violence against their formidable rival.

The late Emperor's last decrees were not well received in Peking, where the newly appointed Regents were unpopular. Memorials were sent in by the Censors, advising that the Princes Kung and Ch'un, as well as the two Empresses, be associated in the Regency. But Su Shun counted on being able to set aside all protests, as soon as he should find himself once more within the walls of the capital. The treasure stored in the cellars of his palace would buy political support in Peking. He hoped also to take advantage of the popular discontent, following on the signature of the Anglo-Chinese and Franco-Chinese conventions. The ink on these treaties was hardly dry, and the fire still smouldered among the ruins of the Summer Palace, yet already the Manchu Princes at Jehol were contemplating a systematic massacre of all foreign diplomats in Peking, as a means of acquiring popular favour and of consolidating the regency. A similar idea recurred again and again, among Court officials, and materialized at last in the attacks on the foreign Legations, by the Boxers, in 1900.

The struggle between Su Shun and Yehonala continued, while preparations were being made to transport the late Emperor's body to Peking. But it was a silent struggle. The adversaries faced one another in attitudes of deference, while performing acts of ritual, prescribed by an ancient etiquette. Clouds of incense floated round them, and chanting bonzes droned the praises of the dead. Questions of life and death hung in the balance, but the ceremonies that follow the passing of an Emperor had to be accomplished in due form and the closing Annals of the reign prepared in the grand manner. Men are fragile mortals. They are born, and die, and are born again. Only the Rites endure for ever. On this creed, Eastern philosophy takes its stand. Truth is that which is accepted as such; wisdom consists in adapting realities to appearances; error in assuming that material things are only what they are.

The Rites offered to Yehonala a strategic advantage of which she was not slow to avail herself. On the journey from Jehol to Peking, the bier, carried by one hundred and sixty bearers, had to be accompanied by the Regents. But the Empresses might travel independently, preceding the coffin, in order to be in Peking in time to receive it at the gates of the town. The funeral procession had to move slowly (the journey might take ten days, or more). But the Empresses could travel fast.

Su Shun realized the danger of allowing Yehonala to arrive in the capital before him, and he took steps to avert it, ordering that the two Empresses be accompanied to Peking by the personal escort of the Prince Chief Regent. With such an escort the Empresses would never have reached their journey's end. The place was decided on, where they were to meet their death: on the lower slopes of the mountains, that open out on to the plain. Jung Lu had orders to remain behind, to command the escort of the funeral cortège.

The bier was shaped like a domed pavilion, curtained with yellow satin, embroidered in gold. It was borne shoulder-high, on a network of poles, lacquered in crimson and gold.

The secondary poles crossed and recrossed each other as the weight was divided up among the bearers. Unless the transport was effected with infinite precautions, the oscillation might have tossed the coffin into the air. The bearers, keeping time under orders from their chief, had to advance three steps, then stop during three beats (struck on a musical wooden gong), then advance three steps, and again stop during three beats without moving—and so on, for a hundred and fifty miles. At each halt, the bearers were changed, and at each resting-place (every fifteen miles) temporary pavilions had been erected, to shelter the dead Emperor and his suite. These pavilions were made of poles and matting, and were called the ' mat-shed palaces '.

All through the long day, Jung Lu rode, silent, at the head of his faithful Bannermen; the procession advanced slower than at foot's pace. As the shadows lengthened, the first of the mat-shed palaces came in sight. When they reached it, all dismounted and knelt in the dust, while the catafalque was housed in its resting-place. Only the bearers might stand at such a moment. All others, headed by the Regents, had to kneel. But even as they knelt, Jung Lu, with raised hand, gave a signal, and the Bannermen sprang to their feet. The quiet evening air rang to the slap of saddles; stirrup chimed against stirrup as the eager ponies, so long held in on the curb, let themselves out for a race. The startled Regents looked round and saw only an empty space where the horsemen had been kneeling. Jung Lu had dashed off into the mountains, a lover to the rescue of his love.

A few hours later, in the darkness of her palanquin, Yehonala heard a thunder of hoofs on the track behind. Another moment, and the frightened bearers staggered and faltered under the poles, as Jung Lu tore aside the curtain, to make sure that the Western Empress was safe. Around her, on sweating horses, closed the guardsmen of her clan.

It may be that, even then, the Regents guessed that in going forward to Peking, they faced the possibility of disgrace and death. But they proudly kept their place in the funeral train, as it lumbered slowly on towards its goal. Of Jung Lu's desertion of his post beside the Emperor's bier not a word was said. Between the Empresses and the Regents as they travelled, messengers came and went with reciprocal enquiries: formal letters from Yehonala to Tsai Yuan, commending him for his care of the imperial coffin; official edicts from Tsai Yuan to Yehonala, to thank her for her kind interest and to assure her that all was well.

It began to rain, and the sticky mud added a new difficulty to the advance of the catafalque. Yehonala sent a present of one thousand taels, to be distributed among the bearers, and once more Tsai Yuan formally expressed his thanks. In that exchange of courtly messages, the antagonists played their parts with dignity and a certain grim deference, like duellists whose rapiers rise and dip to the salute before they seek to kill.

As soon as she reached Peking, Yehonala summoned to secret conclave the brothers of the late Emperor and the two Grand Secretaries of State. She warned them that Su Shun was bringing with him lists of proscription, which meant death to all those who opposed him in the past. It was always Yehonala who took the initiative in these matters. Sakota's part in political events was practically *nil.*

Three days after the arrival of the Empresses, watchmen on the wall of the Tartar City descried the outriders of the funeral cortège on its march towards Peking. The yellow and gold of the imperial brocades rivalled the autumn tints of the countryside. As the catafalque drew near, the child Emperor went out to meet it and knelt at the side of the road. Behind him knelt his uncles, the Empresses and the dignitaries of the Court. The gates of the town were guarded and the streets lined with troops faithful to Yehonala.

After the ceremonial greetings, and when the sacrifices and libations were over, the Regents advanced in the incense-laden air and entered the marquee (last of the 'mat-shed palaces'), which had been set up near the An-ting gate for their reception. According to the dynastic laws, they had to render account to the Son of Heaven of their task of bringing the remains of the late Emperor to the capital. Speaking in her son's name, Yehonala thanked the newly arrived Princes for the faithful fulfilment of their duties, as well as for their zeal as Regents, a charge which they were now permitted to relinquish.

Tsai Yuan answered haughtily, and with threatening mien: Our authority emanates from the late Emperor and cannot be taken from us. The Empress of the Western Palace has no right to be present at an audience, save with our express consent.'

No one answered. The Regents stood for a moment puzzled and nonplussed. Then Prince Kung held out the edicts which appointed the two Empresses as Regents, during the minority of Yehonala's son. This time, the Seal of Legally Transmitted Authority was not missing.

Su Shun turned to his fellow-conspirators and exclaimed in bitter reproach:

'If you had listened to me when I first proposed to do

away with this woman, we should not have come to such a pass!'

That was the only moment when any of the actors dropped his mask. Once that moment had passed, the funeral rites continued as if nothing had happened. But, on coming out of the marquee, to join the cortège which continued on its way to the palace, the ex-Regents took the second place. Later on, when the ceremonies were over, they were tried by the tribunal of the imperial clan, Prince Kung presiding. Another series of edicts was promulgated, giving details of the conspiracy and condemning the conspirators to death, a lingering death by dismemberment. But a special act of Imperial clemency modified this sentence. Su Shun was beheaded in the market-place, and Yehonala confiscated his property. The Princes Tsai Yuan and Tuan Hua were each presented with a silken cord with which to hang themselves.

VIII

You cannot get to the Emperor, to tell him your wrongs.

Chinese Proverb.

MERE 'foreign devils', who resided in Peking before 1887, never saw the Dowager Empress or the Son of Heaven. If they did catch a glimpse of them, it was by chance; one might almost say, by mistake. Even the diplomats were not received at Court. When a foreign Minister expressed a desire to present his credentials, he was told that it was not possible, as long as the Emperor was a minor. All he could do was to frequent the somewhat dingy little pavilions in the Tartar City, and discuss matters with the officials who were supposed to conduct the foreign affairs of the nation.

These gentlemen (none of whom spoke a foreign language)

were cordial and friendly, but they took no pains to conceal the fact that the relations between China and foreign nations were of little importance, when compared to other public matters. It was apparent that many of these officials only learnt of the existence of the various Western States at the moment when they took up their duties and came into contact for the first time with foreign diplomats and their interpreters. A list of the 'Barbarian' nations was then consulted, giving the names of each, with some indication of their relative importance.

The Chinese 'Foreign Office' worked under the direction of Prince Kung and was briefly called the Tsung-li Yamen. Its full title might be translated 'Directorate General for the Affairs of All Countries'. This denomination was intended to convey to the mind of the 'stupid people' (a Chinese expression corresponding to what we would call public opinion) that among Prince Kung's minor duties there was also that of regulating the internal affairs of vassal States. Among the staff of the various Legations in Peking, the Tsung-li Yamen was known as the Office for saying *No* to foreign diplomats.

In a book, written in the eighties and published in 1901, called *John Chinaman*, by E. H. Parker, formerly a British Consul in the Far East, there is an amusing description of the Tsung-li Yamen's personnel:

Possibly things are changed since I was there, and in any case my intercourse with the old boys of the *Yamên* was limited. I only saw Prince Kung once, and that was on October the first 1869, when he came to say good-bye to Sir Rutherford Alcock. Ch'unglun was a curious man with a huge goitrous wen, and naughty, twinkling eyes; he specially shone at the race-course, or in telling a *risqué* story.

Tung Sün was a renowned poet, whose sacred fire was easily kindled by Sir Thomas Wade; I believe he inflicted upon the Peking world a translation of *Childe Harold*. Great men are usually known by a *mot*. Tung Sün's *mot* was: *Pi-fang, yi-t'iao Yü-a!* ('for instance one piecey fish'); the wit comes in through the simile of one fish (England, of course) leading the way, and then others (minor powers) following in a line: also in the word *pi-fang* ('for instance'), a favourite refuge for foreign interpreters when hard-pressed for a word: hence Sir Rutherford's caustic expressing: '*pi-fanging* their way through an interview'.

Cheng-lin seemed to have had the end of his nose snipped off and replaced by a piece of dull red Turkish pipe-clay. The others were Shên Kwei-fên and Paoyün, neither of whom left very definite impressions upon my inexperienced and callow mind.

All Chinamen and Manchus of rank seem to have a 'monstrosity' of some sort: either a fearful goitre; or one side of the face totally different from the other; or a strange squint; or four or five teeth run together in one piece, like a bone; or a big dinge in the forehead; or a beard consisting of six long, stout bristles; or a set of eagle's claws instead of nails. In those days everyone was deeply pock-marked. All men's morals are *plus quam* Turkish, for it is the Peking custom to have them so, and one feels a ghoulish sort of sensation in their presence. Ch'unglun did me the honour to wet his finger and rub my cheek to see if I were painted; Li Hung-chang patted me and put his arm round my neck. It will be remembered that the Emperor Kienlung, who was a notorious old *rip*, similarly patted the head of Lord Macartney's page, Sir George Staunton. Their 'room' is decidedly better than their company when temptation offers, for they are not very strong in virtue, any of them. Perhaps it is 'only their way . . .'

It was great fun talking to them: they seem to loathe business, and to be convulsed with merriment at the thought of the British Lion roaring with rage, just because a missionary had had his eye squelched whilst holding forth from a barrel in the streets. I remember once 'soaring to eloquence' myself in describing in horror-stricken language and earnest tones how the *shih-lao-ju-yü* ('the stones fell like rain') about some preachers' heads. 'Splendid!' said Ch'unglun. 'Not bad at all! You've got it well off by heart! Ha! Ha! —The stones fell like rain!' This was too much for me; I joined merrily in the infectious mirth, and the rest of the interview was noisy, hilarious and anything but business-like. The fact is that the *Yamên* does not want any missionary to be basted, nor any merchant defrauded: the view of life (and government) it takes is quite easy and good-natured: 'Oh! don't bother; let things right themselves: we'll pay the damage some time. What did he want preaching there?' or 'What did he sell things to a man like that for?'

Of all Prince Kung's offices, by far the most important was his position as mentor to the Empresses during their first regency.

Kung and his brother Ch'un were typical Manchus, with heavy, lethargic faces, strangely reminiscent (if one makes allowance for colour and racial characteristics) of a contemporary statesman in England, Lord Hartington, afterwards eighth Earl of Devonshire. One can imagine that Prince Kung, whose mentality was of a somewhat ponderous calibre, must have appeared as a tower of strength to a young Empress, who needed advice and help. But later on, Yehonala came to regard him with the impatience natural to her quicker and more brilliant intelligence.

The collaboration and advice of a man of mature experience, such as the late Emperor's brother, was indispensable to Yehonala, until she had acquired a greater familiarity with the routine of government. Especially in questions of foreign policy was she willing to leave things to him and to his jovial and goiterous underlings.

Prince Kung realized his own usefulness and presumed

on it more than was prudent. He spoke and acted as if he were Chief of the State and he appointed his own personal friends to the more important offices. He was reported to have said that, if the two Empresses occupied the throne, it was entirely due to his favour and support. He made it plain that he considered it his right to be received by the Empresses at any hour that suited his own convenience.

To the Empress of the Eastern Palace, this mattered not at all. Sakota had no ambition to govern. But Yehonala began to resent the over-confident manner of her principal counsellor. Nevertheless, she kept her feelings to herself, biding her time till the opportunity should arise to make clear who it was that ruled within the Palace and throughout the Empire.

The opportunity presented itself on an April night in 1865. During an audience with the Empress of the Western Palace, Prince Kung rose to his feet before he had been dismissed from the Presence. A small matter, but the incident became historical. To understand how this could be, it is necessary to know something about the audiences and the accompanying ceremonial.

No greater honour than an audience could be conferred on a subject of the Chinese Emperor, and as a rule it was no barren honour. An official who had been admitted to prostrate himself before the Dragon Throne felt that he was entitled, for some time afterwards, to sit in the seats of the mighty. The ceremonial was of a studied magnificence, and the difficulties in obtaining an audience were often insuperable, even for those who, as the Austrians say—or used to say—were *Hof-fähig*: qualified to be received at Court. The difficulties were even greater during the regency of an

Empress. Important officials arriving in Peking from the Provinces found the Forbidden City aptly named, since entrance was denied to them, as to any common coolie. One had to know the 'open Sesame' which could set wide the bronze-studded portals, to admit those whom the Empress delighted to honour.

This charm, strange to say, could usually be found (and bought) in certain curio-shops situated to the north of the Coal Hill, on the street that runs between the Drum Tower and the Bell Tower.

Supposing that a *Tao-tai*, i.e. the civil governor of a province, or some equally important official, found himself out of office and wished for a new appointment, his best hope lay in obtaining an audience with the Empress of the Western Palace. So he would take his request to the *K'ai-men-ti* (Warden of the Gates), or better still, to the Chief Eunuch.

If things went well, the *Tao-tai* in search of a job would be confidentially informed, through some minor go-between, that the Chief Eunuch had a great longing to possess a certain pair of vases, that were for sale at such and such a shop, near the Bell Tower. But the price was high: two hundred thousand taels! The Chief Eunuch had not the money to satisfy his artistic craving.

The *Tao-tai* would take the hint, and—if necessary—borrow the money. He would acquire the vases without bargaining over the price, and send them as a humble offering to the illustrious connoisseur, who desired to possess them. A considerable part of the two hundred thousand taels probably reached the privy purse of the Empress herself, and an almost equal part was doubtless appropriated by the Chief Eunuch, and a certain profit accrued to the owner of the shop near the Bell Tower. It was understood, of course, that so expensive an audience would not be barren of good fruit. An Empress, on receiving a request in person, could not refuse or adopt a non-committal attitude. The fact of his being received signified that the petitioner's prayer would be granted. 'The King's face gives grace.'

The ritual observed during an imperial audience was characteristic of a Court which knew all the psychological value of a rigid etiquette. The act of bending the knee, which in our day a westerner performs as if conscious of humiliation, was accomplished by Chinese officials with easy simplicity. When it was necessary to remain in a kneeling position for a long time, they used to strap small wadded cushions on to their knees. These cushions were not visible under the long robe. The obligation of kneeling during an audience was originally a precaution against a sudden attack. Later it became a mere matter of form. At any time and place, a person receiving an imperial order was expected to put his knee to the ground.

Audiences used to take place in the very early hours of the morning and the officials were accompanied into the hall by a eunuch, who showed them at what distance from the throne they should kneel. When he had done so, and had announced the exact hour at which the official had presented himself to be received, the eunuch had to run quickly out of the hall. It would have been a grave misdemeanour on his part to have remained before the Dragon Throne for one moment longer than was necessary. But apparently there was no objection to the eunuchs remaining in the room, behind the Empress, as long as they were not seen.

Princes of the Blood and the two Grand Secretaries of

Photo : Hartung, Pekin.

A COLUMN OF A PAVILION AT THE IMPERIAL MAUSOLEUM

State possessed the right to have a cushion placed for them, on which to kneel. Five of these cushions were always left on the floor of the hall, and they formed a barrier, which might not be removed by those who had no right to kneel on them. This was exceedingly inconvenient, as the greater distance from the sovereign made it more difficult to hear and to be heard. One might not say to an Emperor or to an Empress: 'Excuse me. What did you say? Will you repeat?' Nor would it have been polite to raise one's voice.

The remedy lay in paying the eunuch who accompanied one into the hall. He would surreptitiously remove one of the cushions, leaving room to kneel in its place.

During the audiences given by Yehonala and Sakota in the name of the child Emperor whom Hsien-feng had chosen to be his successor, a curtain of yellow silk was suspended in front of each Empress, so as to render her invisible to the person kneeling in front of the platform on which the throne was raised. In the Chinese phrase 'the Empress dropped the curtain' or 'the Empress governed from behind the suspended curtain'. This formality was observed during the first regency, which lasted from 1861 to 1873. But during the subsequent two regencies (1875 to 1889, and 1898 to 1908) Yehonala acted for an Emperor of her own choosing, therefore with greater authority, and the yellow curtain was done away with. The sovereign will was no longer made manifest through a veil.

The ceremonial of the audience, during the days of the 'suspended curtain', prescribed that whoever was received by an Empress should remain kneeling as long as her voice was heard. The cessation of questions and the prolonged silence behind the yellow curtain were the only signs of dismissal.

During the audience of April 1865 (since become famous), Prince Kung, either out of absent-mindedness, or bravado, or merely because he was tired of kneeling, rose to his feet before the Empress of the Western Palace had finished speaking. The eunuchs, who were watching from behind the throne, informed Yehonala, who immediately ordered them to give the alarm. The audience was suspended, the outer guards were summoned, and Prince Kung was ignominiously hustled out. The long-awaited moment had come for Yehonala to show who it was who ruled in China.

An imperial edict informed the world that Prince Kung had shown disrespect to the throne and had presumed to usurp powers that were not his; also that he had been guilty of favouritism in the distribution of offices. For which reason he was deprived of all his official charges, even of the directorship of Tsung-li Yamen.

But having proved her power and administered a lesson to her haughty kinsman, Yehonala's resentment faded. She was an autocrat by nature, but there was nothing spiteful about her. Once her object had been attained, she would rather use her personal charm to fascinate, then her political power to control. Also she realized that it might not be prudent to keep her influential brother-in-law too long in disgrace. The Manchu Princes were not yet prepared to accept her supremacy in all things.

Other edicts appeared, with further explanations. Prince Kung was made to appear as weeping tears of penitence. Soon after, he was reinstated in all his official charges minus one. On the occasion of the sepulture of the late Emperor, in the costly mausoleum that had been prepared for him at the Eastern Tombs, a final edict decreed that the former ones concerning Prince Kung should be expunged from the Annals of the reign.

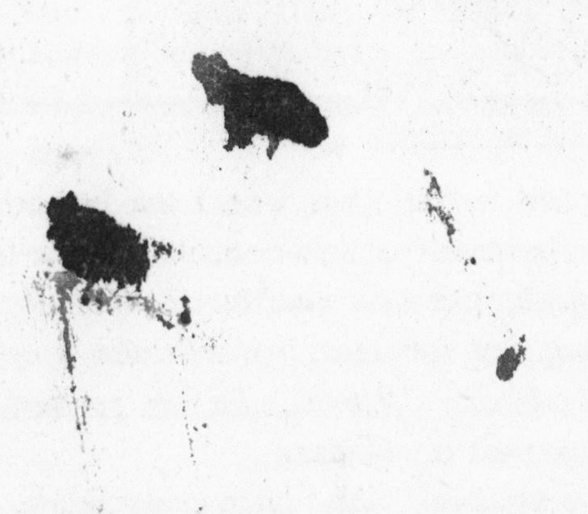

IX

Round her she made an atmosphere of life.
The very air seem'd lighter from her eyes.

BYRON, *Don Juan.*

YEHONALA, during the first regency, was in the flower of her youth and in the plenitude of her feminine charm. How great this charm was, even in later years, is told in many Memoirs, written by foreigners who knew her before and after 1900. The power of attraction, which was hers, has become a legend, and in China the remembrance of her beauty lives on, a joy for ever. It will be told of by Eastern story-tellers, long after the records of her political activity have been consigned to oblivion.

In an article by E. J. Dillon, published in the *Fortnightly Review*, the Empress is described in the following passage:

Prepossessing in person, she was so kindly in manner and suave of disposition that she won every heart, persuaded every hearer, disarmed envy and hatred. All who came in contact with her describe her as a fascinating talker. Her language abounded in witty sallies, quaint notions clothed in racy words, embellished with poetic images, bright with bursts of musical laughter. People loved to listen to her, were proud of her notice, and captivated by her smile. While she spoke, an intense fire lighted her eyes, kindled her mobile tongue, and as one of her own countrymen puts it 'made her lips drip honey'. People of character were drawn towards her despite their will, and clever statesmen were swayed by her, despite their intelligence. A magnetic force seemed to go out of her, hypnotizing her environment and making instruments of all who came within the radius of its operation.

Yehonala was small in stature, but her figure was perfectly proportioned, with a finely poised head, a broad forehead, delicately arched eyebrows and brilliant black eyes, set perfectly straight and not, as with some Orientals of Mongol origin, obliquely in the face. Her hair was jet black. Her small nose was broad between the eyes and formed a straight line with the forehead (there is nothing that the Chinese find more ugly in foreigners than fair hair and large protruding noses). When she became a widow, Yehonala followed the Manchu custom and used no more paint on her cheeks and lips. But she gained by this simplicity, for her complexion was marvellous even in old age; her skin was smooth and soft and unblemished like a child's. She took the greatest pride in it, and when she first came to meet foreigners, expressed contempt for their rough skins, so often blotchy in colour and coarse in texture. She once remarked that no one could be called beautiful, with such poor complexions as foreigners had, and that only when covered with soft downy hair, did their skins have an appearance of smoothness.

Nearly all the soaps and creams for the Empress' toilet were prepared in the Palace under her own direct supervision. She would, herself, stir the creams, when in making, and add a favourite perfume.

Her hands were beautiful, though spoilt (from a Western point of view) by long nails on the third and fourth fingers of each hand, so that she had to wear nail-protectors. These were golden shields, jewelled with rubies and jade and pearls.

Being a Manchu, Yehonala naturally did not follow the Chinese custom of binding the feet. She had a horror of such deformities, and more than once promulgated a decree 'recommending' that the barbarous custom be abandoned. She felt perhaps that she could not prohibit it altogether, as the fashion of the 'lily flower feet' was of great antiquity and connected with the story of the Lady Pàn, who danced before the Son of Heaven, on a floor of gold, where the lotus flowers were represented by clusters of precious stones (see page 20).

The footgear of the Manchu ladies consists of shoes that are raised from the ground by an extra sole, in the middle of the foot, supporting the instep only (like the pattens worn in wet weather by ladies in the days of *Cranford*). These supports are made of cork, covered over with white kid. Yehonala found that the cork soles added to her height, and gave her a more impressive appearance; therefore she wore them very high, so that her feet were raised six inches from the ground. But this lifted the knees, when she sat down. There were always several hard cushions placed on her chair or throne, to keep the knees level.

Her shoes were often richly jewelled and adorned with a hanging fringe of pearls, which fell from the level of the foot to the ground and undulated as she moved. A story was told in Peking, after the Boxer troubles, of one of these jewelled shoes being looted from the Palace and sold in Europe for six hundred thousand French francs (about twenty-four thousand pounds).

Oriental fashions in dress change slowly. The style and cut of the Court robes and even of the unofficial dresses remained practically the same during Yehonala's lifetime. But the colour and the embroideries varied with every garment, save those worn on the more important State ceremonies, in which the colour and the design might not be modified by the individual taste of the wearer. Yehonala used to have paper patterns made, on which the designs for the embroideries were carefully drawn, the colours being indicated only in one corner of the pattern, so that variants might be tried in other places. Yehonala never saw the Court tailors; she gave her orders through the eunuchs. This was because the principal part of the work of dressmaking—that of executing the embroideries—was done by men. Three embroiderers would work on one coat at the same time, sometimes taking many months, or even a year, to finish their task.

No aniline dyes were used in China at that time, and it is difficult to obtain certain colours in vegetable dyes. The embroiderers used to show much ingenuity in producing their colour effects, by combining silken threads of different hues. The outline of a golden dragon on an orange robe (orange was the colour worn, on official occasions, by the secondary wives of the Emperor) would be surrounded by a halo of violet rays, obtained by alternating blue and green threads.

This gave an effect, as the wearer moved, of changing colours. The famous 'Peking stitch', which somewhat resembles a French knot, was much used in embroidering flowers on the Court robes. Some gorgeous effects were produced by placing a golden net over gold leaf—the whole being sewn on to a satin robe. The material known as *kosseu*, which is a mosaic of silk, was fashionable during the eighteenth and nineteenth centuries. Its tones are softer than those of the embroidered silks and satins, and the otherwise unbecoming 'imperial yellow' was thus rendered more pleasing, without loss of splendour to the State robes, adorned with the twelve symbols that only the Emperor might wear.

Japanese kimonos and Chinese coats of various hues and patterns are still made by the thousand in Shanghai and other Treaty Ports of China, with the express purpose of being sold to foreign tourists. Some of them are pretty. But none of these garments can give any idea of the dazzling magnificence of the old Court robes. The nearest approach to the vanished splendour can be admired on the stage: that is to say among the dresses worn by the better-class Chinese actors. But the theatrical costumes, although very fine, do not have the delicate embroideries that were seen at the Court of the Emperor.

In winter, the Court dresses were lined with fur, with a sable collar. The head-dress was an embroidered and jewelled cap, trimmed with sable. Fur-lined dresses were worn indoors as well as out, for the Palace was heated only with braziers, and though there were heavily wadded curtains over the doors, the big halls were draughty. Carpets were not much used; the high cork soles and fur-lined shoes protected the foot from the chill of stone floors. The bedrooms were warm, being small rooms, and in winter the brick foundation of the beds was heated by fires that could be kindled from an opening in the outer wall of the house, so that no smoke could penetrate into the rooms. In these beds, called *kangs*, the warmth of the heated bricks comes up to the sleeper through wadded mattresses, and very little covering is necessary.

The fashions that change more often in the Far East are those of the women's head-dresses. When Yehonala was young, a wing-like construction was in vogue, carried out in the hair itself, which was taken from a coil at the back of the head and spread over a long jade pin, so as to form a raised bow. It was almost impossible to keep this structure in place. Yehonala hated untidiness and she used to get much annoyed at the bedraggled appearance of her ladies' head-dresses, especially in windy weather. It was at her suggestion that flat wings of black satin were substituted for the hair, where it left its parent coil. So black and shiny are the tresses of the Manchu ladies that it is difficult to see, when they wear this head-dress, where the hair ends and the black satin begins. At either side, natural flowers are worn, and jewelled ornaments. Yehonala used to wear a band of large pearls round the black coil of her hair, and, on official occasions, the so-called 'flaming-pearl' on her forehead. This pearl was supposed to represent the jewel, which appears in Chinese symbolical designs, surrounded by tongues of flame and pursued by the double-dragon, who stretches out his talons to grasp it. A setting of seed pearls and coral, round the pearl that was worn on the forehead, represented the flames. The jewel was supposed to symbolize omnipotence, and appeared also in the embroideries of the Court robes. The dragon pursued but could never attain it.

When Yehonala was dressed in her full robes of State, a long tassel, made of eight strings of large pearls, hung from the wing of her satin head-dress and fell to the right shoulder. A cape of pearls, made as a net, fitted her shoulders. The hem of her skirt was fringed with hanging threads of pearls, and she held in her hand an enormous pear-shaped pearl, which was hollowed out and had a little stopper, made of a ruby. She used this pearl as a snuff-box.

Pearls and jade were Yehonala's favourite jewels. She never wore, and apparently did not possess, any diamonds or emeralds. Her jewels were kept in boxes, in a room set apart for them. There were about six hundred boxes full, on shelves along the walls. Each box was divided up into little trays. Not all the jewels were of great value. Many were mere ornaments of coral and gold and ivory. Some of the most beautiful head-dresses were made of the tiny feathers from the kingfisher's breast, or from the wings of butterflies.

When the Court moved from Peking to the Summer Palace, or vice versa, the eunuchs carried Yehonala's dresses, in shallow trays, with wadded covers of yellow silk. She generally had about three hundred dresses in use, and even for a brief stay of two or three days, no less than sixty dresses were taken for her to choose from.

Her clothes being always cut from the same pattern, they could be put away and worn again after many years; the furs and sleeve embroideries of one dress could be detached and used on another.

Yehonala was very careful of her clothes. During meals, she wore a silken napkin, pinned to the front of her dress with a golden pin. A drop of grease or fruit-juice, falling on her dress, would cause her great annoyance, and she would immediately try to remove the stain. But she did not mind getting wet, in rainy weather. She even enjoyed doing so, perhaps because the rain comes as a real relief after the dry winters and the spring dust-storms in the north of China. She would visit her gardens and leisurely pick the flowers and gourds (the yellow, bottle-shaped gourds that are so prized by the Chinese) in pouring rain, while the Court ladies and the eunuchs stood by, in their embroidered robes, getting wetter and wetter.

When Yehonala first saw the dresses worn by foreign ladies, it was in the days of high shoulders and wasp-like waists. She observed that such clothes might look well on young girls with beautiful figures, but for persons of a certain age, they must be very trying. The long-cut Manchu dress seemed to her more practical and becoming.

Miss Carl, to whom we owe the most interesting particulars of the Empress' daily life and habits (see Chapter XXII), when excusing her own 'indiscretion' in writing about the Court, explains how:

> In doing this, I will transgress another long-established rule of Chinese propriety, which makes any comment, favourable or unfavourable, upon the Sacred Persons of Their Majesties, a breach of etiquette. No act of theirs is ever criticized, no report in reference to them is ever explained, no slander about them is ever refuted by loyal Chinese, and the generality of Chinese are loyal. Thus the falsest statements, not being refuted by those in a position to know, gain credence until they are reported as facts.

Yehonala was often accused of extravagance, especially by anti-dynastic pamphleteers in the south. And there may have been some truth in their accusations. But if one takes into consideration the resources of the Chinese Empire and the

Oriental love of splendour, such magnificence as that of the Court of Peking does not appear unjustified. Unfortunately, the cost of this magnificence was multiplied by the depredations of the eunuchs, who took care to treble the price of every luxury and of every necessity.

Yehonala's extravagance was most apparent in the rebuilding, extending and restoring her palaces, but it is nothing when compared to the lavish expenditure of the Emperor K'ang-hsi (1662–1722) who ordered the Jesuit Fathers to build for him a line of palaces in European (baroque) style, so that he might have some idea of how kings lived, in France.[1] Yehonala was also most lavish in the distribution of gifts—no less so than in her charities. In this, however, she merely followed the Chinese custom, celebrating almost every festivity by giving presents to her ladies, to the Court officials, to the eunuchs and to everybody with whom she came in contact. If she was guilty of extravagance in the richness of her presents, it was because her feelings in the matter were similar to those of Tamerlane, who was reproved by his ministers for the same fault, and answered: 'Since all the world is mine, what does it matter what I give?'

She expended large sums on frequent and costly theatrical performances. There were theatres in the Forbidden City and in the Summer Palace. One of these was built over water, this being supposed to improve the sing-song of the actors' voices, and to soften the clash of cymbals which accompanied the recitation. Yehonala had a passion for the stage, which was shared by her subjects, both Manchu and Chinese. She sometimes acted herself, with the higher

[1] See in preface K'ang-hsi's order to bring the town of Albazin to the Western hills for him to see.

eunuchs. Her favourite part was that of the Goddess of Mercy, enthroned on lotus-flowers.

Accusations of extravagance, levelled at a woman, even when they are not tinged with racial antipathy and malevolence, grow easily into accusations of immorality. Much was said about a certain 'false-eunuch', who was no other than An-te-hai, and by whom the Empress was supposed to have conceived a son. Such calumnies can have no other foundation than the malicious spite of their authors. The selection of Court eunuchs in China was regulated by rules, so severe in themselves, and so rigidly applied, that no doubt was possible.

Other stories grew around the Empress, strange erotic stories of lovers who were drawn into her embrace and then put away with a poisoned cup, lest they should presume on, or tell of, favours received. None can prove these stories, or disprove them. But there is a sameness about them all, whether they are attributed to Yehonala, or to Cleopatra, or to other beautiful Oriental queens. This makes one wonder if the scurrilous pamphlets from Cantonese or Shanghai printing presses, purporting to reveal the secrets of the Forbidden City, were not mere adaptations of old tales that have been told round camp-fires in Asia, since the world was young.

X

A name and also an omen (*nomen atque omen*).

PLAUTUS, *Persa.*

PART of the fascination of China lies in its names: The Forbidden City—The Tower of Distant Sails—The Terrace of Great Fragrance—The Garden of Past Favourites—The Island of Fulfilled Desires.

But with the names of historical personages, the trouble (from the point of view of the historian) is that they change so often. During the reign of an Emperor, one never made use of his personal name. It became taboo and ineffable, like the name of God for the Jews. Hence the constant use of the expression Tien-tze, meaning the Son of Heaven, in lieu of a personal designation. When a new Emperor ascended the throne, the fortune-tellers chose a name to designate his era, that is to say the years of his reign. This was called the

Photo : Hartung, Pekin.

A PRIEST

nien-hao (*nien* meaning year). We speak of the Emperor Ch'ien Lung, or of the Emperor K'ang-hsi, as if these were personal names, but in reality they correspond to the years of his reign, as in English 'the Victorian Era'. This custom is still followed in Japan.

At the time we have now reached in Yehonala's history, she and Sakota had titles given them by the young Emperor. Yehonala became Tzu-hsi, 'maternal and auspicious'. Sakota became Tzu-an, 'maternal and peaceful'. Each of these titles was accompanied by an allowance of about ten thousand pounds a year.

It is by the name of Tzu-hsi that Yehonala is known in foreign histories. But both Chinese and foreigners now speak of the Dowager Empress, as if this rank had never been held by others than by her. The common people used affectionate terms, such as The Great Ancestor, or The Old Buddha (*Lao-fo*). This name was given to her by the eunuch Li Lien-ying, after her prayers had been successful in bringing about the cessation of a long period of drought. The sacrifices accomplished by Tzu-hsi, in honour of the Dragon who rules over the waters, were followed by an abundant fall of rain 'as if Buddha himself had intervened'. The Empress liked the name and allowed her ladies and the eunuchs to use it even when speaking to her. To foreign ears it sounds disrespectful; not so to the Chinese. The Emperor was considered an incarnation of the Buddha, and the character *Lao* means, not only old, but also venerable.

Nevertheless the episode of a nickname, given to her by a eunuch, is typical of the intimacy which Tzu-hsi allowed to the guardians of the harem. Indeed the most serious accusation brought against her by historians is that of having shown undue favour to the eunuchs, letting them usurp the powers of government.

The Censors (a body of about fifty men, distributed between the provinces and the capital) did not hesitate to forward memorials to the throne, quoting historical precedents in order to prove that the Ming dynasty, for example, had fallen because the Palace eunuchs had been allowed to become all-powerful.

Tzu-hsi signified her approval of the memorials, but failed to act upon their advice. She expressed gratitude to the Censors who had brought the matter to her notice, and manifested her firm intention of setting her house in order. After which, things went on as before. The outlay of the Court was largely made up of percentages and commissions which accrued to the Palace eunuchs. The meals of the Imperial family (not counting servants and attendants) cost about 2,000 taels a day (at that time, equivalent to about 250 pounds). Tzu-hsi was fond of a popular dish called '*tanwo kuo*' (fruits in gravy), which consisted of poached eggs in chicken-broth. She used to be charged 24 taels for this delicacy, though the price in a good restaurant in Peking would be about the same sum in copper cents. Tzu-hsi was perhaps wise in not making much fuss about this form of 'squeeze', as it is called in China. Her father-in-law, the Emperor Tao-kwang, had taken it much to heart, without having the energy to put a stop to it. Being partial to macaroni soup, he gave orders that some should be prepared for him every day; but the eunuchs objected that this would be possible only if a special kitchen were built, at the cost of 600,000 taels. They added that the yearly expenditure of such a kitchen would amount to 15,000 taels. The Emperor replied that, according to reliable information, a bowl of macaroni soup could be bought outside the Ch'ien Mên for forty copper cents, and he ordered the eunuchs to send out and buy him a bowl every day. A week later, he was told that the only restaurant outside the Ch'ien Mên where the soup could be procured was closed, the proprietor having gone out of business. Tao-kwang was not of the herculean breed that cleans out Augean stables. He let the matter drop, and resigned himself to doing without his favourite soup.

The whole system of administration, which made the eunuchs intermediaries between the Court exchequer and the tribute-bearers of the provinces, was one that seemed especially designed to foster the cupidity of the guardians of the harem and to accentuate the dangerous confusion between their private interests and the interests of the Crown. The eunuchs received no wages, but were allowed to retain about one-tenth of the sums that passed through their hands. This percentage roughly corresponds to the 'squeeze' that is tolerated by foreign employers of Chinese servants. A 10 per cent squeeze is considered honest. More than that is extortion.

But this theoretical rate of payment, to be deducted from the tribute in bullion, represented a small part of the eunuch's perquisites. All the tribute in furs, in silks and brocades, in jade and ivory and porcelain, passed through their hands, and much of it stuck there. No purchase could be made by the Court, no works accomplished, no contact established with the outer world, without the eunuchs making a profit thereon. And this would have mattered little, had not the politics of the country, and its attitude towards international problems, been determined, or at least greatly influenced, by the interests of the eunuchs. Outside the palace, they were unpopular, and their constant interference with public affairs and private business was resented. It was often proposed that the eunuchs should be abolished altogether, and this was attempted in 1622, when the Emperor K'ang-hsi, then still a child, came to the throne. The Regents abolished the harem of the late Emperor, dismissed the eunuchs and set up an iron stele, bearing an inscription to the effect that no eunuch might ever hold public office. The reform was short-lived, for the institution of the eunuchs was considered necessary to ensure, without possibility of doubt, the legitimacy of the imperial succession. It is only fair to add that among the eunuchs were many loyal and devoted servants. The Annals tell of a Chinese admiral, who—although a eunuch—was a daring and able leader, as was Narses in the service of Byzantium.

It was the Chief Eunuch who kept discipline among his subordinates, and this discipline, which was as a rule somewhat lax, could also be very cruel. Wherever the Court went, a large bag was carried, made of yellow silk and containing rods to beat the eunuchs with.

Tzu-hsi used to fly into violent rages with the eunuch whose duty it was to dress her hair. On one occasion, through sheer nervousness, he was unfortunate enough to pull out several hairs which had caught in the comb. His irate mistress complained bitterly to the Chief Eunuch, who calmly suggested that the offender should be beaten to death.

During the first years of her life within the Palace, Tzu-hsi's favourite was the Chief Eunuch, An-te-hai, commonly known as 'little An', by reason of his diminutive stature. It was he who had been, and probably still was, the intermediary between the Empress and Jung Lu. Like many such upstarts, the little eunuch was not able to withstand the temptations and to avoid the dangers of an overwhelming good-fortune. Secure in the favour of the all-powerful Empress of the Western Palace, he failed to propitiate her colleague of the East. Sakota, or, as we should now call her, Tzu-an, was not politically ambitious, but she resented the Chief Eunuch's indifference to her wishes and his half-veiled contempt of herself. Her resentment might have mattered little, had not An-te-hai made a more formidable enemy in Prince Kung. It appears that, on one occasion, when the Prince asked for an immediate audience with Tzu-hsi, he was refused admittance on the ground that the Empress was in conversation with the Chief Eunuch. The brother of Hsien-feng was not the man to forget such an insult or to leave it unavenged.

The dynastic laws of the Manchus did not allow the Palace eunuchs to leave the capital, except when accompanying the Empresses. In violation of this law, An-te-hai went on a journey, during the summer of 1869, into the province of Shan-tung. The object of this excursion (to which Tzu-hsi gave her full consent) was to collect tribute. But the Governor of the province, an old official called Ting Pao-chen, shocked at the violation of the dynastic laws and impoverished by An-te-hai's exactions, wrote direct to Prince Kung, reporting the arrival of the Chief Eunuch, whom he denounced as having usurped the prerogatives of the Son of Heaven, travelling along the canals in gilded barges, under dragon-embroidered canopies of the imperial yellow.

Prince Kung took the incriminating reports, not to Tzu-hsi, but to Tzu-an, and obtained with some difficulty her signature to a decree, ordering the immediate decapitation of the sacrilegious eunuch, who had assumed the pomp of the Son of Heaven. A few days later, An-te-hai was invited to the Yamen of the Governor, at Tsi-nan Fu. He went, all unsuspecting, and was received with the usual formalities as a welcome guest. After an exchange of compliments and enquiries as to the health of the host and of his family, An-te-hai asked the reason of his being bidden to the Yamen. Then it was that the Governor showed him the edict containing the order for his execution. In vain the unfortunate eunuch appealed to the authority of the Empress of the Western Palace, and begged that he might be allowed to send a messenger to Peking. He was taken into a courtyard, where the executioner was waiting with his huge double-handed sword. No block is used for decapitation in China, but the executions are generally conducted with remarkable efficiency. An-te-hai was made to kneel, while a servant, standing in front of him, pulled his pig-tail, so as to hold him steady and expose the neck. One blow and the head was severed from his body.

Some time passed before Tzu-hsi heard of her favourite's death. When she did so, the Imperial countenance 'became divine in its wrath'. She sought her colleague of the Eastern Palace and cursed her with a cold concentrated fury that struck terror into the heart of the trembling Empress.

The above is the most generally accepted account of the death of An-te-hai. But there are other versions, and, owing to the mystery which surrounded events in the Forbidden City, we are left in doubt as to which of various statements comes nearest to the truth. The story was told in quite another way to Signor Ros (a member of the Italian Legation in Peking), by Ting Pao-chuan, Governor of Shan-si and brother to Ting Pao-chen, who, as Governor of Shan-tung, received An-te-hai in his Yamen and caused him to be beheaded.

According to Ting Pao-chuan, a Prince, who was one of the Emperor's uncles (it can only have been Prince Kung), was asked by An-te-hai to give him a ring of dark green jade (an archer's ring, called *pang-tze,* made to be worn on the thumb). The Prince, who detested An-te-hai, answered his request with a contemptuous refusal. Whereupon, An-te-hai told the Empress what had occurred. The next time the Prince presented himself for an audience, Her Majesty herself asked for the ring, which at once was presented to her. But the Empress passed the ring on to An-te-hai, and the latter, wishing to show off and to annoy the Prince, appeared before him with the ring on his thumb, and said: 'That which you would not hand over to me direct, I have received through the Empress'. Enraged at this taunt, the Prince turned savagely on An-te-hai and swore that, before another moon had passed, he would cause him to be put to death.

It so happened that the very next day An-te-hai went to visit a fortune-teller, to have his future predicted. The fortune-teller placed before him a small box full of little squares of paper, on each of which was written a Chinese character, and he told him to extract one of the little squares. Now it should be known that the first character (*an*) in the name of An-te-hai means 'peace' or 'tranquillity' (the same character appears in the title of Tzu-an). It is made up of two other characters, (ideograms), which correspond to our words 'woman' and 'roof'. In the philosophy of Chinese characters, *one* woman under a roof means peace and tranquillity, whereas *two* women under a roof form the character for 'discord', and *three* women under one roof correspond to 'gossip'.

The character extracted by An-te-hai from the fortune-teller's box was the one meaning 'woman' (*nu*): that is to say, the character *An*, minus the top, i.e. minus the roof. The fortune-teller interpreted this as meaning that the Chief Eunuch himself was in danger of decapitation, and he told An-te-hai to be very careful.

nu = 女

an = 安

The episode made a profound impression on the mind of An-te-hai, following as it did on the threat of the powerful Prince whom he had so imprudently offended. He thought that he could best avoid the dangers which menaced him by absenting himself from Peking. Therefore he begged the Empress to allow him to make a journey into Shan-tung. Tzu-hsi consented, but she advised him to leave town in secret, as the palace-eunuchs might not travel farther afield than Liu-ko-chao. In order to justify An-te-hai's absence from the capital, she wrote him an order for a private mission. But spies, whom the Prince kept in the Palace, promptly informed him of An-te-hai's departure, whereupon he presented himself before the Empress, together with several other Princes, in order to denounce the crime committed by the Chief Eunuch. The Imperial order, given by the Empress to An-te-hai, was not sufficient to exonerate him, for Tzu-hsi herself was bound by the dynastic laws which had been so flagrantly violated. Therefore the Empress of the Western Palace could not refuse to put her seal on the order of execution.

But as soon as the Princes had left her presence, Tzu-hsi sent a message to the Governor of Shan-tung, ordering the arrest of An-te-hai, who was to be sent under escort to Peking, for judgment. The messenger, sent off by the Empress, travelled at the rate of 600 *li* a day; but the Princes, having been informed of his departure, sent off another messenger, who could travel 800 *li* in one day (the system of mounted couriers was still, in the nineteenth century, similar to that which had been described by Marco Polo). Of the two messengers, the one who bore the order for immediate execution arrived first, and An-te-hai was promptly beheaded.

In telling this story (which is quoted here almost in his own words) Ting Pao-chuan added the following comment:

> The readiness with which my brother carried out the order of decapitation was determined, not only by his zeal in the public service, but by his personal dislike of An-te-hai, who had once been very rude to him. One day, on the occasion of an audience at Court, my brother (who was old and absent-minded) forgot his hat, outside the throne-room. An-te-hai, with shouts of laughter, seized the hat and told my brother that he must buy it back, otherwise it should be placed on a stand in one of the principal court-yards, with the inscription: 'forgotten by Ting Pao-chen, Governor of Shan-tung'. The price required by An-te-hai was 3,500 taels, and my brother, who had not so large a sum with him, was obliged to borrow it, in order to meet the eunuch's exactions and to avoid the loss of face which the jest would have caused to its victim.

Such are the two versions of the story. It matters little which (if either) be correct. To Tzu-hsi, the death of An-te-hai was a great blow. From that hour, the relations between the two widows of Hsien-feng became formal and strained. The atmosphere of a youthful, pleasure-loving Court grew sombre and dangerous. Prince Kung was reproved less fiercely than the timid Empress, who had dared to sign An-te-hai's death-warrant. The senior Prince of the Celestial Empire did not allow himself to be browbeaten, even by the Empress of the Western Palace. But from this time onward, Tzu-hsi began to leave aside the Manchu Princes and to turn to other counsellors, such as the more important officials, who had been brought into prominence by the political events in the south.

When the question arose once more of finding an heir to the throne, Tzu-hsi took care to exclude Prince Kung's lineage from the succession. The history of China was altered, to avenge a eunuch's death.

XI

They swore the Huns should perish,
They would die if needs they must,
And now five thousand, sable-clad,
Have bit the Tartar dust.

Along the river bank their bones
Lie scattered where they may,
But still their forms in dreams arise,
To fair ones far away.

'*An Oath*', *by* CH'ÊN T'AO, *translated by* PROFESSOR GILES.

WARD and Burgevine were two American adventurers, whose names are inscribed in Chinese History, for having organized, in 1860, a small company of volunteers of various nationalities, to defend Shanghai against the Tai-pings. This first nucleus of an international force grew in strength and in importance until the Chinese Government decided to make use of it, to suppress the Tai-ping rebellion. It then became known by the high-sounding name of 'The Ever-Victorious Army'.

Ward and Burgevine had the qualities and the defects of typical buccaneers. They were good fighters, but bad soldiers, with scant ideas of discipline and none of strategy. They were among the first to realize that the Chinese might make formidable combatants, if led by capable foreign officers. Ward's idea of a *corps d'élite*, which should act as a spearhead, has been applied on many subsequent occasions. All foreign military advisers of the Chinese Government (such as the German Colonel Bauer) have endeavoured to create 'shock troops', which they could place in the forefront of the battle, to inspire confidence in the rest. This method of warfare proved most useful against the Tai-pings, who had raised their heads once more when the Anglo-French expedition to Peking and the Tsai Yuan conspiracy distracted the attention of the Court from events in the South. It was then that the ill-suppressed revolt broke out with renewed vigour and threatened to overthrow the Manchu dynasty.

By that time the rebellion had lasted almost fifteen years, and had destroyed 600 cities. In 1850 the population of China was reckoned at 400 millions. In 1862 it had shrunk to 267 millions. The civil war in America broke out at the same time, but according to Chinese ideas it could hardly be called a war. So few people were killed. In his *Textes Historiques*, the Jesuit Father Wieger writes that the Tai-ping rebellion, in the province of Kiangsu alone, caused the death of twenty million souls. To realize how such figures can be correct, we must bear in mind that China has an area which is larger than that of Europe, and its population represents almost a quarter of the human race (calculated, in 1929, at two milliard souls).

We are always being told that China is an over-populated country. It is true that nowadays there is not enough to eat for the 450 millions of her population. It follows that banditry and civil wars, while they hinder those preventive measures that a stable government might carry on to avoid the recurrence of droughts and of floods, yet combine with such plagues as these in bringing to the tragic situation a remedy that never fails. They reduce the number of those who must be fed. One of these blood-lettings was the Tai-ping rebellion.

A Cantonese of the Hakka tribes, named Hung Hsiu Ch'uan, having failed to obtain a degree, became a village schoolmaster and then a witch-doctor. He read some Protestant missionary tracts and took service for a time with Mr. Issachar J. Roberts, an American missionary, who directed the Baptist mission at Canton. Hung Hsiu Ch'uan became a diligent student of the Bible, and these studies led him to the discovery that he was none other than the second son of God the Father, and a younger brother of Jesus Christ. He had been commanded to descend into the world to become the one true lord of all nations. He preached this doctrine in the market-places and gained a considerable following. Later on he attached to himself some pirates, who had been harassed by the English gunboats, and with them he took an oath to destroy the Manchu dynasty, or perish in the attempt. It was in the year 1850 that he raised his standard in the south and assumed the title of Heavenly King. This event was followed by a natural portent (whether the omen was good or evil none could say); the Yellow River, known as 'China's Sorrow', changed its course.

The Tai-ping rebellion was the first State problem that the youthful Yehonala helped to solve. From the day when she brought pressure to bear on the Emperor Hsien-feng, urging him to reappoint General Tseng Kuo-fan to command the imperial troops, until the year 1865, when the rebellion was finally crushed, the Manchus were in constant danger of being swept away, like the Mings before them, and this cast a shadow over the Court.

The Heavenly King was no great leader, but to the movement which he had initiated he gave a semi-religious, mystic appeal. Some of his followers, such as Li Hsiu Ch'eng (known as 'the Patriotic Prince'), were men of great ability and admirable character. The strength of the rebels was increased by frequent desertions *en masse* of the imperial troops, sent to exterminate them.

Like all such wars in China, the campaign dragged on, year after year. It is probable that the Manchus could not have held their own, and might have retired into their native Manchuria (anticipating by seventy years the creation of Man-chu-kuo), had not the imperial forces been supported by foreign adventurers, such as Ward and Burgevine, and later by army officers placed at the service of the Chinese Government by the foreign powers. Students of Far Eastern affairs have expressed the opinion that, in the long run, China would have benefited had the Manchu dynasty been allowed to fall at that time, before the more progressive elements in the south were ready to make constitutional experiments on Western lines, unsuited to the Chinese character and civilization.

The task of bolstering up the falling dynasty fell principally on three people: on Yehonala in Peking; on Li Hung-chang, in supreme authority on the spot, and on Charles George Gordon, commander of the Ever Victorious Army.

Yehonala gave to the military commanders her unswerving, unfailing support, and this was all the more remarkable as it had been a fault of the later Manchu Emperors to leave to their subordinates all responsibility, with scanty means to attain their end. The constant, personal interest of the Empress was a guarantee of ultimate success. Tzu-hsi's methods were very different from those of the Manchu Princes and Chinese officials. Whereas the latter were nearly always guilty of procrastination, and preferred to let their thoughts and their opinions be inferred rather than expressed, Tzu-hsi could decide promptly, and express herself in brief phrases which left no doubt as to their meaning.

Li Hung-chang was a man of letters and a member of the Han-lin Academy. Despite his literary tastes, he had raised a regiment of militia and dedicated himself to the despised profession of arms, in order to defend his native district from invasion by the Tai-pings. He attracted the attention of Tseng Kuo-fan and became his lieutenant and right-hand man. It was through Tseng that he became known to the Empress of the Western Palace.

When Li Hung-chang first made use of the Ever Victorious Army, it was commanded by Ward and Burgevine. But it was with Ward's famous successor, Charles George Gordon, that he finally succeeded in suppressing the Tai-pings.

The celebrations, in January 1933, for the centenary of Gordon's birth served to concentrate public opinion once more on the life-history of the most popular of the Eminent

Victorians. In the new biography by H. E. Wortham, the story of 'Chinese Gordon' is retold, with new data, taken from Gordon's correspondence with his mother and sister.

Gordon regarded the Chinese as heathen and was loath to accept from them any monetary reward for his services. But he was anxious to help in putting an end to a rebellion that was responsible for so much misery. In time, he got to like the Chinese peasantry, whom he described as 'the most obedient, quiet, industrious people in the world'.

At first Li Hung-chang was doubtful as to the wisdom of employing an officer who had been officially placed at the disposal of the Chinese Government by his own national authorities. Nor could he understand Gordon's offer to serve without remuneration. Li's experience taught him that what is offered for nothing is often worth that and no more. In the end, Gordon's salary, first fixed at three thousand two hundred pounds a year, was reduced at his own request to one thousand two hundred. Of this sum Gordon spent only a small part on himself.

From their first meeting, Li Hung-chang fell under the charm of Gordon's manner, and they became great friends. Yet it is the famous incident of their quarrel that is best remembered. The episode is perhaps too well known to need re-telling, but the following version, given by Father Wieger in his *Textes Historiques*, is interesting if only by reason of the comments of an impartial foreign historian:

Gordon captured, one after the other, the enemy positions which defended Soo-chow. In these daily encounters, his heroic bravery procured for him, among the Chinese, an almost legendary fame. Unarmed, and holding in his hand only a small riding-whip, he would indicate the point to be attacked. Though always under fire, he never received a wound. In the intervals, he was kept busy by acts of disobedience among his officers and acts of treason among his soldiers. It is impossible to set forth all the bitterness of spirit which this loyal, big-hearted man must have endured.

Meanwhile, inside the beleagured city, the minor captains of the rebels had murdered their Chief. They offered to capitulate, and Gordon promised that their lives should be spared. But Li Hung-chang caused them to be beheaded. . . . For the first time since the beginning of the campaign, Gordon armed himself and went out to seek Li Hung-chang, determined to shoot him with his own hand. But Li effaced himself during several days. Gordon sent in his resignation.

An imperial Edict gave all honour to Li Hung-chang for the taking of Soo-chow. Gordon was offered a remuneration of ten thousand taels, which he naturally refused. However, he let himself be persuaded to withdraw his resignation, in order to accomplish his task.

The beheading of the Tai-ping chiefs, after they had been given a safe conduct, appeared to Gordon to be an unpardonable act of treachery; whereas, in Li's estimation, it was a necessary act of policy, and fully justifiable in the case of officers who had murdered their own chief.

Fate could hardly have thrown together men who were more diverse in their attitude towards life in general, and to each other, than these two. Differences of race, of temperament, of education and of mental outlook, tended to accentuate the disagreements which unavoidably arose between the two men during their collaboration. Yet, when his anger had cooled off, Gordon returned to fight the Tai-pings and, when he met Li again, neither of them mentioned the execution of the rebel chiefs.

To Li Hung-chang, the experience of dealing with Gordon

brought in time the revelation of a truth that neither he nor any other Chinaman appeared to have guessed or suspected, namely, that the 'outer barbarians' actually possessed a religion and certain spiritual ideals of their own, which might compare, not unfavourably, with those professed by Confucius.

To have given Li Hung-chang some knowledge of the moral forces that inspire our Western civilization was a task which perhaps only Gordon could have accomplished, in Gordon's own peculiar way. That he should have done so constitutes a fact of historical importance, for Li Hung-chang was destined, after the Tai-ping rebellion had been crushed, to represent China in her dealings with foreign nations, during many years. The Tsung-li Yamen, although expressly created to deal with foreign affairs, was practically useless for that purpose.

When his task in China was nearing completion, Gordon wrote a letter to his mother, in which he said that the Chinese 'have no reason to love us, even for the assistance we have given them, for the Rebellion was our work indirectly'. Gordon accepted the current opinion that the Tai-pings had received encouragement and support from Protestant missionaries, who believed that the Heavenly King would help them to propagate the Gospel in China. The Tai-ping chiefs printed a translation of the Bible into Chinese, and kept the Sabbath day and prayed to the Heavenly Father, but they would not consent to give up polygamy. To quote Mr. Wortham:

For all his liberalism in things doctrinal, Gordon never acknowledged any sort of Christian brotherhood with the Tai-pings. Indeed, no one in Shanghai ventured to do so after the prolonged visit which Mr. Roberts paid in 1860 to his old pupil at Nanking. Mr. Roberts' stay in the rebel capital enabled him to learn at first-hand the extraordinary doctrines to which the rebels subscribed. A shocking tenet of their theology was the attribution of wives to the First and Second Persons of the Trinity. . . . Finally, Mr. Roberts, who had hoped that the Tien Wang's provision of eighteen chapels in every large city was the beginning of a nineteenth-century Reformation in the Far East, fell into great disfavour and narrowly escaped with his life.

Somewhat against the wishes of his superiors, foreign and Chinese, Gordon demobilized the Ever Victorious Army in the late spring of 1864. Special Envoys from the Court in Peking brought to the foreigner, who had so valiantly supported its cause, the Yellow Jacket which was the highest honour that the Empire could offer. When dressed in the full uniform of a Mandarin of the highest class, with silk skirt, hat, fan, girdle, necklace and the 'archer's' thumb-ring of green jade, Gordon was photographed, and his likeness sent to the Empress of the Western Palace.

Then, he left China, so quietly and modestly that it seemed as if his one desire was to be forgotten.

One of the effects of the Tai-ping rebellion was to disorganize completely the Chinese custom service and to close the custom office in Shanghai. The collection of duties was then undertaken by the British, French and American Consuls, who appointed an official for the purpose. In 1863, the office of collector was entrusted to an Irishman in the British Consular service, Robert Hart. He made of the Chinese Maritime Customs an organization of world-wide repute. In the passing from the Old China to the New, Hart and his foreign staff did more useful work for the country that they served than can ever be sufficiently appreciated. They furnished the Chinese Government with the only source of revenue that could be offered as security for loans; they organized the first efficient postal service, and they gave to Chinese officialdom an example which might well have helped them to realize the most sanguine hopes of a regeneration of China on modern lines. Unlike the loquacious reformers, who have voiced the aspirations of New China in later days, Sir Robert Hart's collaborators were realists. To use an American expression: they held their tongues and sawed wood. The foreign-drilled staff of the Maritime Customs acted as a spear-head for the Chinese civil administration, much as the foreign-drilled troops for the Chinese army.

Sir Robert Hart was a friend of Gordon's, and in the early spring of 1880, when China seemed to be on the point of an armed conflict with Russia, over a question concerning the grasslands bordering the river Ili in Central Asia, he telegraphed to Gordon to come out to China once more. Gordon accepted and remained for some months in Tientsin, renewing his ancient friendship with Li Hung-chang. He was also consulted by the Grand Council in Peking, as to the policies to pursue. Gordon's advice was of a conciliatory character. But there was no work for him in China, and in August he returned home.

At that time, Li Hung-chang was Viceroy of Chihli, and had his official residence in Tientsin. There he was visited by foreign diplomats, who found that by dealing with him they could arrive at a solution of problems, which the tactics of procrastination habitually adopted by the government officials appeared to render insoluble.

Li Hung-chang became one of the most faithful adherents of Tzu-hsi, and was in high favour with her, being second only to Jung Lu. He was a scholar, a soldier and a diplomat: if not a great man, a big man, in stature, in mental outlook, in reputation. He was also, as we have pointed out, the first Chinaman of the governing class who showed any comprehension of, or sympathy with, the mentality and ideals of the West.

Among the havoc wrought by the Tai-ping rebellion should be mentioned the destruction of the town of Nanking, with its magnificent palace, dating from the days of the earlier Ming Emperors. When the Republic of China, in 1928, decided to transfer the capital from Peking to Nanking, there was a great waste of marshy land within the enclosure of the ancient walls, with here and there some groups of habitations, like villages, and a small foreign centre of modern houses, besides a dirty, malodorous suburb between the walls and the river. The inhabitants of Nanking, during the prolonged siege that the town underwent in the years of the rebellion, had destroyed the buildings in order to clear the ground for the planting of crops.

But the greatest loss was caused by the destruction of the famous porcelain pagoda, which was one of the wonders of the world. It had been designed by the Emperor Yung-lo (1403–28) to honour the memory of his mother, and it took nineteen years to build. In shape it was an octagon, 260 feet high, with nine stories, divided by overhanging eaves. The outer walls were cased with a shell of finest white porcelain; the eaves were of green porcelain tiles. On the summit was an iron rod, bearing a gilded ball, encircled by nine iron rings. On chains that hung from the apex to the eaves were 'pearls of good augury', ensuring happiness and prosperity to the city. And from each of the nine series of eaves hung lanterns and little golden bells, that tinkled in the breeze.

XII

N the fifteenth of November, 1872, in the eleventh year of his reign, the Emperor Tung-chih, who was then seventeen years old, was declared to be of age. An edict, signed by the two Empresses, passed over to him the reins of government.

Following on this event, the representatives of the foreign powers in Peking expressed a desire to be received by the Emperor. So many difficulties were raised that, in order to obtain an audience, the foreign Ministers had to make a formal demand, in the shape of a 'collective Note', asking that a date should be fixed for the presentation of their credentials. The reply took the form of an edict, which ran as follows:

The Tsung-li Yamen has presented a memorial to the effect that foreign Ministers in Peking have implored us to grant them an Audience, in order that they may present letters from their governments. We decree that an audience be indeed granted to the foreign Ministers, who have brought credentials from their governments.

Hear and Obey!

Protests were raised at the use of the word 'implore', but it was not withdrawn. The Court would not admit that the foreign Ministers represented monarchs whom the Emperor of China could consider as his equals. But it was only after the ceremony was over that it became known that the representatives of the great powers had allowed themselves, through inadvertence, to be received in the hall where envoys of vassal States, such as Tibet and Mongolia, used to prostrate themselves before their suzerain. The Ministers were not asked to perform the *ko-tow*, but their respectful behaviour during the ceremony was favourably commented on by a member of the Tsung-li Yamen, who remarked that it was evidently due to their long residence in China that the foreign diplomats had become so civilized.

After the ceremony, printed leaflets were distributed among the people, giving an entirely imaginary account of the effect produced on foreign Ministers by the majesty of the Son of Heaven. The following is a translation:

The Ministers were introduced into the Presence by the higher officials of the Tsung-li Yamen. They wore swords. When they had all entered, the doors were closed. They saluted the Emperor without prostrating themselves, but only bending the head. On one side of the throne was a small table, near which each Minister in turn was told to stand, while he read out his credentials. The British Minister came first. But he had not spoken more than a few words when he was seized by a fit of trembling which prevented him continuing his speech. The Emperor kindly asked him some questions, but it was no use, there was no answer.

Then the other Ministers came up, each in his turn, but they were all seized with a panic and dropped their credentials, without being able to read them. Prince Kung gave orders to the Palace servants, to help the Ministers down the steps, holding them under the arms. So abject was their terror that they were incapable of standing up, and sank to the ground, damp with perspiration and gasping for breath. They could not even partake of the banquet that had been prepared for them.

Prince Kung said: 'I warned you that the act of entering the Emperor's presence should not be taken lightly. You would not believe what I said. Now you realize that I was right!'

And yet the reception had been prepared without much pomp. The foreign Ministers now admit that a transcendent virtue emanates from the Emperor, filling humbler mortals with alarm. . . . Such are these vainglorious men, braggarts from afar, cowards when at hand!

Audiences with the Emperor ceased once more, during the brief reign of Tung-chih and the minority of his successor. But in 1876 the first Chinese diplomatic representative ever sent by the Emperor to a foreign country arrived in Great Britain. He was a scholar, by name Kuo Sung-tao. His mission lasted three years and undoubtedly contributed to improve the relations between the Court of St. James and that of Peking. He was recalled in 1879. In paying his farewell visit to Lord Salisbury, he said that he liked everything about the English very much, except their shocking immorality!

In the ordinary course of events, the story of the Empress Dowager might well have ended at this point, with the coming of age of her son and the transfer of power to the young Emperor. But the making over of authority, in an

Eastern Court, is no mere formality. There is no essential, uninterrupted continuity, as is expressed in the phrase *Le Roi est mort. Vive le Roi !* In the East we find a very different saying: 'Who rides the tiger, cannot dismount!' To abdicate from power in China might mean to step down from a throne into a grave. The coming of age of Tung-chih marked the beginning of a struggle, none the less bitter because it was conducted in secret; none the less terrible because the rivals were mother and son.

Before handing over the government to the young Emperor, the Dowager Empresses provided him with a wife and several concubines. The rank of first imperial consort was given to a girl belonging to an aristocratic Manchu family. Her name was A-lu-te. The first of the concubines, called 'The Discerning Concubine', was a daughter of Feng Hua, a friend of Jung Lu. According to a story told in the diary of one of the Court eunuchs, the Empress Tzu-hsi wished the nominations to be made in the opposite order; she meant Feng Hua's daughter to be principal consort, and A-lu-te to be merely a concubine. But some disagreement having arisen on this matter between the two Empresses, it was decided to allow the Emperor himself to express an opinion. Tung-chih promptly showed his preference for A-lu-te. At which Tzu-hsi, who had confidently expected the Emperor to conform to her wishes, was much annoyed, and made no attempt to hide her disapproval.

It was well known in Court circles that the young Emperor had little affection for his mother. Even as a child he had always shown preference for the Empress of the Eastern Palace, and after his marriage matters grew worse. Neither did A-lu-te get on with her mother-in-law. Thus it became clear that the ascendancy, which Tzu-hsi had always exercised at Court, might vanish, as a new generation came into power.

One of the first acts of the Emperor Tung-chih, after the regency had been abolished, was to give orders that State documents should no longer be submitted to his mother.

In the old days at Jehol, while the Emperor Hsien-feng lay dying, the youthful Yehonala had fought for life and power, and she had wrested the Empire from the usurping Regents. Now that her turn had come to give up the regency, she realized how ominous was the outlook.

Those must have been anxious months at Court, when the rivalry between the old order and the new first became apparent. Would youth be served and the Emperor succeed in supplanting his formidable mother? Would Tzu-hsi allow herself to be put on the shelf? To guess the answer to these questions, and to guess in time, might mean success and high fortune for an official who looked forward to an honourable old age, secure in the favour of the great.

Tung-chih and his young consort (she was fifteen, two years younger than her husband) were imprudent in revealing their hostility towards Tzu-hsi before consolidating their own position, which was still far from secure. In a conflict with age, youth could well afford to wait. But youth is impatient. Had Tung-chih bided his time till the succession to the throne was assured, A-lu-te, as mother of the heir, would have assumed a far more important position (as had happened to Tzu-hsi herself, after the birth of her son) and Tzu-hsi's numerous honorific titles would no longer have given her the same authority. Just after the end of the regency, in the first year of her son's direct reign, she was still the most powerful person within the Forbidden City, and her personal charm and high prestige still held the highest officials bound to her interests. Jung Lu was within call, and Li Hung-chang was at Tientsin, with loyal troops at his command.

But the person on whom she relied most was Li Lien-ying, the Chief Eunuch, who had succeeded An-te-hai in the direction of the household service of the Court. No less than his predecessor, Li was faithful to the Empress of the Western Palace, and to her alone.

All the corruption in high places, all the arts of diverting public funds from their legitimate uses, all the pressure brought to bear on officials or on private individuals, to extort money, or service, or a tacit consent to illegitimate practices, found in Li Lien-ying their principal and most fearless exponent. His was one of those grim figures, all the more formidable for having no official responsibility, who move among the shadows behind an Oriental throne. An-te-hai had been a devoted servant to his imperial mistress, but he was domineering and imprudent. Li Lien-ying's suave manner and affectation of deference served to cloak a will of iron. Within the precincts of the Forbidden City, he was servant only in name, and his enmity was to be feared by the Emperor himself. No one might give him orders, save the Empress of the Western Palace. In his hold over Tzu-hsi lay the secret of his power.

It is difficult to realize how a woman, whose personal magnetism was so potent in influencing others, could have fallen so much under the sway of her Chief Eunuchs, of An-te-hai and Li Lien-ying. To explain the ascendancy which these two obtained over their imperial mistress, one must take into consideration that the Forbidden City and the

Summer Palace were entirely served, and therefore almost entirely controlled, by eunuchs.

An Empress of China never saw her subjects. Only the highest officials and the most exalted nobles might approach her. When she passed through the streets of the town the shops were closed and the people might not show themselves. Even the Court painters had to rise and hurry away when the Empress crossed the courtyard or the hall where they were at work.

Yet Tzu-hsi liked to see people. From the hill-side at the Summer Palace it was possible to look down upon the road that stretched away towards Peking. The Empress used to sit and watch the traffic. She amused herself by guessing who might be travelling in the palanquins and carts, and was always the first to descry the Emperor's chair, coming from Peking (perhaps, if anyone saw it before she did, they were careful not to say so). Great was her astonishment when she learned that Queen Victoria might be seen by any of her subjects, as she drove in an open carriage through the streets of London.

Facts like these implied a mental isolation such as a foreigner could hardly imagine, and they explain how Tzu-hsi came to rely on the Chief Eunuch. Through his eyes she saw the world that lay beyond the palace walls; he stood between her and the countless millions who acknowledged her sovereignty.

Legends grew up about Li Lien-ying, legends of his cupidity, his cruelty, the fear that he inspired even in Princes of the Blood. Most of these legends have some foundation in fact. The Devil was almost, if not quite, as black as he was painted.

In appearance he was unprepossessing: tall and thin, with heavy features and a protruding lip; shrewd eyes in sunken sockets; a wrinkled yellow skin, like old parchment; a sinister expression, but a pleasant voice and gentle, insinuating manners. Like most eunuchs, he looked older than he was. The common people spoke of him as 'cobbler's wax Li', in allusion to what is supposed to have been his profession before he qualified for employment at Court, or —to use the Chinese expression—before he 'left the family'. There was also a strange rumour, at one time current in Peking, and which found an echo in *Mesny's Chinese Miscellany* (February 1905). According to the author of this article, Li Lien-ying, in the opinion of many of his contemporaries, was no other than 'the long-lost brother of Li Hung-chang, who, as *Tao-tai*, was in the early sixties summoned to audience by the Empress Dowager, and shortly afterwards disappeared from ordinary mortal view'.

Whatever his origin, Li Lien-ying was a power to be reckoned with, and in him were embodied most of the dangers that lurked behind the walls of the Forbidden City. The younger generation possessed no such powerful adherents. The eunuchs who served Tung-chih and A-lu-te took orders in secret from the senior guardian of the harem. Not theirs to control events, or to direct policies, but only to guide the Son of Heaven along paths that others had traced for him.

It was Tung-chih's own imprudent hostility which forced his mother to defend the Dragon Throne from the dangers of an unfettered rule by the young Emperor and his consort. Such dangers were by no means imaginary. The young couple were hardly qualified to hold the reins of government in a great Empire, in times of transition and of revolt. China had already suffered much from her *rois fainéants*.

Tung-chih was a sickly, dissipated youth. His favourite amusement was to go incognito, to seek adventures in the less reputable quarters of the town. A small private door was made in the outer wall of the Forbidden City, in order that he might go in and out, unbeknown to the guards who were stationed at the gates. A eunuch, named Chou, used to wait for him outside, with a closed cart, to which was harnessed a fast-trotting mule. Like any truant schoolboy, the Son of Heaven would slip out through the side door, into the covered cart, and away to the obscure *hu-tungs*, where, under flowery names, are practised the vices of the East. In his use of a disguise as a means to break away from the restraints of his position, Tung-chih resembled the Harun el Rashid of the legend, but in other ways he had little in common with the Caliph of Bagdad.

The eunuch who accompanied him on his nocturnal escapades was supposed to take care that the Emperor should return to the Palace at dawn, that is to say, in time for the audiences. But more than once it happened that the Grand Councillors waited in the side-pavilions long after the sun's rays had 'chased the session of the Stars from Night'. So the secret leaked out, and wise men shook their heads, and spoke with regret of the days when the Dowager Empresses ruled the Empire wisely from behind the suspended curtain.

It was no secret, even at the time, that Li Lien-ying and his underlings were in part responsible for the Emperor's evil ways, and that they encouraged him in his vices. One courageous member of the Imperial household attempted to interfere. His name was Kuei Ching, and he even took it upon himself to cut off the heads of several eunuchs who had accompanied the Emperor to various brothels and opium dens. But Tung-chih resented the implication that he was not able to look after himself, and Kuei Ching left the Court in disgrace.

Many deaths have been laid at Tzu-hsi's door, and her guilt accepted as probable if not proven. But none of the crimes of which she has been accused stands out with such a sinister significance as her mere inactivity during the time when her son was treading the downward path that, for a man of his weak constitution, could only lead to the grave. She well knew what was going on. It must be that she approved.

The mother-love, which during Tung-chih's childhood was not lacking in Yehonala, had withered as her son grew up and became estranged from her. He had clearly shown that he meant to thrust her aside. But not for his sake would she accept defeat. In what was virtually a struggle for life, she did not mean to become the loser. Let the eunuchs see to it!

The Chinese have a strange superstition: they believe that small-pox brings good luck. In December 1874 an edict announced that the Emperor had been 'fortunate' enough to contract small-pox. This was not the only piece of good fortune that he had brought back with him from his excursions into the underworld. The edict went on to say that, during the Emperor's illness, the two Dowager Empresses had shown great solicitude for his person and that they had consented to examine all documents of State.

It is generally assumed that Tung-chih contracted small-pox by accident. But it is not to be excluded that the infection was given to him intentionally, with the object of bringing about his death. There is a tale, that recurs every now and then in the tea-house gossip of Peking, of some great man who has been got rid of by means of those small rough towels, heated with steam, that are offered in Chinese theatres and restaurants, as well as in private houses, for passing over the hands and face. Before giving the warm towel to their master, the servants (in this eastern 'detective story') pass them over the ulcerated face of a man with small-pox. And so the infection is given.

This same story was told, as late as in 1929, of Colonel Bauer, a German who acted as military adviser to the most prominent of the Chinese generals. Bauer died of small-pox, after three days' illness. He was then occupied with the task of reorganizing the Chinese army. It is possible that the favour he enjoyed with the government may have provoked jealousies and procured him enemies. But it is impossible to say if there were any truth in the legend of the infected towels, as told after his death.

Conditions at the Court of Tung-Chih were no less perilous than those which surrounded the foreign colonel, who had offered his services to China after the Great War. And this makes one wonder if the Emperor's 'good fortune', as mentioned in the edict, did not come to him through the little steaming towels that were handed to him, every half-hour or so, under the watchful eyes of Li Lien-ying.

XIII

Le Roi est mort. Vive le Roi !

TUNG-CHIH died on the 13th of January 1875.

During his earthly existence, he had often violated the Rites and provoked scandals by his licentious conduct. But in dying, he conformed to the austere ritual prescribed for the passing of an Emperor. His attendants dressed him in the ceremonial 'Robes of Longevity', and he awaited the end in the presence of the Court, with his face turned towards the south.

And then arose the question: Who next ?

It was the custom in China for an Emperor, who felt his end approaching, to compose a valedictory decree, in which he took leave of his people and appointed a successor. The necessity for such a designation was all the more apparent, when the Emperor left no son to succeed him. But, at the time of Tung-chih's death, no valedictory decree was published.

An anti-dynastic pamphlet, which had a large circulation at the time of the fall of the Empire (in 1911), contained a detailed, if somewhat improbable, account of how a valedictory decree had indeed been prepared by Tung-chih and confided to his old tutor, Li Hung-hao. But the latter, on receiving the decree from the dying Emperor's hands, imprudently took it to the Empress of the Western Palace, who flew into a violent rage and tore it up, giving orders that no more food or medicine should be taken to the Son of Heaven. According to the pamphlet, Tung-chih nominated as his successor the son of Prince Tsai-chih, Pu-lùn; and this despite the fact that the Emperor's consort, A-lu-te, was with child, so that a male heir to the throne might well have been born within the next few months. The fact that Tung-chih, in designating a successor, deliberately ignored the claims of his own unborn son, was attributed by the author of the pamphlet to A-lu-te's patriotism. She expressed a desire to avoid another long regency, during the minority of the reigning Emperor: a state of affairs that might have been dangerous to the country.

Though it cannot be said that the events, as described above, are in any way incredible, the source of information is untrustworthy in the extreme. Whatever the reason for Tung-chih's apparent omission to nominate a successor, the situation after the Emperor's death was obscure and fraught with danger.

There were three principal candidates for the throne: the son of Prince Kung; the son of Prince Ch'un, and the son of Prince Tsai-chih (the Prince Pu-lùn, mentioned above).

The son of Prince Kung was then seventeen years old, and his claims to the succession were stronger than those of any other Manchu Prince of his generation, for Kung was the elder brother. But Tzu-hsi had excellent reason for opposing such a candidature. Although six years had passed since An-te-hai had been executed at Tsi-nan-fu, the heart of the Western Empress was still bitter against those who had caused his death. Also, the son of Prince Kung was nearing maturity. He might assume at once, or after a very short time, the responsibilities of government. This meant that Tzu-hsi would have to give up the regency, whereas the election of a younger Emperor would have assured it to her, for many years to come. Tzu-hsi had a candidate in mind, a child of four years old, son of her own sister, who had married Prince Ch'un, called the Seventh Prince, because he was the seventh son of the Emperor Tao-kwang.

Leaving aside for the moment Tzu-hsi's preference for the child of her sister, as opposed to the son of Prince Kung, there was an objection to both these candidates in the fact that they belonged to the same generation as the late Emperor, being his first cousins. According to the dynastic laws of the Manchus, one might not worship as an ancestor one who belonged to the same generation as oneself. Thus the sons of Prince Kung and Prince Ch'un were legally excluded from accomplishing the annual sacrifices to the shade of Tung-chih.

This objection did not apply to the son of Prince Tsai-chih. Three generations, and not only two, separated the young Prince Pu-lùn from the common ancestor, Tao-kwang. His claim was invalidated to a certain degree by the fact that his grandfather had been adopted into the family from a collateral branch, and could not take precedence of lineal descendants. But the obstacle of an adoption was less serious than the disqualification from rendering ancestral worship. This was indeed a sacrilege, for it meant that the Emperor

Tung-chih must go desolate in the land of spirits: a tragedy inconceivable!

The ancestral cult had to be assured to the dead, in order that the succession might be considered legitimate. But Tzu-hsi was not to be swayed by such considerations. Nor was she disposed to put off a decision in view of the fact that Tung-chih's widow was expecting a baby. Had a male child been born to A-lu-te, in time to be chosen as Emperor, A-lu-te herself would have assumed the rank of Dowager Empress, with greater right to take part in a regency than any member of the former generation. The claims of A-lu-te's unborn child represented for Tzu-hsi a new danger of being relegated to a position of undesirable obscurity. For this reason she wished the matter of Tung-chih's succession to be settled before the birth took place.

In the absence of any indication of the late Emperor's will, the question of choosing a successor had to be submitted to a meeting of the Grand Council, to whose members were added, for the occasion, several Princes of the Imperial clan, and three important Chinese officials from the southern provinces. In such a meeting, Tzu-hsi counted on her own personal ascendancy to ensure the election of her choice. There is nothing to prove the story, which was current at the time and which since then has been generally accepted: that Tzu-hsi summoned Li Hung-chang to her aid, and that he sent his loyal An-huei troops, by forced marches, to Peking, where they seized the outer gates and held them until the new Emperor had been chosen. On the other hand, there is nothing improbable in this legend. Tzu-hsi was never one to leave things to chance, and her actions in that difficult moment show that she had laid her plans for every contingency. Jung Lu's men held the outer wall of the Forbidden City, and he himself attended the meeting of the Council.

So many particulars are known of events on that famous night in January, 1875, when a new Emperor was chosen in Peking, that the moment stands out with a vivid distinctness, among the mists of uncertainty that veil the greater part of similar episodes in Chinese history. The whole scene can be reconstructed with sufficient accuracy to be impressive, without being fanciful.

In accordance with custom, the Grand Council met by night, and we know that the night was stormy. It was bitterly cold, and a 'yellow wind' swept over Peking, bringing the sand of Mongolian deserts. At the hour when the Council was summoned, the storm had not reached its full strength, but the dark night was made oppressive by a great pillar of sand, that advanced from the Gobi desert, heralded by gusts of dry, cold air. The street dust rose in miniature whirlwinds, as if to give a foretaste of what was to come. The corner-towers of the Forbidden City loomed up, gigantic shadows among the darker shadows below. A few lights showed here and there in the quarter reserved for the concubines, and other lights moved across the open spaces, as the members of the Council arrived, preceded by their torch-bearers.

The meeting was held in the pavilion known as 'the Palace of Mind Nurture'. Before the door were two lines of palanquins, the chairs resting on the ground, while the bearers sought shelter and a cup of hot tea in the porter's lodge. As the Princes and other Councillors arrived, they were carried up, according to their rank, to the door of the inner pavilion, or only as far as the outer courtyard. Before

Photo : Hartung, Pekin.

A CORRIDOR AT THE SUMMER PALACE

they entered the meeting-room, the servants brushed their coats with little dusters, made of strips of blue cotton on sticks of bamboo. No one took off his coat or head-dress, for the big hall was only heated here and there by braziers. Most of the coats were of sable, belted with silk, with priceless buckles of jade and ivory. The fur caps were surmounted by ' buttons ', denoting the rank of the wearer, and made of rubies, or coral, or lapis-lazuli. Some wore the ' peacock feather ', a short straight plume that fell on to the left shoulder.

The Dowager Empresses arrived in closed palanquins, like the others, for the ' Palace of Mind Nurture ' was situated far from their private quarters. But A-lu-te did not come to the meeting. In a distant pavilion, she knelt in night-long vigil, at the foot of the bier where the late Emperor's body was laid out. This was in accordance with instructions given by the Empress of the Western Palace.

During the meeting, the Councillors knelt in two rows, facing each other, and at either end was a throne; on these thrones the Dowager Empresses took their place.

The hall was lighted by lanterns, suspended from the ceiling or hung on lacquered poles; other lanterns rested on three-legged stands, close to the ground; they were placed beside the doors and on the steps that led down to the courtyards.

When the meeting opened, the Dowager Empress of the Eastern Palace proposed the nomination of Prince Kung's son. But no one ever paid much attention to Tzu-an's suggestions, and her proposal carried no weight. Others put forward the candidature of Prince Tsai-chih's son, Pu-lùn. Prince Kung, after the usual formal declarations of unworthiness, with respect to the nomination of his own son, suggested that the death of the Emperor be kept secret until his posthumous child were born. But Tzu-hsi objected. In a situation rendered uncertain by legal difficulties and conflicting interests, she knew exactly what she wanted, and was determined to brush aside all opposition. After years of patient study, Tzu-hsi had at her fingers' ends all the historical precedents which count for so much in framing political action especially in the East. If indeed Li Hung-chang's guards held the City gates, they were there only as a last resource. Tzu-hsi counted on her dominant personality to impose her will in the Council Chamber. She pointed out that rebellion was yet rife in the south, and that the throne must not be kept vacant to await the birth of a possible heir: 'When the nest is destroyed, how many of the eggs remain unbroken?' Whenever the succession had been held up, to favour an unborn heir, the subsequent reign had been full of sorrow and disaster. Cutting through all counter-proposals, she insisted that the only course to follow was to nominate, without further loss of time, the child of Prince Ch'un and of her own sister.

Prince Kung boldly opposed her wishes, appealing this time to the rights of primogeniture, in favour of his own son. But when the question was put to the vote, the majority of the Councillors declared themselves in favour of Tzu-hsi's choice. As usual, she got her own way.

The meeting had lasted far into the night, and meanwhile the storm had gathered strength. In Donn Byrne's *Messer Marco Polo,* there is a description of a dust storm in the Gobi: '. . . and a burning wind came, and the sand arose, and the desert heeled like a ship, and the day became night'. Even such a storm swept over the mountains and down on to the plain of Peking, as the new Emperor was chosen. The lanterns flickered in the Council chamber and the yellow dust filtered in through windows and doors. The rice paper on the windows creaked and split under the pressure of the wind, which moaned over the curved roofs, and broke off loose tiles, that fell and splintered on the marble flags below.

Anyone but Tzu-hsi would have been content to wait until next day, before sending to her sister's house to have the new Emperor brought to the Palace. No one would take a child out in a dust storm, unless in unavoidable necessity. But part of this strange woman's success in life came from her promptitude and thoroughness in any action that might ensure the safe and complete execution of her plans. Before leaving the Council chamber, she ordered Jung Lu to bring the little son of Prince Ch'un from his father's house in the Western City.

Eunuchs ran to fetch the golden palanquin, with dragons embroidered on the yellow satin curtains. The Manchu Bannermen saddled their ponies, so like little bears in their long winter coats. The riders wore great bows across their backs, and quivers of arrows hung from their saddles. Jung Lu mounted his pony and halted under the arch of the doorway, while he drew down the fur peak and flaps of his cap, to protect his eyes and ears from the bitter wind. The brass-studded doors opened slowly and the horsemen clattered out over the bridge that spanned the moat. For a moment the light of the torches shone on the ice below. Such a scene might Marco Polo have witnessed, at the Court of Kubla Khan.

And so the ill-omened reign began, in storm and intrigue.

The baby cried, when they lifted him from his warm bed and called him Emperor. And an occasional sob still shook his small person, while he lay in his mother's arms, in the chair that moved so swiftly through deserted streets. A few wayfarers, who were abroad in the bitter weather, saw the gorgeous palanquin sweep past in the dust-laden air, with outriders, guards and torch-bearers. They must have wondered who it was, travelling in such state, at such an hour. Next day, when they heard the news of Tung-chih's death and the nomination of his successor, they may have guessed that they had seen the Son of Heaven himself on his way to take possession of the Empire.

XIV

Tarquinius made no reply to the messenger, but walked up and down in the garden, striking off the heads of the tallest poppies.

Early Roman History.

SHE must have realized what it meant to her — poor widowed A-lu-te!— when, towards the end of her long vigil beside the bier of Tung-chih, she saw the doors fly open and Jung Lu, in a long sable coat, bring in the new child Emperor to perform the first ceremony of his reign. For the Rites prescribed that the Son of Heaven, on entering into his heritage, should do homage to his predecessor.

There was little chance, now, that A-lu-te's own child should live! There would be no place for him on the Dragon Throne. Better that he should not be born at all, and that the late Emperor's consort should follow her lord to the last trysting-place, beside the Yellow Springs. A few days later, A-lu-te died, with her child still unborn. In the market-places and in the tea-houses, people asked each other: 'Was it suicide or foul play?' Only Tzu-hsi and her eunuchs could answer that question, and they maintained that the young Empress' grief had not allowed her to survive her imperial consort. Tzu-hsi did not war with the dead. The *Peking Gazette* (an official newspaper that had appeared regularly since the days of the Tang dynasty A.D. 618–905) published an Imperial rescript containing the news of A-lu-te's death. It spoke of her as 'The filial, wise excellent Queen, who governed her actions by the laws of Heaven, and whose life added lustre to the teachings of the sages'. *De mortuis nil nisi bonum.*

The new Emperor impersonated an era, to which was given the name of Kuang-hsu, meaning 'glorious succession'. He took the place of Tung-chih as worshipper at the ancestral shrine of Hsien-feng. But Tung-chih's own shrine remained without a ministrant, and the mysterious death of A-lu-te helped to focus public opinion on the illegality of the new Emperors succession. The Censor's presented memorials to the Throne, protesting at the sacrilege. And Tzu-hsi, who realized that the reign had begun inauspiciously, betrayed her feelings in a certain irritability, that was apparent in her answers to the memorialists. But in order to reassure public opinion, it was announced that, as soon as the reigning Emperor should have a son, the latter would be appointed to make sacrifices to Tung-chih.

As far back as the year 1627, the Jesuits, anxious to convert China to Christianity, raised the question whether ancestor worship might not be considered simply as conforming to the fourth commandment. But the Vatican decided in the negative. Indeed the cult, as practised in China, far transcends any ordinary interpretation of the duty to honour one's father and one's mother. The full significance of ancestral worship was never more apparent than in the case of Tung-chih.

In 1879, on the occasion of the Emperor's final sepulture in the mausoleum that had been built for the purpose, a scholar and ex-Censor, by name Wu-ko-tu, wrote a memorial to the Throne, pointing out once more that no heir had been given to Tung-chih. As a last unanswerable protest, he committed suicide in the region of the imperial tombs, as near as possible to the grave of the Emperor, whose spirit had been left disconsolate.

The idea of what an Emperor's tomb should be comes down to us from the times of the self-styled 'First Emperor', who reigned about two hundred years before the birth of Christ. The tale is told of how he chose a mountain and caused it to be hollowed out, and his Empire reproduced within: cities of jewels and rivers of quicksilver on a floor of polished bronze. In the centre stood the sarcophagus, where he was ultimately laid to rest, and on each side were enormous bowl-shaped lamps, containing oil of dolphins sufficient to keep the flame of a wick alight for two hundred years. The chasm was vaulted by a ceiling on which were reproduced the heavens, with golden stars and silver planets on a background of dark blue. The Emperor's wives, concubines and servants were buried with him, crucified to the walls, lest in death they should assume an attitude disrespectful to their lord.

After the burial, the entrance to the mountain-side was closed and covered up with earth. Trees and grass were planted over it. And all those who had hollowed out the mountain, or worked at the tomb, were put to death so that none might tell where it lay.

Later Emperors have been buried in the mountain-side, facing south, or in great mounds, grown over with trees, and called 'Jewelled Cities'. The wives and concubines did not accompany their late lords, except in effigy.

The successive Emperors of the Manchu dynasty were buried alternately at the Eastern and Western Tombs (Tung-ling and Hsi-ling) situated in two different mountain ranges, to the east and to the west of Peking. Each group of tombs had a governor of its own, living in a village within the sacred forest, and each tomb had its own guard of archers and halberdiers. In the Eastern and Western Tombs, each mausoleum had a marble-flagged road leading up to it, with colossal marble figures on either side: warriors, sages, elephants, camels, horses and supernatural animals who are no longer seen on earth. In front of the mountain, or the 'Jewelled City', which contained the tomb, were built pavilions like those of a temple, with carvings of sandalwood, whose scent mingled with the pine-scent of the surrounding forest. Thrones of yellow satin, embroidered with golden dragons, were placed beside banqueting tables where, on the day of the annual sacrifice, the departed Great Ones might come and feast.

There was an extraordinary spiritual appeal in the eerie silence of that realm of the dead, where the only sign of life was the cooing of pigeons among the eaves, or the quick scamper of a squirrel across the marble flags of a triumphal way. In those secluded valleys, the Emperors slept on, close to the heart of nature. The imagery of a life immortal lay around them, less in the complicated symbolism of their costly tombs, than in the slow-moving shadows of the hills and in the ever recurring pageant of starlit nights.

But what of Tung-chih ? His tomb was no less magnificent than those of his predecessors. But it was deserted.

The north wind blew the dust from his altars and the moon illumined his courts with her silvery light. But no mortal descendant might make sacrifice to his spirit, nor burn incense before his shrine. What wonder that, in distress for such a betrayal of his Emperor, a loyal scholar chose to die ?

There is something Roman in the figure of Wu-ko-tu, if indeed there is not something even more characteristic of the civilization that he, and such as he, represented more worthily than the degenerate Emperors whom they served. He hung himself in the region of the Tombs, near a bridge which takes its name from the God of Horses, in the grounds of a temple called the Temple of the Threefold Duties. He left a sum of money for the Temple priest, with instructions to buy a plain lacquered coffin and a small plot of ground to bury him in. He was dressed in new clothes and, in his written instructions, gave orders to cut off the outer sole of his shoes, so that nothing soiled should accompany him to the grave. In fear lest some passer-by should see him hanging and cut him down before death had set in, he took a strong dose of opium as an added precaution. At the end of his long memorial to the Throne are these words:

'Once a scholar went to the place chosen for suicide, and his knees trembled, so that a friend asked him: "If you are afraid, why not turn back ?" And he answered: "My fear is a private weakness, but my death is a public duty."'

Such was the spirit that animated Wu-ko-tu: the spirit of

Old China that was passing away, with the passing of her proud old scholars. He may have trembled as he placed the noose round his neck. But death came to him, as he wished that it should come, 'in fitting and harmonious dignity'.

Tzu-hsi does not appear to have suffered from qualms of conscience, but she was superstitious and realized that disaster might well accompany a reign so inauspiciously begun. Although conscious of her mistake, she could not, at the time, do anything to remedy it. Meanwhile, she continued to consolidate her own position and to get rid of those who formerly had taken part with her in the government of the country. Prince Kung was put on the shelf, with several other members of the Grand Council. When she had need of help or confidential advice, Tzu-hsi turned to Li Hung-chang, who often came up from Tientsin to be received in audience, and took an active part in the administration of the Empire. He was of a very different stamp of counsellor from that of the old Manchu Princes. If the foreign politics of China had been left entirely in his hands, he might have saved the country from much humiliation.

Jung Lu also fell into disgrace. It appears that he took advantage of the charge of Comptroller of the Imperial Palaces to enter the Forbidden City at unusual hours, in order to make love to a woman belonging to the harem of the late Emperor. Tzu-hsi was informed of this intrigue by Weng Tung-ho, tutor to the young Emperor and a personal enemy of Jung Lu's. It is said that Tzu-hsi wished to ascertain for herself whether the accusation was well-founded, and that she actually found Jung Lu in the apartments reserved for the women. *Inde iræ* . . .

In her anger at the discovery of this *liaison*, Tzu-hsi deprived her cousin of his official posts at Court and gave him a military command at Hsi-an-fu. There he remained, practically in exile, for seven years. Time mellowed the first bitterness of her anger, and in the end, Jung Lu was pardoned. But with that inconsistency which characterizes human actions in matters concerning the heart, Tzu-hsi concentrated her rancour on a person who really cannot have had much to do with it, namely on Tzu-an. The eunuchs declared that the Empress of the Eastern Palace had been aware of the intrigue, and out of spite towards her colleague, had done her best to smooth the path of untrue love. Tzu-hsi was only too willing to find some extenuating circumstance for Jung Lu's misconduct, and she accepted this explanation of what had happened.

A certain amount of rivalry between the two Empresses was perhaps inevitable, but their mutual jealousy and dislike, instead of growing less, became more intense as they grew older. When they first entered the Forbidden City, as concubines of Hsien-feng, the two girls had clung together, as young things will. One recalls the whispered conversation over the bowl of goldfish at Jehol, and the hurried flight from Peking, when Yehonala sought her child and found him in Sakota's palanquin, and the two women smiled at each other in silence over the sleeping babe.

As the little Emperor Kuang-hsu grew older, a new cause of friction arose in his marked preference for the Empress of the Eastern Palace. Towards Tzu-hsi, who had placed him on the throne, he was distrustful and rebellious. So it had been, in former days, with Tung-chih. This may have been a consequence of the fact that Tzu-an let children do as they pleased, whereas Tzu-hsi recognized the necessity for some discipline, even for the little Son of Heaven.

At the Court of an absolute monarch, the likes and dislikes of a child may have political importance. It was easy to foresee that, as the years passed, Tzu-an might have found in the young Emperor a powerful ally against Tzu-hsi.

In the growing estrangement between the two Empresses, the eunuchs did not hesitate whose part to take. Li Lien-ying preferred one mistress to two, and he gave his allegiance to the Empress of the Western Palace.

In 1881, during the annual ceremony at the Eastern tombs, there arose a question of precedence. Tzu-an insisted on maintaining her rank as first consort of the late Emperor, and endeavoured to relegate Tzu-hsi to a second place. A violent scene followed, and the quarrel between the two Empresses brought confusion to the whole Court. Not long after, another quarrel arose over the conduct of the eunuchs. Tzu-an accused Li Lien-ying, as in other days she had accused An-te-hai, of assuming the powers of the Emperor, and of insolence towards herself. It was not always safe, even for an Empress, to fall foul of the First Eunuch.

Fourteen years before, when Hsien-feng lay dying at Jehol, a story was told about a written order that he was supposed to have made out, to prevent the Empress of the Western Palace from having any part in the government of the country after his death. According to one version of this story,[1] the written order was entrusted to Sakota. She was to use it only if her colleague of the West should presume to interfere in affairs of State. In this case, the Grand Council was to be summoned, the order exhibited, and Yehonala was to be

[1] Another version is given at the end of Chapter VI.

assisted to commit suicide. But the Empress of the Eastern Palace never availed herself of the powers accorded to her. Only in 1875 did she bring out the order and show it to Tzu-hsi. This was an imprudent attempt on the part of Tzu-an to prove that by having kept the matter secret during so many years she had been inspired by sisterly affection. But although the order was then burnt, in the presence of the Empress whose death it might have caused, the latter showed no gratitude. On the contrary, she seems to have been both frightened and enraged. It was hateful to her to realize that her fate had hung so long in the balance, and that she, who had thought herself all-powerful, owed her life to poor insignificant Sakota. Some days later, the Empress of the Eastern Palace ate some sweet cakes that had been brought to her by a eunuch at Yehonala's behest. After which she fell ill and died.

Once more, the suspicions of the 'stupid people' pointed at Tzu-hsi, as being the authoress of a crime, but such suspicions could neither be proved nor dispelled.

Tzu-an's death was accompanied by all the formalities prescribed by the Rites. The Empress of the Eastern Palace took leave of her people in an Edict, which expressed, in modest but dignified terms, her goodwill towards the world she was about to leave. At the time of her death, Tzu-an was forty-two years old. She was buried in the mausoleum of Hsien-feng.

And Tzu-hsi remained sole regent of the Empire.

XV

The chronicle tells us of Timur's bride that her beauty was like the young moon and her body as graceful as the young cypress. She must have been about fifteen years of age, because she had been allowed to ride to the hunts with her father. Her name was Aljai. . . .

Tamerlane, by HAROLD LAMB.

IN spite of the rule that excluded all foreigners except diplomats and their families from residing in Peking, there were a few alien business men and tradesmen who actually lived in the capital. And there were even one or two unpretentious shops, of which one was kept by a Dane, named Kierulf, who in his variegated stock had on sale some toys from Nuremberg.

The Palace eunuchs, who were attached to the person of the Emperor, having scoured the Chinese markets for playthings to amuse the Son of Heaven, happened to notice Kierulf's shop, tucked away in a sort of outhouse, close to the German Legation. Here they bought some mechanical toys, which were so much appreciated by Kuang-hsu that the shopkeeper was told to procure more. It was from such imported trifles that the little Emperor acquired a taste for things exotic. And this was the beginning of his downfall.

When he grew older, he had a telephone installed and a narrow-gauge railway-track laid down along the shore of the Palace lakes. He used to invite the Court ladies to go up and down with him in a miniature railway carriage, drawn by what was little more than a toy steam-engine. This boyish curiosity concerning foreign mechanical contrivances was a healthy symptom and should have borne good fruit, encouraging him, in his maturer years, to develop his Empire on lines of Western progress. Such indeed became his aspiration and his ideal. But Kuang-hsu was born under an evil star. He lacked guidance during his boyhood, so that he never had a chance to develop the well-balanced mind, the just sense of proportion and above all the prudence and moderation, which are indispensable to the successful reformer. Even had he been naturally endowed with these qualities, he must surely have lost them, with such a training as the Rites prescribed for little Emperors.

Brought up among women and eunuchs, in the seclusion of a palace, he could hardly be expected to acquire any manly qualities, even had his physical disabilities not made him naturally a weakling. In order to dissuade him from giving himself a stomach-ache by gobbling up large quantities of some sweetmeat, of which, as a child, he showed himself most greedy, the eunuchs would prostrate themselves at his feet and implore him to stop. His teachers, during lesson-time, would remain on their knees before him. It was only when Kuang-hsu, as a grown man, was forcibly removed from power and kept prisoner in one of the Lake Palaces, that the servility of the courtiers disappeared and the eunuchs showed their indifference to the wishes of the Son of Heaven.

Like many stronger and more experienced men, Kuang-hsu went in fear of Tzu-hsi. His mother, Tzu-hsi's sister, was a bond between them while she lived. But she died young, and after her death there was no one who could have prevented the almost inevitable estrangement.

In February 1889, a Decree was published, to announce the forthcoming marriage of the Son of Heaven to his cousin, another Yehonala (known later by the title of Lung Yü, 'Honorific Abundance'). Thus the clan consolidated its position at Court. The bride was a daughter of Kwei-hsiang, known also as Duke Chow, who commanded one of the eight Banner Corps. He was brother to Tzu-hsi and to the Emperor's mother, so that bride and bridegroom were first cousins. They had been affianced since they were children. These 'engagements' are considered so binding in China that the happy couple are spoken of as husband and wife long before they are of an age to marry. Should the bridegroom die before the ceremony, his bride is considered a widow and should not marry again, but lead a life of retirement and never again use paint or powder on her face.

The decree that announced the coming nuptials spoke of the future Empress as 'a maiden of great virtue and becoming and dignified demeanour'. People who knew the Empress Lung Yü describe her as small in stature, very patrician in looks and manner, and very charming. Hers cannot have been a happy life. No real family ties were possible, as wife of Kuang-hsu. It was known that the Emperor was afflicted by certain physical disabilities, which rendered him unfit for married life. A French doctor, who visited him nine years later, when he was ill and likely to die, said that his physical conformation excluded the possibility of his ever having children, but that the consummation of marriage was not impossible. If this diagnosis was correct, it may account for Kuang-hsu's habitual ill health and physical exhaustion.

The Emperor never made any mystery of the fact that he disliked the bride, who had been chosen for him. After the marriage, they had frequent quarrels, in which Kuang-hsu was wont to come off badly. It was commonly believed that Tzu-hsi had deliberately chosen a wife who should watch over the Emperor and keep her informed of his doings. She did not desire that the new Empress should be on such good terms with her husband as to render possible another alliance against her, such as that of Tung-chih and A-lu-te.

Two concubines were also chosen for Kuang-hsu. These girls were sisters and aged respectively fifteen and thirteen. They were known as the Pearl Concubine and the Lustrous Concubine. Kuang-hsu became very fond of the Pearl Concubine, and she of him, a fact that brought upon them the somewhat unreasonable jealousy of the Empress Lung Yü. But he disliked the Lustrous Concubine, who was fat and tactless.

The marriage was celebrated at great cost to the State, all the provinces being expected to contribute, according to their size and importance. The palanquin in which the bride was carried can still be seen in Peking. It is kept in the tower above the northern gate of the Forbidden City, together with the musical instruments that were used on that occasion. On the yellow satin curtains of the palanquin was embroidered the character *Fu,* meaning happiness. Being repeated twice over, it signified 'conjugal happiness'. The bride wore a beautiful head-dress of gold filigree, representing five phœnixes with tails and wings outspread. Each bird held in its beak a tassel made of little strings of pearls, which hung down and veiled the bride's face.

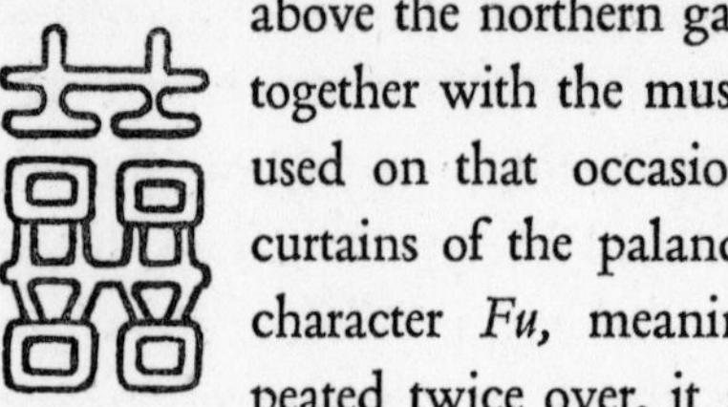

If ever there should arise a second Gibbon, to write The Decline and Fall of the Chinese Empire, he will find in the marriage of Kuang-hsu a symptom of a moral, no less than of a physical, decay (and as he writes, he may conjure up, in sheer contrast, visions of the wedding of Tamerlane).

Kuang-hsu's marriage was arranged for him by the eunuchs, in conformity with the Rites. Everyone knew that the only person to benefit would be Li Lien-ying. No hope for the birth of an heir, who might save the tottering dynasty.

Then, for the second time, Tzu-hsi gave up the regency. She passed the government of the Empire over to Kuang-hsu, and retired to live in the new Summer Palace, which she had caused to be built, after Lord Elgin had burnt the old Palace in 1860. She reserved to herself the right to appoint and to remove public servants. This gave her considerable political power and justified the impression that China still retained the accustomed hand at the helm. On the occasion of her retirement, she received another batch of honorific titles, with considerable benefit to her privy purse.

Photo: Hartung, Pekin.

THE SUMMER PALACE AT PEKIN

Beautiful as the buildings are, it is not in them that lies the charm of the Summer Palace, but in the fact that they harmonize so well with the surrounding Nature. Pagodas, temples and pavilions merge into the landscape and rest within the encircling arms of the friendly hills. The limpid stream that bubbles forth from springs round the Jade Fountain runs into other streams and lakes, on which it is possible to navigate. The hills and wooded valleys offer cover to a wild life that forms the very antithesis to the formal pageantry of a Court:

> And I will build a palace,
> Fit for you and me,
> Of green days in forests
> And blue days at sea!

Tzu-hsi's love of nature found an outlet in landscape gardening, among surroundings that were pastoral. The flowers and blossoms, that figure on Chinese scrolls, bloomed on the hill sides and in the forest dells of her domain. Peach blossoms heralded the spring. Peony and lotus ushered in the summer. In autumn, the chrysanthemums filled the palace gardens. In winter the *prunus* flowered above the snow.

The imperial barge, attached by silken ropes to the boats that towed it, would glide over the still waters of the Kung-hing lake, with the graceful pride of a swan. Even in a boat, the Empress had a yellow satin chair, but her ladies reclined Turkish fashion at her feet. The eunuchs stood behind her, ready to offer tea, or a comfit, or a fan. Other eunuchs sang in a minor key the weird songs of the East, and their voices followed the stroke of the oars, as the flutes in Cleopatra's barge upon the Nile. Something in the atmosphere of those summer days recalls the *Lotus Eaters* and

> Music that gentlier on the spirit lies,
> Than tir'd eyelids upon tir'd eyes.

During the ten years of Tzu-hsi's retirement, the Emperor used to come out to visit her at least once a week. He travelled in a palanquin, by road, taking about two hours and a half to cover the sixteen miles that separate the north-western gate of the town from the outskirts of the Summer Palace. More rarely, he came in a barge, along the canal. On his arrival, he had to kneel before the gate, like any ordinary postulant, while the eunuchs announced his presence and asked permission to admit him. The Chief Eunuch, Li Lien-ying, hated the Emperor, ever since the latter, in a fit of temper, had caused him to be beaten. Therefore it often happened that Kuang-hsu would be kept waiting a long time at the outer gate.

The feasts that accompany the changing seasons were duly observed at the Summer Palace: the Chinese New Year, the Beginning of Spring, the Feast of the Lanterns, the 'Excited Insects', the 'Corn Rain', the Beginning of Summer, the Dragon Boat Festival, the 'Sprouting Seeds', the Feast of Heavenly Gifts, the Beginning of Autumn, the 'White Dew', the Frost's Descent, the Great Snow.

Of all the celebrations, the most picturesque was the Mid-Autumn Festival, or Harvest Moon. It took place in the evening and began with a theatrical performance, in which the Chinese legend of the Maiden in the Moon was dramatized for the occasion.

This legend tells how, one day, the Emperor received the visit of a Fairy, who made him a present of a small root, and told him that, if he ate it, he would become immortal. When the Fairy was about to depart, the grateful Emperor accompanied her as far as the Palace door, leaving the magic root upon the table. While he was away, a little handmaiden entered the room, carrying in her arms a white rabbit. She perceived the root and, in girlish curiosity, picked it up and tasted it. Finding it good, she proceeded to eat it, all except a small morsel which she gave to the rabbit.

Soon the Emperor came back and looked for the Fairy's gift. Not finding it, he questioned the little handmaiden, who confessed to have eaten it. The Emperor flew into a terrible rage and, calling the eunuchs, ordered them to cut the girl open and to seek the root in her stomach. But meanwhile, the spell had begun to work. On the wings of immortality, the little handmaiden rose up and sought refuge in the moon, where she has remained ever since, along with the white rabbit, who helps her to prepare, with mortar and pestle, a magic potion which confers immortality.

The dramatized version of this legend concludes like Mascagni's *Iris*, where the soul of a young girl is wafted upwards into a Paradise of flowers. A gilded Buddha, with a serene, impassive face, is seated on the lotus throne, and around him stretches a lake on which, one after the other, luminous flowers open out, like incandescent lilies. In the sky above, flying storks represent the messengers of the gods. This is Nirvana, where the soul is absorbed into Nature.

At the Summer Palace, after the performance at the theatre, the spectators formed a procession with lanterns, and the Court proceeded to a terrace, high up on the hill-side. Here the

Emperor and Empress Mother made obeisance to the moon and placed floral offerings on the altar before the temple of Ten Thousand Buddhas. Two couples of eunuchs recited a poem in alternate stanzas; incense and paper images were burnt, and an inflammable wine was poured on to the altar so that the flames leapt up towards the sky, where the full moon hung above her worshippers.

When the fires died out and only the incense-smoke rose to meet the woodland scents in the evening air, the Empress and her suite descended once more to the lake, where barges were waiting. Eunuchs holding lanterns knelt on the steps that led down to the water's edge, and lanterns shone in the boats, which moved off to the strains of music and silvery peals of laughter.

So the night wore on among songs and lights, till both died down in the distance *per amica silentia lunæ*.

XVI

Di qui nacque che tutti li profeti armati vinsero e li disarmati rovinarono.

MACHIAVELLI, *Il Principe*, Chap. 6.

PERFECT contentment is not given, in this world, even to an Empress, and the quiet serenity of the Summer Palace was often disturbed by events in the outer world.

All through the second half of the last century, China was continually faced with problems similar to that of Manchuria in recent years. Her outer dependencies fell away from her: lands over which she possessed a more or less shadowy claim, which was recognized by the inhabitants until circumstances arose that made it necessary for them to exchange the enfeebled yoke of the Celestial

Empire for that of some less celestial but more efficient power.

Siam, Tonking, Annam and Burma all passed out of the radius of China's sovereignty. The loss of these regions did not create much resentment among the Chinese. The flow of emigration abroad was, at that time, unrestricted; the whole world was open for them to live in. Had not the Burlingame Treaty with the United States recognized 'the inherent and inalienable right of man to change his home and his allegiance'?

In 1894, Korea, Land of the Morning Calm, was about to exchange the protection of the Son of Heaven for that of the Mikado.

Indirectly, it was the action of the United States that first brought Japan and China face to face over Korea. In 1882, Commodore Shufeldt, U.S.A., having been invested with diplomatic powers, concluded (with the good offices of Li Hung-chang) the first treaty made by the Hermit Kingdom with a Western power. In doing so, he led to the enforced admission, on China's part, that Japan's rights in Korea were on an equality with hers. Twelve years later (1894), Japan descended into the arena to defend these rights.

When the war broke out, China's navy was superior, in number and in tonnage of ships, to the navy of Japan. The Chinese fleet included two armoured battleships of 7,000 tons displacement, whereas the most powerful Japanese man-of-war was a belted cruiser of 4,000 tons. But instead of using their superior force to strike at Japan's maritime communications, on which depended the very existence of her forces in Korea, the Chinese used their battleships as convoys of troops, and only accepted battle when forced to do so. This excess of prudence was caused by the knowledge that the Chinese battleships had insufficient ammunition for their 10-inch guns. Corruption in high places had sapped the strength of the navy.

To anyone who has lived in the Far East and who has dealt with Chinese officials of the old school, William F. Tyler's account of naval operations in the Sino-Japanese war must bring back memories of many tragi-comic situations, similar to those described in his book of Memoirs, *Pulling Strings in China*. I give some characteristic extracts:

The way of the Chinese constitution was to govern by and through the Viceroys of the provinces; so it was Li Hung-chang of the northern province of Chihli—the most powerful satrap of that time—who owned a fleet. Nanking and Canton also had their fleets, but their craft was obsolete. Li Hung-chang's was very different. His ships were up to date—two battleships with ten-inch guns, armoured cruisers, light cruisers and torpedo boats—and he had engaged an English naval officer—Captain Lang—to train the officers and crews. Ting Ju-chang was the Admiral; Lang also had that rank, but in an ambiguous Chinese form which might mean anything from his second-in-command to an adviser with the rank of admiral. Lang believed it was the former, so, when Admiral Ting was called to an audience in Peking, he claimed to take his place; but Liu Poo-chin, the senior Commodore, maintained that Lang was only an adviser, and that the post was his. Peking supported Liu, and Lang resigned. It did not seem a matter of much importance at the time; but it was. It was the decadence of the fleet after Lang had left it that caused the Japanese to venture on their war with China. . . .

. . . At Tientsin I dealt with Detring and von Hanneken. The appointment of the latter as co-Admiral was needed, among other things, to save Admiral Ting from summary decapitation, in case of a reverse; for that is what, in accordance with ancient practice, the Empress Dowager would order. A soldier engineer to be an admiral? That did not bother Li Hung-chang, for Ting himself was a cavalry officer and made no pretence of knowing anything about a ship. As for von Hanneken, it is doubtful if anyone else—say an English admiral—could, in the circumstances, have better filled the post. To complete this burlesque setting of the stage, I, a Naval Reserve Sub-Lieutenant, was appointed Naval Adviser and Secretary to von Hanneken; so there we were. . . .

. . . Perhaps next to Li Hung-chang and the Imperial entourage, came Detring as a factor in the war. He was a German and Customs Commissioner at Tientsin; there he had consolidated himself as Li's adviser and thus became partly independent of Sir Robert Hart, who presumably did not like it. Detring thought he looked like Bismarck, and doubtless the fact affected him. . . . He adopted a Bismarckian manner and had a certain grandeur of conception; but obviously in such a matter as war he lacked the elements of judgment and execution, and played with it as a boy might play at being a Red Indian. He had accompanied the Viceroy on the review, when war was in the air. A schoolboy would at once have thought of ammunition; yet that elementary need was unattended to.

(*Note to the last paragraph quoted*): Regarding what I say about Detring, Sir Francis Aglen, the late Inspector General of Customs, writes: 'Detring's swans were nearly always geese, but in many respects he was a big-minded man. If he erred in believing in the Chinese bubble, he was in good company, for at the beginning Sir Robert Hart himself thought that China would win. I have no doubt that such advice as Detring gave to Li Hung-chang was sound enough; and so awe-inspiring was Li's position that Detring was the only man who dared to tell him unpalatable truths. But Detring had no sort of power in connection with naval or arsenal affairs, and I do not think he can be saddled with responsibility for the shortage of shell.'

After reading these paragraphs it is a pleasure to turn to an extract from Mr. Tyler's diary, in which he expresses his admiration and devotion for the man he served: the Chinese Admiral Ting Ju-chang:

He has, since the attack on this place (*Wei-hai-wei*) was made, always been in the place of most danger. When we bombarded the South forts he was always on the bridge, while the Commodore was slinking in the conning tower. He was, of course, on board when the *Ting Yuen* was torpedoed. Since then, when there was any fighting, he has always been in the *Ching Yuen* in the foremost place; and to-day he was on board of her when she sunk.

Though the information contained in it is not of any historical interest, I cannot resist giving one more extract from Mr. Tyler's book. It describes so exactly the mentality of a Chinese official in an outlying port:

In a sense it was Li Hung-chang and not China that was fighting, and it may well have been that the majority of the Chinese people knew nothing about the war. But in the north they knew, of course, about it, and at Newchwang, the northernmost treaty port of China, an old Major was considering the situation. He had charge of the fort commanding the entrance to the Liao River. The fort was old and dilapidated; it was only made of mud, and its armament consisted of a few old cast-iron guns. But it was a fort and there was war; so on his shoulders rested great responsibilities; quite plainly he must pull up his socks, eschew opium and keep his weather eye lifting. Yet he hoped with earnestness that great issues would not fall on him for settlement. But luck was not his way; for on the wide mud flat which lay between his fortress and the sea, on which hitherto he had rarely seen a soul, there now appeared each evening a group of foreigners, whose actions were undoubtedly mysterious and suspicious. He watched them with his telescope, and in the morning when the place was clear, he scrutinized the little holes and the larger banks which they had made and the flags that they had left behind. Then he sat down and wrote a formal letter to the Tao-tai, reporting what had happened.

He would have felt it his duty to report in any case, but doubly so in these crucial times. The foreigners had made small cylindrical holes in the ground and carefully and skilfully lined them with metal; they had dug short trenches here and there—a most suspicious fact. They were each armed with various shaped weapons, with which they propelled white projectiles for long distances. The whole proceeding was most mysterious and he could form no opinion as to what it meant. He could not say for certain that these operations were connected with the war, but he begged the Tao-tai to instruct him what to do.

On receipt of this letter, the Tao-tai sent it to the Senior Consul, with a covering despatch, referring to the war and the need for utmost caution. He concluded by saying that whatever might be the purpose of the operations on the mud flats, they must now be stopped. Would the Senior Consul please take note and the necessary action.

The Senior Consul was an Englishman. He would reply very formally and politely: . . . 'What my co-nationals are doing is playing a well-known game which is played at every other port. It is usually done on grass, but as none exists here they are making the best they can of the deserted mud flat. They are merely amusing themselves; that is all.'

The Senior Consul's letter was now sent to the Major with instructions from the Tao-tai for a further report by the light of the information given in it. So once more the old man took his brush in hand and wrote those upright columns of complicated characters: 'I am an ignorant soldier, and this problem is beyond me. If these operations have no military significance, I have wondered whether they might not be connected with prospecting for minerals. It is the only suggestion I can make. As for the Senior Consul's so-called explanation, I have admitted that my ignorance disables me from saying what they are doing; but it is not so great as to disable me from saying, quite positively, and without a shadow of doubt about the matter, that they are not amusing themselves.'

After a series of crushing defeats on land and sea, China found herself without a fleet, with Wei-hai-wei in the hands of the enemy and even the metropolitan province of Chihli threatened with invasion by 'the dwarfs of the East'.

Popular clamour was inclined to make Li Hung-chang a scapegoat for the national disaster, for it was he who, as 'Warden of the Northern Seas', had taken in hand the reorganization of the navy. After the defeat, Li Hung-chang sought to replace the lost ships, and he made an offer to buy, or failing that to lease, the whole Italian Navy (which was then the fourth navy in the world). But his offer was not accepted.

Li Hung-chang had foreseen the war and had done his best to avoid it, realizing the superiority of the Japanese. But his hand had been forced by his subordinates, no less than by his superiors. The responsibility for the naval defeat rested, in part, on Tzu-hsi and on Li Lien-ying, for they had appropriated most of the funds, earmarked for naval expenses, and had spent them on building the Summer Palace. It was well known at Court that the marble terraces and costly pavilions, mirrored in the waters of the Kung-hing lake, had been paid for with the money that should have furnished the Chinese ships with shot and shell.

Admiral Mahan's studies on *The Influence of Sea-power on History* had been published only four years before the outbreak of the Sino-Japanese war. Readers of that famous book may wonder to-day what might have been the consequences if, in 1894, the Chinese had obtained a victory such as the number and tonnage of their ships should have assured. But in Peking, at an emasculated Court, the war spirit was lacking. One of the eunuchs, to whom the misappropriation of the naval funds was mentioned, answered with the following comment: 'Even if the money had been spent on the navy, the Japanese would have beaten us all the same. As it is, at least we have the Summer Palace!'

Tzu-hsi was by no means disposed to admit her own fault. Indeed, her resentment was very bitter, because the unfortunate war with Japan had obliged her to put a stop to the costly celebrations that were being prepared in honour of her own sixtieth birthday. The festivities for this jubilee were to have been on a scale unrivalled on any former occasion, even during the reigns of Kang-hsi and of Ch'ien-lung, both of whom had been Emperors for more than sixty years. The most exalted personages in China gathered round the Old Buddha, and her benevolence was extended also to those who, in recent years, had been considered more or less in disgrace. Prince Kung's fine figure, stately in old age, lent dignity to the Court of Tzu-hsi, as in youth it had added strength to the Court of Yehonala. Jung Lu, recalled from exile, was given the command of the gendarmerie and a high military post at Tientsin. Triumphal arches spanned the road to the Summer Palace. All public officials offered (not quite spontaneously perhaps) 25 per cent. of their annual pay, as a birthday present to Her Majesty.

But evil tidings from Korea spoilt the apotheosis in Peking, and the prestige of the Manchus was shaken. Times were not favourable for costly celebrations. Much against her will, Tzu-hsi had to give them up. She laid the blame on the Emperor, whose poor statesmanship had involved the country in war without her consent.

In those days, the personal antagonism between Tzu-hsi and Kuang-hsu had become acute, and in some ways it seemed to crystallize, at Court, the rivalry between North and South China, between Peking and Canton. The North was conservative and reactionary; the South represented modernist tendencies. The northerners invoked a return to the old traditions, which had made China so great in the past. The southerners preached reform.

In many cases, the would-be reformers became suspect and had to leave the country. The most formidable of these exiles was Sun-yat-sen, son of a poor farmer on the island of Hsiang Shan, near Macao, who was a convert of the London Missionary Society. As a young man, Sun-yat-sen took a degree at the medical school at Hong Kong. He belonged to a secret society, which planned to overthrow the Manchu régime in China. In 1895, he had to fly for his life, after which he lived in England, in Japan and in the United States, and organized from abroad various attempts at revolution. He was considered so dangerous that a price of £100,000 was placed upon his head. In 1896, when residing in London, he was asked to come to the Chinese Legation in Portland Square, and on entering, was arrested and confined to an upper room of the house, whence he managed to throw a letter into the street, addressed to Sir James Cantlie, and this letter was brought to its destination by a passer-by. A question was asked in Parliament and Sun's release was demanded and obtained with some difficulty, after Lord Salisbury had taken the matter up as one of abuse of diplomatic privilege.

This incident revealed to the outer world how great was the tension between the Chinese imperial authorities and the advocates of reform. The latter did their best to overthrow the monarchical régime, until it became clear that they had an ally in the enemy's camp. This ally was the Emperor himself!

Kuang-hsu hated the venerable formalities so dear to Chinese bureaucracy: the long, dull audiences, during which he sat enthroned on high, while aged Councillors knelt before him and made long reports on the situation in far-off provinces. He received the Council at two in the morning, and because of his shy retiring disposition, he would not allow the hall to be sufficiently lighted. Thus, in the dead of night, and in a semi-obscurity, he would sit, a dim pathetic figure, and wearily follow an administrative routine that was as old as the hills. Meanwhile, his brain fermented with vague aspirations towards novelty and change.

That same curiosity which had inspired his childish passion for foreign toys, caused the young Emperor to devour with avidity all procurable translations of foreign books, including a Chinese version of the Bible. Such disordered reading could hardly help him to assimilate the culture of the West. But, in many ways, his reasoning was sound. Kuang-hsu well understood that his country's defeat by the Japanese constituted a sure proof that China needed reorganizing on new lines in order to ensure to her a status of equality with other powers. This laudable ideal, coupled with his love for things exotic, induced the Emperor to rush headlong down the path of reform, without stopping to consider the dangers into which it might lead him.

His tutor, Weng Tung-ho, was not able to keep pace with Kuang-hsu's desire to acquire knowledge of foreign institutions. But he suggested that a friend of his, a Cantonese of notoriously advanced views, be summoned to the Palace.

The friend's name was Kang Yu-wei. His official position did not justify the honour of an Audience, but Kuang-hsu willingly consented to receive him. And in this fiery zealot he found a political Mentor.

Within the space of three months, the Emperor, acting on the advice of Kang Yu-wei, promulgated a series of edicts which, if the world could be changed by such means, might have transformed China completely. Public instruction, petrified in forms of hoary antiquity, was reorganized on modern lines, and in accordance with systems prevailing in Western lands. To facilitate instruction in the sciences, many temples were transformed into schools. A special institute was established at Shanghai for the translation and distribution of foreign books. The scions of princely Manchu houses were encouraged to travel abroad for purposes of education. Many offices were abolished, as being no longer necessary, in Peking and in the provinces.

Thus a numerous and powerful bureaucracy saw its privileges, acquired through a millennial prescription, cancelled by one stroke of the Vermilion Pencil. Men who had served the Emperor long and faithfully according to their lights resented the hasty reforms, which threatened their vital interests. To the opposition of a ruling class was added the irrational fear of a superstitious people, and in both, the instinct of self-preservation inspired a common abhorrence of all change.

Kuang-hsu's attempts at reform have been variously described. Some sinologues speak of them as the tragedy of a noble effort cruelly thwarted. Others as a childishly imprudent attempt to transform, in one hundred days, the very nature of a people so numerous that none can count their teeming millions, and so established in their ancient order that in the market place one may still spend coins that were current in the days before there was an England, and before Carthage had been humbled by the rising power of Rome.

Visions of a rebirth of China have inspired the statesmanship of more experienced and more fortunate men than those who first realized that any change was possible or necessary. The obstacles that stood in the way of such a rebirth have revealed themselves more clearly with the passing of the years.

In the old days, the Chinese government rested on the central authority of the throne, upheld by an immense prestige. The administration was decentralized, and on the patriarchal organization of the family was founded the whole political structure of the State.

At the Altar of Heaven, the Son of Heaven prayed for humanity. He stood between his subjects and the Gods above. No abstract constitutional idea could serve as a substitute for that solitary figure upon the Dragon Throne.

To modify the ancient structure of the State and to adapt it to foreign ideals appeared to most Chinese as a sacrilege. The eternal struggle between the old order and the new was envenomed, as such struggles often are, by personal antipathies.

Prince Kung was one of the tories, but he used his great influence to inspire counsels of moderation among the anti-foreign die-hards of the Manchu clans, as well as in the mind of the Emperor himself. Prince Kung's death, in the spring of 1898, was a great loss to China, for it made the chances of agreement more remote, and thus cleared the way for the Boxer troubles of 1900.

At a later date, it became customary to number Jung Lu among the reactionaries, but in the beginning he showed a certain friendliness to Kang Yu-wei, and did not oppose the projects for reform.

The hopes of the conservative, or northern, party lay with Tzu-hsi, but she was in no hurry to assume the leadership of the anti-reformers, although she rebuked the Emperor for listening to Kang Yu-wei's accusations against herself. She also manifested her displeasure by bringing about the dismissal of the Emperor's old tutor, Weng Tung-ho. To Tzu-hsi's credit be it said that, despite repeated appeals from Princes and Grand Councillors to reassume the regency, she took no steps to do so until she felt herself directly menaced by the Emperor's projects.

It has not been sufficiently emphasized that Kuang-hsu's plans for reform found the most formidable obstacle in his own limitations, in his inability to persuade others, and to find adherents for his cause. The personal factor was lacking. Even an Emperor needs the qualities of leadership, if he wishes to lead. There was nothing inspiring about Kuang-hsu, no charm, no personal magnetism and no driving power. That such a man should have taken up such a burden was pathetic. And it was tragic that, in so doing, he should have provoked the antagonism of the one person whose help might have removed most of the difficulties from his path.

In his charming and learned book, *Twilight in the Forbidden City,* Reginald F. Johnston draws attention to a point of what might be called Chinese constitutional law. He compares the retirement of Tzu-hsi, after relinquishing the regency, to the abdication of the Emperor Ch'ien-lung in 1795:

> The words 'abdication' and 'retirement', when applied to the action taken by Ch'ien-lung in 1795 and by the empress-dowager in 1872 and again in 1889, are likely to create a false impression in Western minds. After celebrating his jubilee with great pomp in 1795, Ch'ien-lung exchanged the position of emperor *(huang-ti)* for that of super-emperor *(t'ai shang huang)* in virtue of which he took precedence of his successor on the throne for the remainder of his life. Ch'ien-lung was indeed a more august and splendid personage in the Court and in the Empire after his 'abdication' than before it. Nor was his exalted position a purely honorary one. Though relieved of the routine functions of the throne, he had the right and the power to reserve to himself the final decision in all matters of importance and to over-rule and set aside, if he felt so disposed, the mandates of his successor.
>
> . . . .
>
> Now if the position of the empress-dowager after her 'retirement' was hardly as exalted as that of the venerable Ch'ien-lung, it was superior, not only in practice but in theory, to that of the emperor. There was nothing extraordinary about the honours conferred on or assumed by the 'Venerable Buddha'. They were hers in virtue of her place in the genealogical table of the imperial family; and even if she had never acted as regent during two minorities, she would have taken precedence of the emperor Kuang-hsu, not merely because she was the mother of his predecessor, but also because she belonged to the senior generation.

In these circumstances, it is evident that a reform movement in China, even if directed by the Emperor, could hardly have been successful unless conducted with exceptional qualities of tact and prudence (such as Kuang-hsu certainly did not possess) in order not to offend the susceptibilities of the Old Buddha.

Had it been possible for Kuang-hsu and the Empress Tzu-hsi to have worked together in mutual sympathy and understanding, the Empire would never have fallen, and the Chinese of to-day might be happier than they are.

XVII

A man thinks he knows, but a woman knows better.

Chinese Proverb.

UANG-HSU'S reforms seem moderate enough in the light of later experience. With a little patience, it should have been possible to carry them through. Public opinion in the north (especially in the capital) was alarmed, but not openly rebellious, and in the southern and central provinces a policy of radical reform had many powerful sympathizers. One of the Viceroys had published a pamphlet on the advisability of acquiring foreign learning. Innovations in the matter of education might have created little opposition, if they had been merely constructive, that is to say, if they had been limited to the creation of facilities for the acquisition of foreign knowledge. But the zeal of the would-be reformers inspired them with a desire to destroy before they began to construct, and what they destroyed, though antiquated and inefficient, had still a greater educational value than anything they had ready to offer in its place. The Emperor began his reforms by abolishing the State examinations in classical subjects which had always formed the necessary test for the acquisition of a degree.

Dwellers in Peking, who walk along the Tartar wall, between the Hata-mên and the old observatory, can still look down on the remains of a strange hive-like construction, with many rows of tiny cells, which are now visible from above, as the roof has fallen in. This ruined building, nestling in a corner of the old walls, is all that remains of the Examination Halls, connected with the once famous 'Forest of Pencils' or Hanlin Academy. In those little cells, the candidates from all over the Empire were shut up for several days, until they had produced the essay from which their knowledge might be judged. It was not an ideal system, and there can be no doubt that the old knowledge was insufficient to the needs of the hour. But it was to the ancient philosophy that China owed her stability through the centuries, her moral cohesion, her dignity and prestige. To throw aside the old learning, before there was an alternative curriculum, was an error that Kuang-hsu was the first to commit. His example has been followed by later reformers.

The constant stream of edicts that flowed out from the Emperor's study during three short months, gave public opinion no time to get used to the many innovations, and created the uneasy impression that nothing of the old order was sacred and that nothing was safe.

Of the two principal representatives of the reform movement, Sun-yat-sen and Kang Yu-wei, the former lived in exile and believed that no success was possible until the Manchu dynasty had been overthrown, whereas Kang Yu- wei frequented the Court and put his trust in the Emperor. But even Kang Yu-wei was convinced that no reform had any chance of being carried out as long as the Empress Dowager maintained her influence in public matters. Tzu-hsi represented the principal obstacle to any change. There was only one way to overcome her opposition. She must be forcibly put aside.

Therefore, Kang Yu-wei advised the Emperor to have Tzu-hsi arrested and kept in confinement on a small island in one of the Palace lakes. Such an act was nothing less than a *coup d'état,* and the forces necessary to carry it into effect were not at the Emperor's command. Kuang-hsu's adherents were few and of small account, as compared with those of the Empress Dowager. In the ten years of his reign without tutelage of regents, Kuang-hsu had not been capable of inspiring the devotion of any one personality of real political importance. Realizing the weakness of his position, he endeavoured to obtain the support of some powerful military commander. His choice fell upon Yuan-shi-kai.

In the years that preceded the Sino-Japanese war, Yuan was the Imperial Resident in Korea, and his mismanagement was considered, by some critics, as responsible for the loss of that dependency. In his reports to Li Hung-chang, he expressed the firm conviction that, in the event of an armed conflict with Japan, China would receive assistance from Great Britain. When the war broke out, this assistance did not materialize, except in a minor episode. Yuan-shi-kai

Photo: Hartung, Pekin.

THE SUMMER PALACE

himself found refuge on a British gunboat, when he hastily quitted his post, before the arrival of the Japanese at Seoul.

In the summer of 1898, Yuan held a military appointment under Jung Lu in the metropolitan province of Chihli, and had acquired the reputation of being an efficient commander of well-disciplined, well-drilled and well-armed troops. Thus Yuan-shi-kai appeared to be a suitable instrument for carrying out the act of violence necessary to put an end to the dualistic régime then in force.

The Emperor sent for Yuan and in two successive audiences endeavoured to ascertain his views concerning the recent edicts and the prospects of future action along the same lines. It is evident that Kuang-hsu felt that Yuan was to be trusted, for in a third and final interview he charged him with the execution of his plans.

We can only guess at the impression produced on the mind of Yuan-shi-kai by the Emperor's views in the matter of reform, and on the methods proposed for carrying them into effect. It may well be that Yuan's courteous and courtly acquiescence in the opinions expressed by his sovereign were mistaken by the latter for genuine sympathy. But even if Yuan-shi-kai declared himself to be imbued with the new doctrines of reform, it was imprudent of Kuang-hsu to have immediately entrusted him with so grave a mission as the arrest of the Empress Dowager. To any well-brought-up Chinaman of the old school, what Kuang-hsu proposed to do represented a grave infraction of the rules of filial piety, and the infamy of such an act would have been shared by anyone who participated in it. Serious scruples must necessarily have arisen in the mind of an elderly official, and doubts as to whether it could really be in the interest of the Empire to place all the power of the State in the hands of a weakling like Kuang-hsu, with his hurriedly conceived schemes of regeneration.

But there was another weak point in Kuang-hsu's plan of action. Li Hung-chang was no longer Viceroy of Chihli. With the object of removing him temporarily from public affairs, after the unhappy ending to the war with Japan, Tzu-hsi had sent him to represent China at the coronation of the Tsar, after which he was to visit the principal foreign capitals. And he had been replaced, at Tientsin, by Jung Lu.

It was easy to foresee that, in the event of any danger threatening the Empress Mother, Jung Lu would spring to her defence, as he had done thirty-seven years before, on the road to Jehol. Therefore, in order to strike at the Empress, it was necessary to begin by suppressing Jung Lu.

Yuan-shi-kai was given a written order appointing him to succeed Jung Lu in the command of the troops. At the same time, the Emperor handed him a small golden arrow, as a symbol of authority.

Like many rulers who govern only in name, Kuang-hsu was ignorant of many things which it would have been useful to have known. He was not aware that Yuan-shi-kai's personal relations with Jung Lu were exceedingly friendly; a few years before they had taken an oath of friendship, which made them 'blood brothers'.

Thus Yuan found himself in the position of having to choose between two acts of treachery: one towards his Emperor, and one towards his friend. And to sacrifice his friend meant also to sacrifice the whole régime which centred round the Empress Mother, to betray the Old China to the New.

Yuan-shi-kai preferred to betray the Emperor.

On reaching Tientsin, about midday, he went straight to Jung Lu and warned him of the danger that threatened him and the Empress Mother.

Tientsin and Peking had only recently been linked up by a railway (the Government authorities, after much hesitation, had consented to the laying of a line that would facilitate the transport of coal from the Kaiping mines). Jung Lu ordered a special train and reached Peking late in the afternoon.

Tzu-hsi happened to be in the capital, spending the night in one of the Lake Palaces, after the annual sacrifice to the God of Silk Worms, a sacrifice which had to be accomplished by the Empress. Jung Lu, having heard of the Old Buddha's whereabouts, hastened to the Palace and, violating all precedents, entered unsummoned and unannounced. Prostrating himself at Tzu-hsi's feet, he appealed to her for sanctuary.

'What danger threatens you,' asked the Empress, 'that you force your way in here, where you have no business to be?'

And then Jung Lu repeated the story, told him by Yuan-shi-kai.

Tzu-hsi was ever prompt to take action. Before many hours were past, the Grand Council had been secretly summoned to her presence. Its members willingly lent their authority to the proposal that she should take up the reins of government. In that meeting of the Grand Council, without the Emperor, one might see Old China at bay. The Councillors met at night, as usual (the fifth night of the eighth moon), and knelt before the throne, where Tzu-hsi presided. She was the last hope and refuge of those who sought to keep the Empire uncontaminated by the new policies, the new ideals. Young China was preparing to strike, but the lion's whelp was less to be feared than the old lion, dying.

Some news of what was happening reached Kuang-hsu in time for him to send a warning to Kang Yu-wei. He wrote:

'I have a very great sorrow in my heart, which cannot be described with brush and ink. You must at once proceed abroad and devise means to save me.'

Shortly before dawn, the Emperor was studying a litany, which he had to recite later in the day, at the annual sacrifices in honour of the tutelary gods of the dynasty. A group of eunuchs burst into the room, headed by Li Lien-ying. Kuang-hsu was seized and taken to an island, known as The Ocean Terrace, on the southernmost of the three lakes that grace the imperial domain, within the walls of the capital. Here Tzu-hsi came to him and vented the vials of her wrath. When angry, she still spoke in quiet tones, but her voice lost its sweetness. Strong men feared her ironic words more than any violent outburst from such as themselves. We can only guess what she said to the unfortunate Emperor. She left him with the impression that he had not long to live. Meanwhile, fifty-three of his favourite eunuchs, who had aided him in the preparation of the edicts of reform, were beaten to death in the courtyards of the Palace.

Kang Yu-wei, warned in time, fled by way of Tientsin to the sea. With the help of the British Consul-General in Shanghai, he eventually succeeded in reaching Hongkong. On the day of Tzu-hsi's *coup d'état*, there was a rumour in Peking to the effect that the Emperor Kuang-hsu, realizing that he was in danger, wished to take refuge in the Italian Legation. The reason given was that Baron Vitale, Chinese Secretary and First Interpreter to the Legation, was a friend of Kang Yu-wei. Baron Vitale himself considered the rumour as well-founded and spoke of it to his Chief, the Italian Minister, Marchese Salvago Raggi, to whom the Emperor's request for sanctuary would doubtless have caused serious embarrassment. But the matter was not heard of again. Another rumour, that the Emperor actually sought refuge in the British Legation and was refused admittance, had no foundation.

Thus commenced the third of Tzu-hsi's regencies, if one may use the word regency for the rights of government, fully exercised by the Empress Mother, while her unfortunate nephew retained the bare title of Emperor and continued to accomplish only the sacrificial ceremonies prescribed by the Book of Rites. During two years, Kuang-hsu remained virtually a prisoner on the Ocean Terrace. The Pearl Concubine was taken from him. The first imperial consort might approach her husband, but it was known that their relationship was anything but cordial.

Kuang-hsu's prison was a beautiful one: a palace on an island, connected with the mainland by a bridge of white marble and red lacquered woodwork.

The buildings are closely grouped, so that the roofs of glazed tiles, yellow, purple, green and blue, rise up like flowers among the encircling foliage. The terrace, which gives the island its name, juts out over the waters and is mirrored in them, except when a passing gust of wind blurs the reflections. It is almost impossible to believe, on approaching such a fairy palace, that beyond the century-old willows and behind the encircling wall, are the crowded streets of a big town.

Even in winter, the Ocean Terrace is beautiful, never more so than on a misty January morning, when the trees are white with hoar-frost and the sky is reflected on the frozen surface of the lake in changing tints of opal. In summer one crosses the water in barges that thread their way among the lotus; in winter one uses sleds, pushed by attendants who run and slide over the ice. In the Emperor's day, the sleds were lined with fur; their runners were lacquered in crimson and finished off with dragons' heads in ivory and gold.

The charm of Kuang-hsu's prison lay in externals only. Comforts he had none. Tzu-hsi's eunuchs took a malicious pleasure in denying to the fallen monarch all the luxuries to which he had been accustomed. The rice paper on his windows broke and fluttered in the wind. His rooms were left dirty and insufficiently heated. His clothes, even, were neglected and, some say, full of vermin. One of the eunuchs, more kind-hearted than his fellows, brought the Emperor a fine fur coat that he had asked for. When Li Lien-ying heard of it, he said nothing, but took care that the eunuch's name should be omitted from the list of those who were to receive presents from the Empress Mother on the occasion of the New Year.

Only on ceremonial occasions was Kuang-hsu brought out and robed in all the splendour of the Son of Heaven, with the great Pearl of State on his official hat and a priceless buckle of jade at his belt.

It would have been in conformity with historical precedents, as also with Chinese ideas of what was fitting and seemly, if, after having ceased to rule the Empire in his own name, Kuang-hsu had fallen ill and died. So it caused no surprise when an edict announced that the Emperor was in bad health, and that he could find no alleviation for his sufferings. The most esteemed physicians of the Empire were summoned to Peking, where they knelt before the throne in the presence of the invalid and of the Dowager Empress, who explained the symptoms from which her nephew was suffering. The doctors were allowed to touch the patient's hand, but they might not presume to raise their eyes to his face. After this ceremonious examination, they spoke oracularly about vapours at work on the Emperor's person, under the influence of occult causes. They concluded that he might get worse or better. If he got better, he might get well. If he got worse, he might die. A French doctor also visited him (a little more thoroughly) and made a diagnosis that filled the Chinese physicians with astonishment and contempt. But his conclusions were much the same as theirs.

Thus the Chinese public was prepared for the promulgation of a valedictory decree and the announcement that the Son of Heaven had mounted on the Dragon for the journey to the Yellow Springs.

But opposition arose from an unexpected quarter. The British Minister made known to the Tsung-li Yamen that the Emperor's health was a matter of concern to the foreign representatives and that the consequences of his disappearance might be serious. This tactless (from a Chinese point of view) communication was unconsciously seconded by one of the Southern Viceroys, who informed the Empress Dowager that the removal of Kuang-hsu from power had made an exceedingly bad impression in the South, and that the news of his death might provoke revolution. Tzu-hsi was much annoyed with the authors of these two warnings. She could do nothing to the British Minister. But the Viceroy, informed in time of her gathering wrath, retired hurriedly into Portuguese territory at Macao and only returned to his post when he felt sure that the danger was over.

It would seem that Kuang-hsu's health benefited by so much interest being taken in it, from near and far. He was soon well enough to be present at a reception (the first of its kind), given by Tzu-hsi to the ladies of the Diplomatic Body in Peking. The guests were all much impressed by the Dowager Empress's dignified manners and great personal charm.

XVIII

CHINAMAN: You allee chop-chop me now. But welly soon forrin devil chop-chop forrin devil.

Cartoon in 'Punch', June 27, 1900.

CAGED on the Ocean Terrace, Kuang-hsu pined away, a lonely, broken-hearted man, while the Empire was governed by Tzu-hsi and her eunuchs. As time passed, he was accorded a little more liberty, and the Empress Mother used to take him about with her wherever she went.

It was now officially admitted that Kuang-hsu could have no progeny to succeed him, and in January 1900 an heir to the throne was chosen in the person of Pu-chun, son of Prince Tuan, who was adopted as a posthumous son of the Emperor Tung-chih, thus fulfilling the promise given at the time of Tung-chih's death, to find a successor who could make the prescribed sacrifices at his altar.

The Heir-Apparent was known as the Ta A-ko (a Manchu term meaning Great Elder Brother), and he was expected to succeed to the throne at no very distant date. But he was a riotous, undisciplined boy, and frequently got into trouble with the Empress Dowager, who used to have him whipped by the eunuchs, much to the indignation of his father, the Prince Tuan (son of Prince Tun, fifth son of the Emperor Tao-kwang). Prince Tuan was a big, blustering man, very full of his own importance, but he stood in great awe of Tzu-hsi, and though he might intrigue against her, he rarely ventured to oppose her will. The fact that his son had been chosen as heir-apparent to the throne encouraged Prince Tuan in certain vague dreams of one day taking the place of the redoubtable Empress and becoming arbiter of the destinies of China.

The *coup d'état* by which Tzu-hsi had once more assumed the government of the country did not attract much attention abroad. Public opinion was occupied with the war in South Africa. The European powers continued to further their own interest in China, but (with the exception of Russia) they took little interest in Chinese internal politics; thus they remained strangely unconscious of the clouds that heralded a coming storm.

In 1897, the German fleet seized the port of Tsin-tao and the adjacent territory of Kiau-chau in the province of Shan-tung, nominally to seek reparation for the murder of two German missionaries. During the negotiations that followed, it was arranged that the bay and the land on both sides of the entrance should be leased to Germany for ninety-nine years, with the right to erect fortifications.

This was the starting-point for a 'forward' policy by all the foreign powers. In 1898, the British leased Wei-hai-wei. In 1899 the French occupied Kuang-chin-wan, in the peninsula of Kuan-tung. The Italians contemplated the occupation of the Bay of San Mun, but the project never materialized.

By far the most dangerous of the 'imperialistic' powers was Russia, whose designs on the northern provinces of the Chinese Empire were rapidly maturing.

Since the end of the nineteenth century, Manchuria has been what Owen Lattimore has called a 'cradle of conflict'. The Chinese were pushed aside as having only a secondary interest in the country whence their Manchu conquerors had descended upon them three centuries before. After her defeat by the Japanese, in 1894, China had ceded to Japan the peninsula of Liao-tung, with Port Arthur. But Japan's easy victory provoked the jealousy of the other powers. Russia, France and Germany brought pressure to bear on the Government at Tokio, to restore the conquered territory and to accept, in its place, the payment of an indemnity.

German action in the Shan-tung province forced the hand of the Russian Minister for foreign affairs, Count Michael Muraviev, obliging him to quicken the pace of his own similar policy. Thus the Russians obtained, in 1898, the lease of that same territory which Japan had been obliged to restore to China a few years before. Russian Viceroys in the Far East dreamt of creating another Muscovite Empire on the shores of the Pacific, such as Rome had created on the shores of the Bosphorus.

Meanwhile it was rumoured in China (not without some foundation) that negotiations were on foot between the principal powers, for the delimitation of their respective spheres of influence. The Chinese believed that the foreign devils contemplated a dismemberment of the Empire. Missionaries began to be regarded, not unreasonably, as political emissaries and forerunners of military aggression.

It was then that people began to speak of 'the Boxers'.

In his latest book (already quoted in these pages) Reginald F. Johnston makes an unexpected comparison between the Chinese Boxers of 1900 and the German Nazis of to-day:

> Had the Boxers appeared a generation later, they would have learned much from the principles and practices of Hitlerite Germany. They would have sought justification for their anti-foreign activities on grounds almost identical with those on which anti-Semitism is based to-day. As to the swastika, they would have had at least as good a right as the Germans to make it their badge, for their religion was Buddhistic, and the swastika was and is a familiar object in all Buddhist temples. The Boxers made a mess of things because of their ignorance and superstition. . . . If Germany may expel 'non-Nordic' elements from her body politic, we cannot complain if the Chinese claim a similar right to rid themselves of those aliens (European or Asiatic) who threaten, or seem to threaten, their national integrity. Nor can we justly blame them if they deliberately set themselves to acquire the power that will enable them to enforce that right. Already there are Chinese writers and speakers who in their demand, not only for the return of lost territories, but also for the cancellation of foreign concessions and the abolition of foreign consular jurisdiction, are using arguments directly and admittedly drawn from the utterances of the spokesmen of Hitlerite Germany. Just as Soviet Russia provided them in recent years with useful slogans to encourage them in their struggles against Western imperialism and capitalism, so will Hitlerite Germany equip them with a new theory of Nationalism and a new technique.

It was the 'technique' that was primitive in the old manifestations of anti-foreign feeling in China.

Before the year 1900 the Boxers were simply known to be members of a secret society, organized in Shan-tung and calling itself I-ho-tuan (Band of Patriotic Union).[1] They were tolerated, if not encouraged, by the authorities, who only qualified them as 'rebels' when their activities became locally inconvenient. Like all Chinese secret societies, they changed their name and their character according to circumstances. At one time they were known as the Plum Blossom Fists; later it became customary to speak of them as *Chuen-fei,* that is to say Bandits of the Fist, or more briefly 'Boxers'. They claimed to be invulnerable, enjoying the protection of China's tutelary gods, who wished to make use of them to rid the country of foreign devils. The latter were accused of having forced the Chinese government to give away territories and ports, and to offend the spirits of Wind and Water (*Feng-shui*) by allowing the building of railways and the exploitation of mines.

Eastern peoples are always ready to listen to a prophet, to welcome a Messiah (even though, later on, they may crucify him) and to declare a holy war. The movement set afoot by the Boxers can be classified in the last category. Although they preached the extermination of all foreigners and killed them whenever the opportunity offered, their most numerous victims were the so-called 'devils' disciples', or Chinese converts to Christianity. Of these they murdered no less than 16,000. The most sincere among the Boxers were of the poorer classes and incredibly ignorant, so much so that they could be persuaded, by the clumsiest of conjuring tricks, that their leaders were really invulnerable and could make

[1] The characters for I-ho are the same as E-wo, the *hong-name* of the well-known firm of Jardine & Matheson. The translation *Patriotic* would not be suitable for a commercial designation. But it may do for the Boxers.

them so. They were filled with a contagious fanaticism, not unlike that which inspired the followers of the Mahdi in the Sudan.

The acknowledged military chief of the Boxers was the Chinese General, Tung Fu-hsiang, who commanded the 'braves' from the province of Kansu. Tzu-hsi had summoned these troops to Peking, after her *coup d'état* in 1898, and they stayed on in the vicinity of the capital. Tung Fu-hsiang's standards were of black velvet, with Chinese characters in red. In the spring of 1900 they were raised for the first time on the hills behind the Summer Palace, as well as over a small encampment on the open space between the Temple of Heaven and the Temple of Agriculture, in the Chinese City. The sight of those black banners, flaunting their crimson characters, like splashes of fresh blood, made people realize that the Boxers must enjoy the favour of the Court, or their chief would never have been allowed to pitch his camp in such privileged positions.

Within the Forbidden City, the Boxers were represented by Prince Tuan and by his brother, the Duke Lan. With the help of the Chief Eunuch, Li Lien-ying, they strove to influence the Empress Dowager, urging her to take up the new doctrine that promised to rid the country of any foreign ascendency and to bring back the good old times.

Tzu-hsi had always been superstitious. More in superstition than in reasoned belief, she admitted the claims of the Boxers to possess supernatural powers, which would enable them to destroy the foreigners. But while in her heart she wished the Boxers all success, her support was hampered by ever-recurring doubts. The Boxer leaders were the men whom the Empress delighted to honour, should they prove successful, but to whom she would offer the silken cord of suicide, should they fail.

The Emperor was all for protecting the foreigners, but his wishes counted for nothing. Jung Lu was opposed to the Boxers and did everything in his power to dissuade the Empress from giving them her support, and especially from allowing attacks on the official representatives of the foreign powers. Yuan-shi-kai was also anti-Boxer. Having been appointed Governor of Shan-tung, he quelled all disorders in his province and obliged the Boxer leaders to carry their activities elsewhere. Li Hung-chang was in Canton and took no part in the events until the Boxer movement had ended in failure and China had been invaded by foreign troops, bent on inflicting punishment. Then he was called upon to represent the Chinese government in the negotiations for peace.

At that time, the Tsung-li Yamen was directed by Prince Ching, an amiable old gentleman and a distant cousin of Kuang-hsu, through their common ancestor, the Emperor Ch'ien-lung. Even with the best intentions, the Minister for Foreign Affairs could do nothing to control the Boxers, as long as they received support and encouragement from the Court. During the months of April and May, 1900, the foreign Ministers made continual representations to the Chinese Government, denouncing the attacks on individual foreigners and on the foreign missions, but all they could obtain were some vague assurances that the matter would receive careful attention.

A characteristic of foreign communities in Eastern lands is their incredulity concerning the danger of an attack from the population among which they live. Residents in China get easily accustomed to the events that appear so sensational when reported in the press of Western lands. It is strange that, even to-day, the foreign community in China shows a tendency to minimize rather than to exaggerate the importance of the Boxer movement and the siege of the Legations in Peking. It would almost appear that people are jealous because nothing so exciting occurs in their own day. They will point out that many similar and equally dangerous outbreaks of xenophobia have occurred in the East (in India, in Burma, in Japan; even in China itself) and that the events of 1900 were insignificant in comparison with the impression they created. All of which may be true. But the importance of historical events is not measured by their scale; if it were, the importance of the Tai-ping rebellion would be greater than that of the Napoleonic wars. The siege of the Legations was, in some ways, a ridiculous episode, and its failure (from the Chinese point of view) was absurd. And yet it marks, as much as any single episode can mark, a turning-point in history, and in the life of Yehonala, a climax and a final disillusion. The date, 1900, is symbolical, not only of a century ended and of another begun, but also of the Old China that passed away and of the New which came into its own.

No one doubted, in the spring of 1900, that the missionaries in the interior were in danger, but this was because of their disinclination to come away while there was still time to seek safety in the Treaty Ports. In those days, foreign governments were by no means unwilling to make political capital out of the murder of a missionary. They carried this policy to such lengths that finally the Vatican had to make known its unwillingness to accept blood money (*pretium sanguinis*) for the murder of a missionary.

To most of the foreigners in Peking it seemed impossible that plans could be laid, with the approval of the Court, for the massacre of foreign residents in the capital, and that the diplomatic representatives of the foreign powers could be attacked by a band of fanatics without any effort being made by the Chinese government for their protection. The diplomatic body in Peking received frequent warnings of a coming danger, and many were the criticisms levelled at the foreign Ministers for not having repeated such warnings, with sufficient emphasis, to their respective governments at home. Some of the most violent of these criticisms were directed against the British Minister, Sir Claude Macdonald.

Sir Claude's position was extremely difficult. He was responsible for the safety of the British community and therefore it was his duty to take all possible precautions and to forewarn his Government of the dangers that menaced his compatriots and himself. On the other hand, he had to avoid giving any unjustified cause for alarm, especially at a moment when his country was involved in a serious colonial war. Sir Claude relied to a great extent on the advice of Sir Robert Hart, whose knowledge and experience of China and the Chinese were considered superior to those of any other British subject. Sir Robert Hart's biographer in the *Encyclopædia Britannica* admits that 'the faith he put in the Chinese made him turn a deaf ear to the warnings, which he received of the threatening Boxer movement in 1900'. To a query of Sir Claude Macdonald's, who had asked whether it would not be advisable to send his (Sir Claude's) children away to Japan, with some relations who were about to leave

China, Sir Robert Hart answered that it might be prudent to bring them in from the Western Hills, where they had been staying, but that no town in China was so safe as Peking, and no part of Peking so safe as the Legation Quarter. The British Minister communicated Sir Robert Hart's opinion to various of his colleagues of the Diplomatic Body.

The French and Italian Ministers had other informants. The French Minister, Monsieur Pichon, was warned of a very great danger by a letter from Monseigneur Favier, the French Bishop in Peking, who asked for military protection for his Mission at the Peitang, in the northern part of the Tartar City. The Italian Minister, Marchese Salvago Raggi, was told by one of his nationals, the missionary, Padre d'Addosio, that the Chinese meant to exterminate all the foreigners in Peking, diplomats included.

Padre d'Addosio had a church (the Tung Tang) and a mission in the Tartar City. He was a well-known character in Peking; an old man with a flowing white beard and a far-away look in his eye. People spoke of him as a kind, harmless old thing, and did not take him very seriously, on account of his strange, exaggerated gestures and declamatory manner of speaking. His prophecies, in the spring of 1900, were all of murder and sudden death.

On the occasion of a visit paid him by the Italian Minister, in company with his secretary, Don Livio Caetani, Father d'Addosio assured them that in a few days they would all meet in Paradise and receive their recompense for having carried the Word of God to the heathen. His visitors did not share this enthusiasm at the prospect of receiving a martyr's crown, and they suggested that Padre d'Addosio and his Chinese converts might take refuge within the compound of the Italian Legation.

News from outside Peking showed that armed bands of Boxers were drawing near to the capital, killing as they came. Even more alarming was the fact that some regular Chinese troops, who were stationed along the railway line, having attacked the advancing Boxers and repulsed them, were punished and transferred elsewhere.

In 1898, at the time of Tzu-hsi's *coup d'état*, the Legations, wishing to allay a certain alarm among the foreign community, had brought up a small force of sailors from the ships lying at anchor outside the Taku Bar. This precedent was invoked at the end of May 1900, and the consent of the Chinese government was obtained to the arrival, by train, of a small detachment of foreign soldiers and sailors, in all 389 men and 16 officers of different nationalities.

A few days later, all railway communication was interrupted between Peking and Tientsin. The Boxers began by destroying the railway tickets. It was only when they discovered that this was not sufficient to stop the traffic, that they proceeded to seize the locomotives and to tear up the rails.

It soon became evident how inadequate to the needs of the hour was the first small detachment, sent up for the protection of the Legations. On the 10th of June, the so-called 'Seymour relief column' started from Tientsin, with the object of repairing the railway and of bringing help to the foreign community in the capital. The column consisted of 2,064 men of seven different nationalities. But at that moment, conditions in Tientsin were no less critical than those in

Peking, and in endeavouring to reach the capital, the relieving column attempted more than was possible. They had to retire and to take refuge in the Tientsin arsenal, where they remained for some time, until they succeeded in cutting their way back to the town, having sustained losses to the number of seventy killed and about two hundred wounded.

The Seymour relief column was expected to arrive in Peking, by train, on the 12th of June. Various Legations sent carts to the station of Ma-chia-pu, outside the walls, in order to facilitate the arrival and to bring the officers' luggage. A few members of the diplomatic corps rode out to see the arrival. Among these was the Chancellor-Interpreter of the Japanese Legation, Mr. Sujimura, who drove out in a Chinese cart.

The wait at the station was a long one, for the railway officials declared that the trains containing the relief column were close to Peking and might arrive at any moment. This, of course, was not true; it was merely one of the false rumours which added to the doubts and anxieties of the foreign community.

Among those who had ridden out to Ma-chia-pu was the Italian Minister. He tried to persuade a German engineer, belonging to the railway staff, to take him and his secretary on an engine, to meet the relief column along the line. The German was quite willing, but so drunk that he could not get started. This was fortunate, as the country was overrun with Boxers, seeking whom they might destroy.

The Japanese Chancellor, Sujimura, waited on at the station, with characteristic Oriental patience, long after the others had given it up and ridden home. But at last he too started homewards in his Chinese cart, following the main road, whereas the others had ridden over the fields. A few